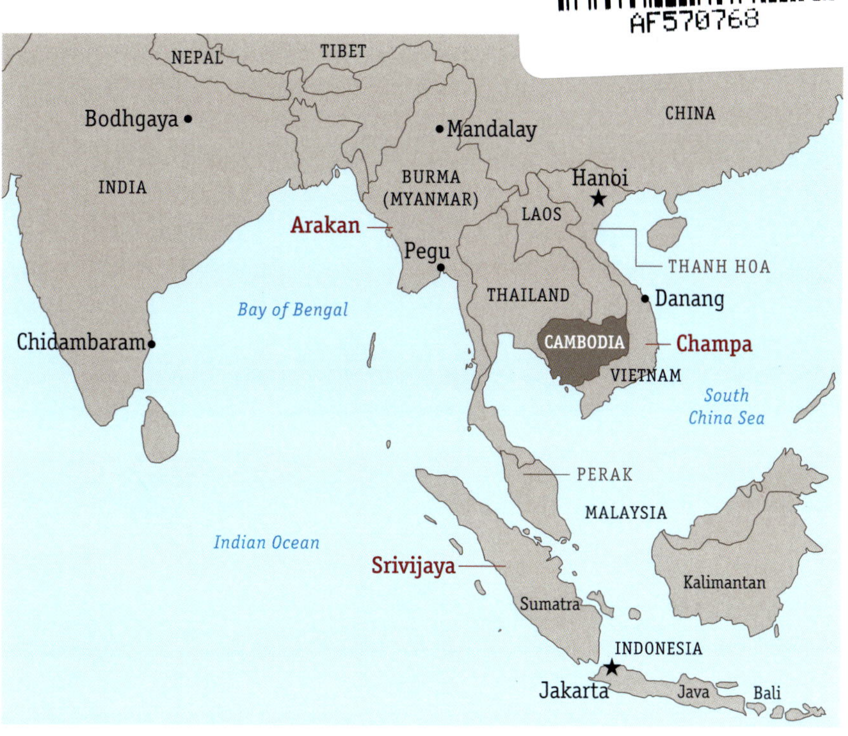

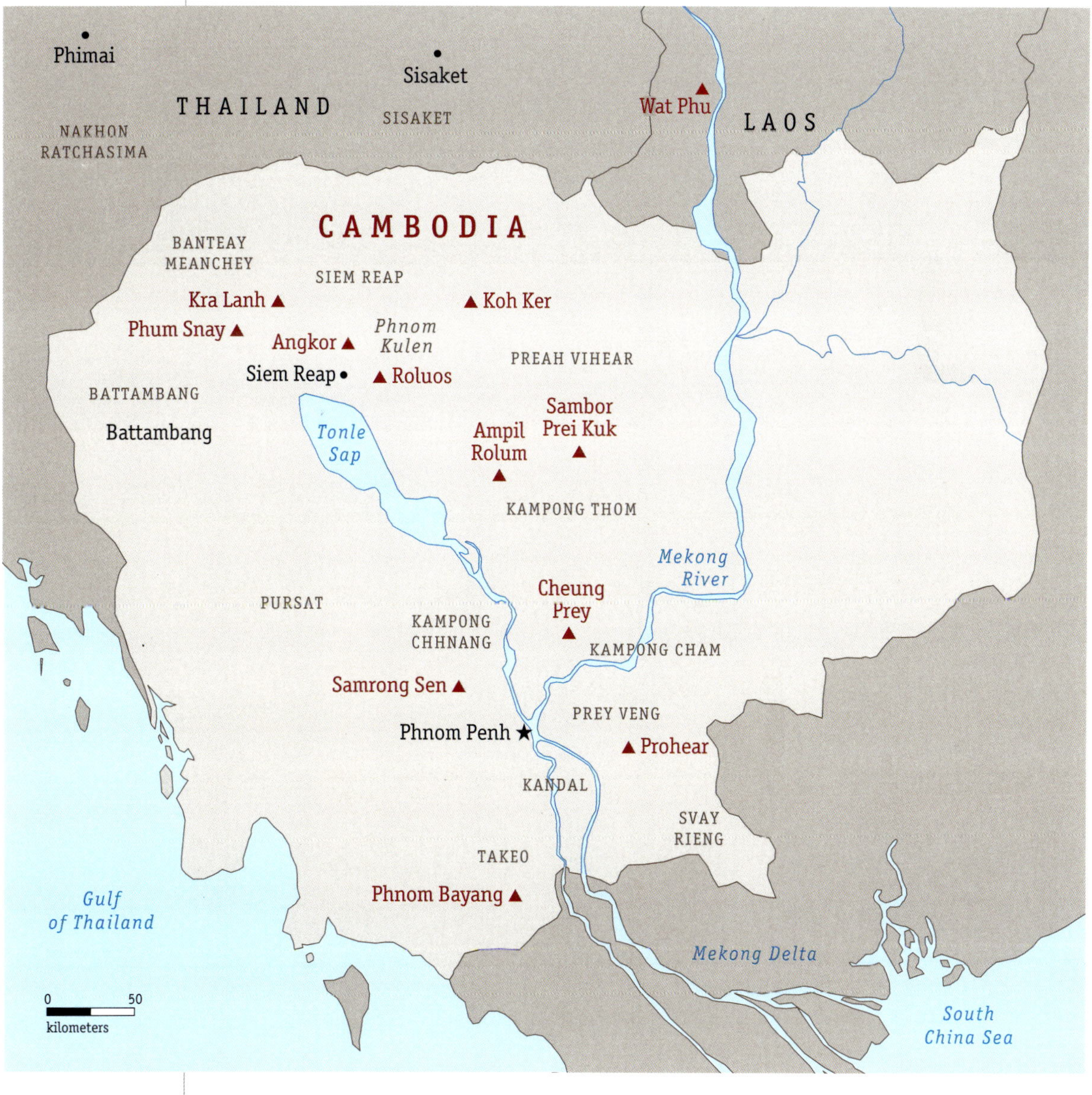

Phimai
Sisaket
THAILAND
SISAKET
Wat Phu
LAOS
NAKHON
RATCHASIMA
CAMBODIA
BANTEAY
MEANCHEY
SIEM REAP
Koh Ker
Kra Lanh
Phum Snay
Angkor
Phnom
Kulen
PREAH VIHEAR
Siem Reap
Roluos
BATTAMBANG
Battambang
Sambor
Prei Kuk
Tonle
Sap
Ampil
Rolum
KAMPONG THOM
Mekong
River
Cheung
Prey
PURSAT
KAMPONG
CHHNANG
KAMPONG CHAM
Samrong Sen
PREY VENG
Phnom Penh
Prohear
KANDAL
SVAY
RIENG
TAKEO
Phnom Bayang
Gulf
of Thailand
Mekong Delta
0 50
kilometers
South
China Sea

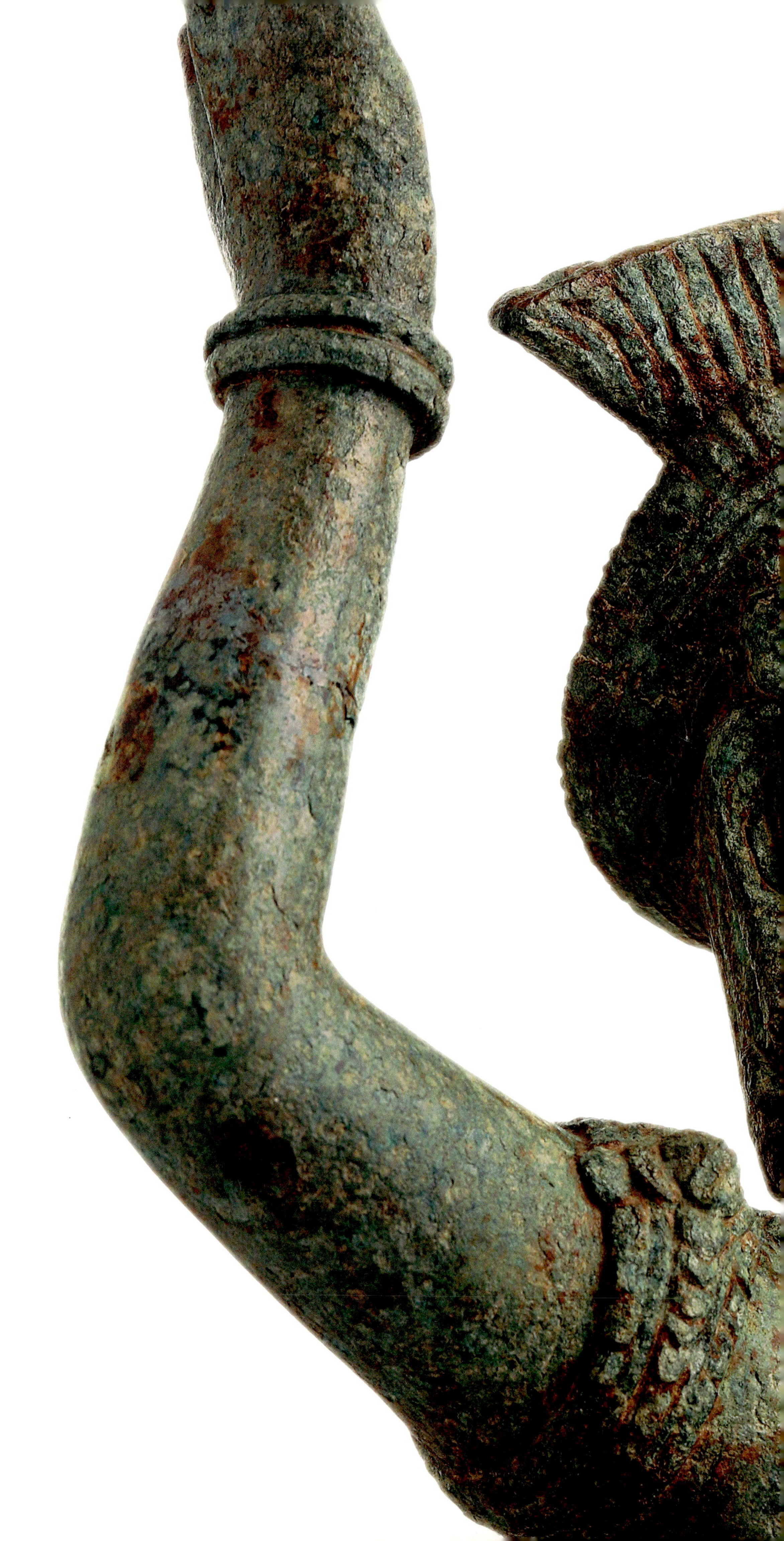

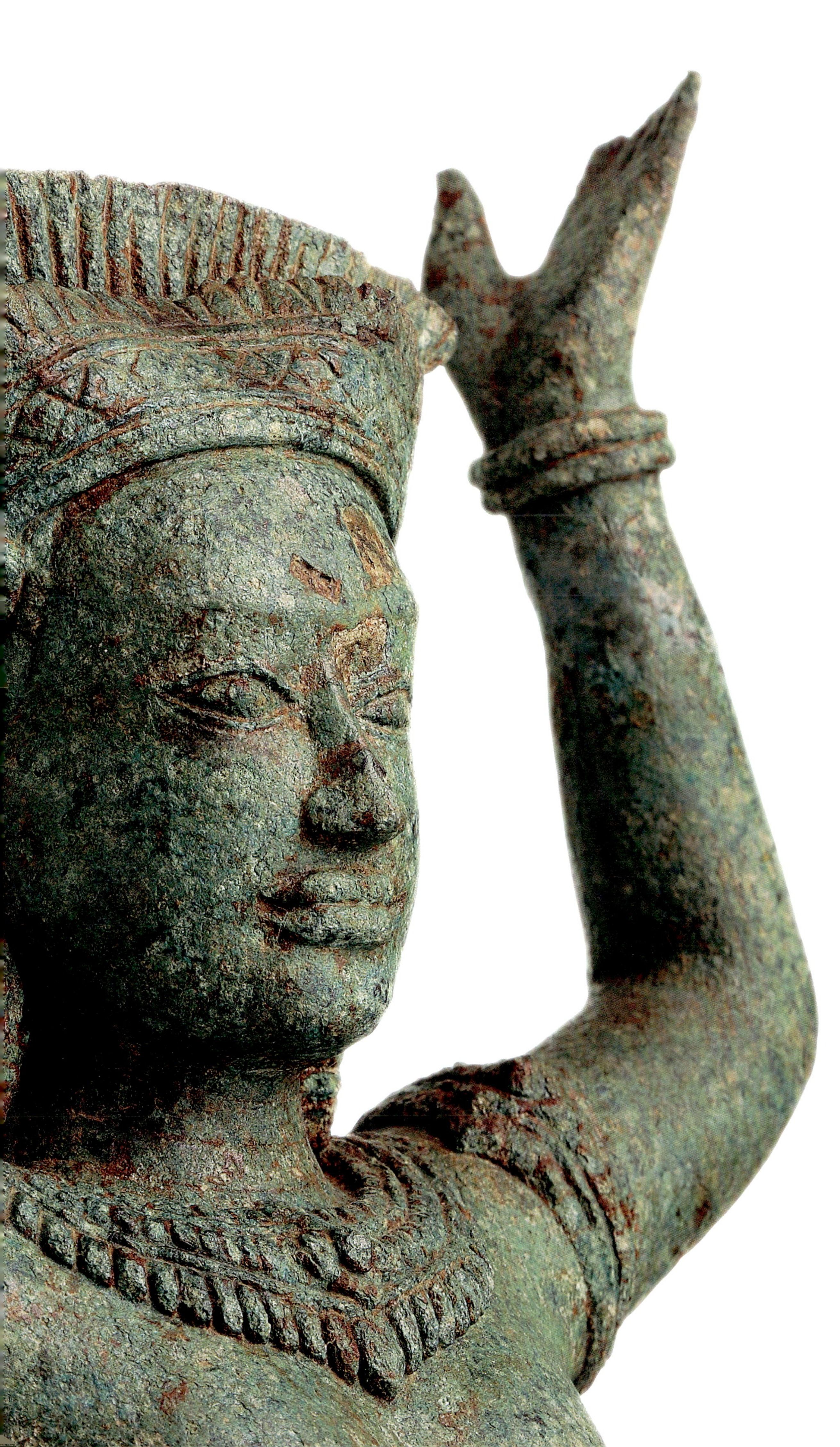

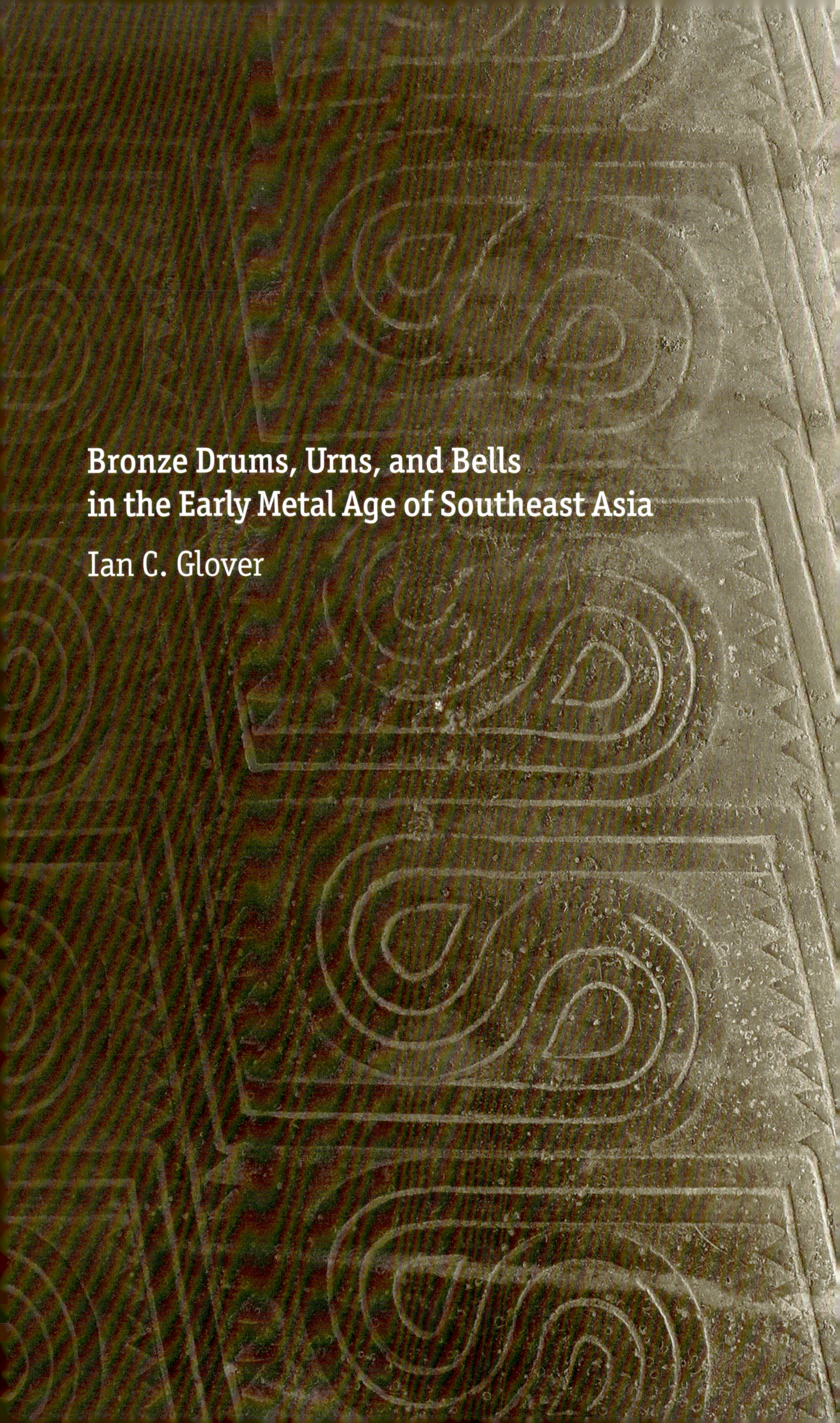

Bronze Drums, Urns, and Bells in the Early Metal Age of Southeast Asia

Ian C. Glover

Given the present state of archaeological knowledge of early Southeast Asia, we can speak of a Bronze Age only for northern Vietnam and northeast and central Thailand, roughly from circa 2000/1700 BCE to circa 500 BCE, when iron started to replace bronze for tools and weapons. The earliest finds of bronze—or, more correctly, copper alloy objects—are small thin bracelets and personal ornaments (mainly lost-wax or open stone-mold castings) and a few small socketed axes, arrowheads, and spearheads, which were cast in sandstone bivalve molds. The immediate source of the bronze technology is most probably from southern China, where very similar objects and casting techniques are known in the early to mid second millennium BCE, clearly before their appearance in Southeast Asia.[1] Larger and more complex bronzes, both for ceremony and for ornament, appeared only some five hundred to one thousand years later, toward the end of the Bronze Age and especially in the Iron Age.

Dating the Bronze and Iron Ages in Southeast Asia has long been—and still is, to some—controversial, disputed, and occasionally confrontational.[2] Nonetheless, there seems to be a general agreement that iron came into regular use throughout much of Southeast Asia between 500 and 400 BCE, introduced perhaps from India. Vietnamese archaeologists, however—on the basis of rather few C-14 dates—place the earliest bronze production in northern Vietnam in the early second millennium BCE, with the production of drums starting around 600 BCE, and iron coming into use from Han China around the second century.

Composition and Casting of Bronzes in Southeast Asia

Bronze is an alloy comprised primarily of copper, with variable amounts of tin and lead. In Southeast Asia, from the very earliest period, tin was introduced into the metal to reduce the melting point and increase its strength. Lead was regularly added to large castings, such as drums, to increase the flow through the mold, and the tin content of drums was generally lower than that of tools and weapons. As Louis Malleret describes, three bells—one from the National Museum of Cambodia, one in Hanoi, and one from Perak, Malaysia, and now in the British Museum—are all bronzes with tin content varying between 13.4 percent and 15.1 percent, but the lead content varies greatly—between 0.1 percent and 12.3 percent.[3]

Southeast Asian metalsmiths created their artifacts for the most part by both lost-wax and bivalve-mold casting. There is debate about whether some of the earliest drums found in China were made by piece-mold[4] or lost-wax casting.[5] The latter method was surely employed for decorated urns, situlae, and bells.

Bronze in Cambodia

Two sorts of major prehistoric bronze objects are found in Cambodia: drums, which appear to have been produced in northern Vietnam or adjacent areas of China, and urns and bells, more probably of local production, since the finds of urns are confined to Cambodia, Thailand, and some parts of Indonesia. The wide distribution of both drums (recorded in large numbers in southern China, southern Vietnam, Laos, Thailand, Malaysia, and Indonesia) and urns suggests that they were most probably circulated as items of prestige rather than as items of regular trade.

There has been too little systematic prehistoric research in Cambodia to determine whether the development of bronze metallurgy was in any degree independent from that of nearby countries. Descriptions and analyses of casual finds of bronze tools and ornaments from the few reasonably excavated sites of Samrong Sen (Kampong Chhnang province), Phum Snay (Banteay Meanchey province), and Prohear (Prey Veng province) show that the local metal workers of the second and first millennia BCE and their contemporaries in Thailand and Vietnam shared the same basic techniques for alloying and casting leaded tin bronzes.[6]

Cambodia appears to lack all nonferrous metal sources. It is most probable that the early copper, tin, and lead were mined in and imported from the mines at Phu Lon in northeast Thailand or from the Wong Prachan Valley in central Thailand.

Bronze Drums

As early as 1705, the naturalist Georg Rumpf (Rumphius) mentioned the famous drum known as the "Moon of Pejeng," from central Bali, where it remains, honored in a temple. Later centuries saw the discovery of many more drums. In 1902, Franz Heger classified all the Southeast Asian and South Chinese drums then known into four main regional and chronological varieties, called Heger Types I–IV.[7] The literature on these drums in multiple languages probably exceeds that on all other aspects of Southeast Asian prehistoric archaeology put together. Not only do the drums exhibit great technical skill in the casting of large objects, but the wealth of iconographic information on the tympani and sides of drums and some related large ceremonial situlae provides vital images of aspects of daily and religious life in vivid detail—expeditions of armed warriors in boats carrying the very sorts of drums on which they are portrayed; domestic activities such as rice pounding, food preparation, and feeding animals; musical performances; and religious ceremonies and dances.

An archaeological source of these drums was not known until 1924, when a fisherman chanced upon a number of bronzes at the Dong Son village on the Ma River, Thanh Hoa province, northern Vietnam. Emile Pajot then excavated the site on behalf of the École française d'Extrême-Orient in Hanoi and the publication of Pajot's finds by Victor Goloubew caused a sensation in Orientalist circles.[8] Some scholars, such as Bernhard Karlgren, ascribed the drums found in Vietnam to the Han Chinese of the first century CE or to the earlier Warring States period (475–221 BCE);[9] others sought their origins in the Eurasian steppes, from where bronze working was thought to have been brought to Southeast Asia by nomadic migrations starting near the Black Sea. Although it is now more or less accepted that the earliest traditions of bronze working in eastern Asia came from the west across Central Asia, the bronze drums are acknowledged to be a local development in the region from southern China to northern Vietnam.[10]

There has been speculation as to whether the drums were made only for religious ceremonies, such as harvest rituals, or had a more secular role, such as rallying men for war. Perhaps they served many roles, for the drums were traded widely, and it is unlikely that they had the same value and purpose for all the communities who treasured them through the vast region from China to Burma and southeast to the islands of eastern Indonesia, where local styles were developed.

The collection of the National Museum of Cambodia includes several drums (see fig. 1), although none was found within Cambodia. A drum recently discovered in the village of Prohear, Prey Veng province, between Phnom Penh and the border with Vietnam is the first documented excavation of a drum in Cambodia.[11] The full publication of the drum and other materials from the excavation will help answer many unresolved questions about the chronology and purpose of these drums in Cambodia.

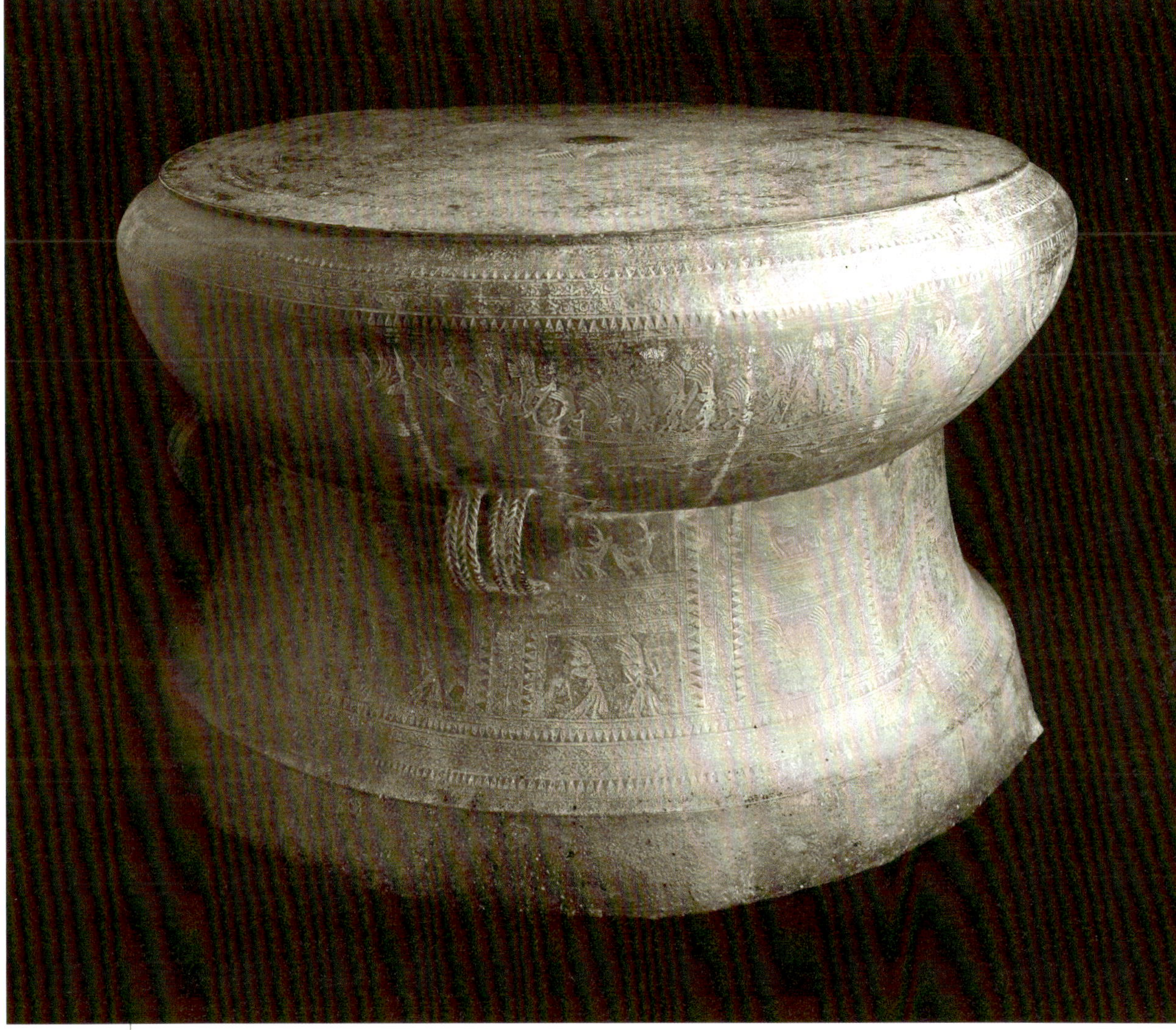

1

1 Drum. Northern Vietnam or China. Prehistoric, 3rd–2nd century BCE, Bronze; 57 × 96 cm. National Museum of Cambodia, Ga5741.

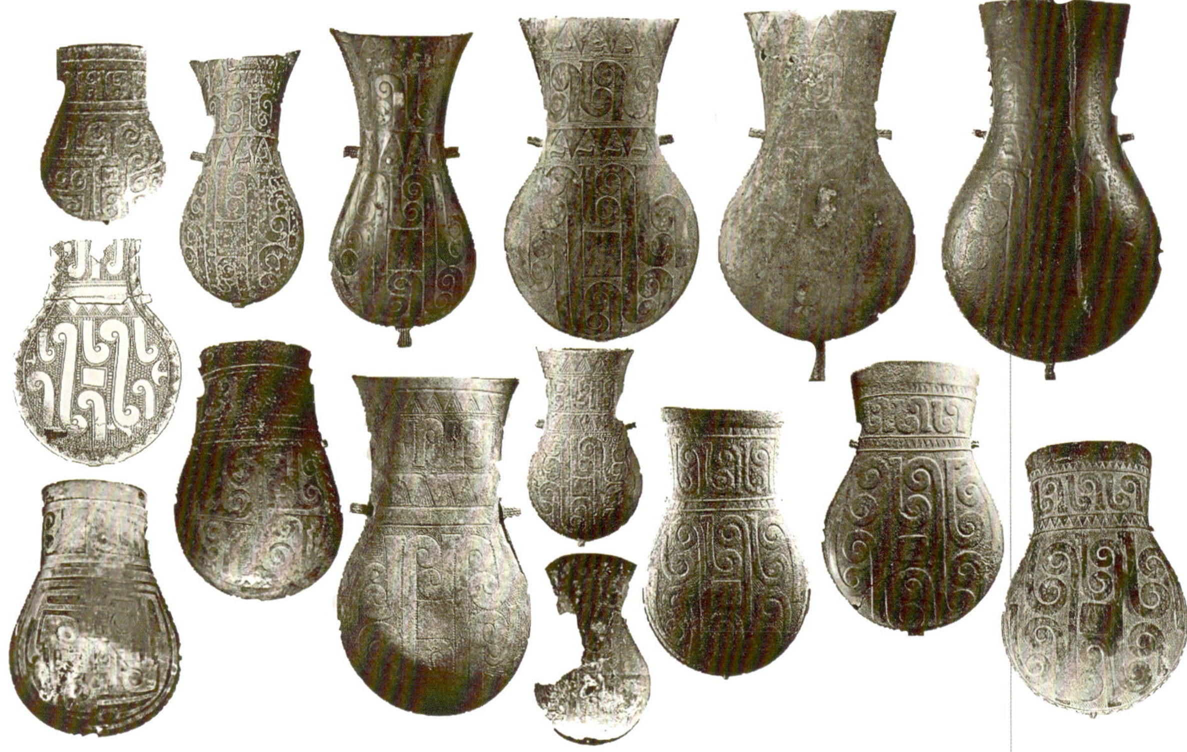

2

Bronze Urns

Among the bronzes of the southern parts of Southeast Asia, two forms stand out as distinct from anything found in the Dong Son culture sphere of northern Vietnam, the source of so many of the large bronze drums. They are elaborately decorated bronze urns and large and similarly (though not identically) decorated bells.

The large decorated bronze urns, or flasks, constitute a distinctive type of ceremonial, ritual, or prestige vessel in Southeast Asia. Remarkably little is known about their function or locations of manufacture. In 1922 Frederik Bosch reported the discovery of the first urn at Mindopo Lolo, south of Lake Kerinci in South Sumatra; it is now in the National Museum in Jakarta. Over the next eighty years more vessels of this category have come to light (fig. 2), mainly as casual finds by farmers but also, in recent years, uncovered by treasure hunters using metal detectors. The total currently known to me is fifteen. Most recent finds are in private collections or museums in Switzerland, Thailand, the United States, and Belgium.

The second urn to be reported (figs. 3A, 3), the one in the exhibition, is referred to as the Kandal urn, for the Cambodian province where it was recovered in 1948. A third urn, very similar to the Kandal urn, was found by a farmer on Madura island off the northeast coast of Java. Possibly the finest example of all, said to have been found in a cave near the Thai–Burmese border, is now in the collection of George Ortiz in Geneva.[12] One of the very few with a known findspot (the bed of an old canal near Nakhon Pathom, central Thailand) recently was given to the Nakhon Pathom National Museum.

All the urns are in the form of a round-based, waisted flask varying between thirty-eight and eighty-five centimeters in height. They have three rather small loop handles, two on the sides just below the neck and the third at the base. A complex geometric low-relief decoration covering both faces is dominated by pairs of large opposed "J" hook motifs arranged around a smooth undecorated square. At least four of the vessels—the Kandal, Madura, Ortiz, and one in the collection of Dr. Joel Greene in San Francisco[13]—also bear stamped designs of animals and, sometimes, men in boats on the neck and upper part of the body and down the sides. All the urns appear to have been cast in one piece, probably by the lost-wax method with the handles cast on later, and are comparable to the Dong Son drums—from which they differ in many respects—as masterpieces of Southeast Asian late prehistoric bronze casting.

The Kandal urn is heavily corroded and shows signs of damage and repair in antiquity. Its decoration (fig. 3A) includes five stylized long-necked birds with short plumes on their heads, within triangular stamped depressions. Below three raised parallel lines, a band of three pairs of opposed J hooks stands against a square-stamped background. Below the hooks are more horizontal raised lines and four triangles, slightly smaller than those containing the birds and this time filled with deer in profile. From the positioning of the antlers, it seems probable that they represent *Cervus eldi*, brow-antlered deer.

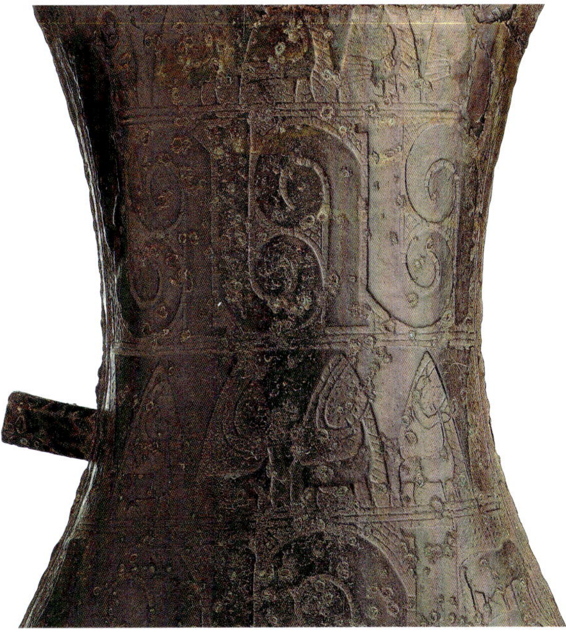

3A

2 Fifteen vessels of this type currently known.

3 and 3A Ritual vessel, the "Kandal urn"
detail above and pages 24–25
Probably Cambodia, prehistoric, 4th century BCE–2nd century CE
Bronze; 55.2 × 28.7 × 13 cm
National Museum of Cambodia, Ga2083

The seller explained that it had been in his family for three generations and had been used to carry water on long journeys.

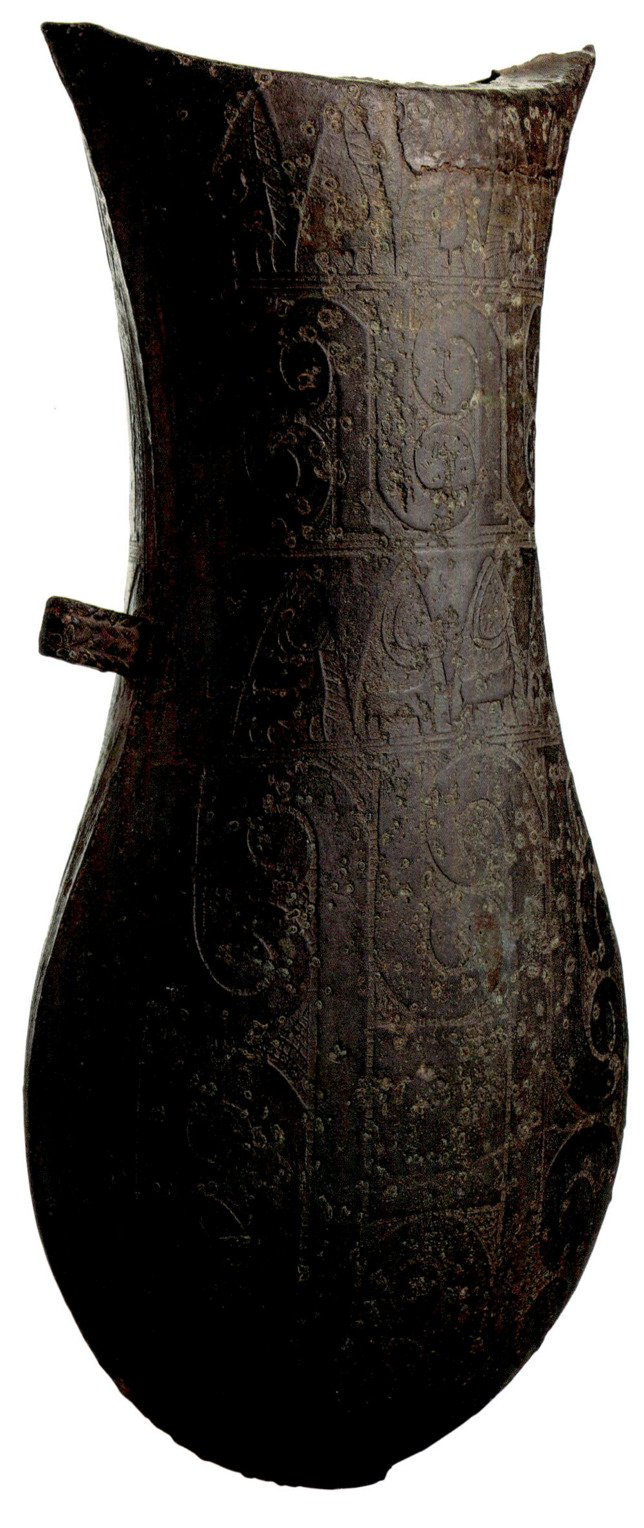

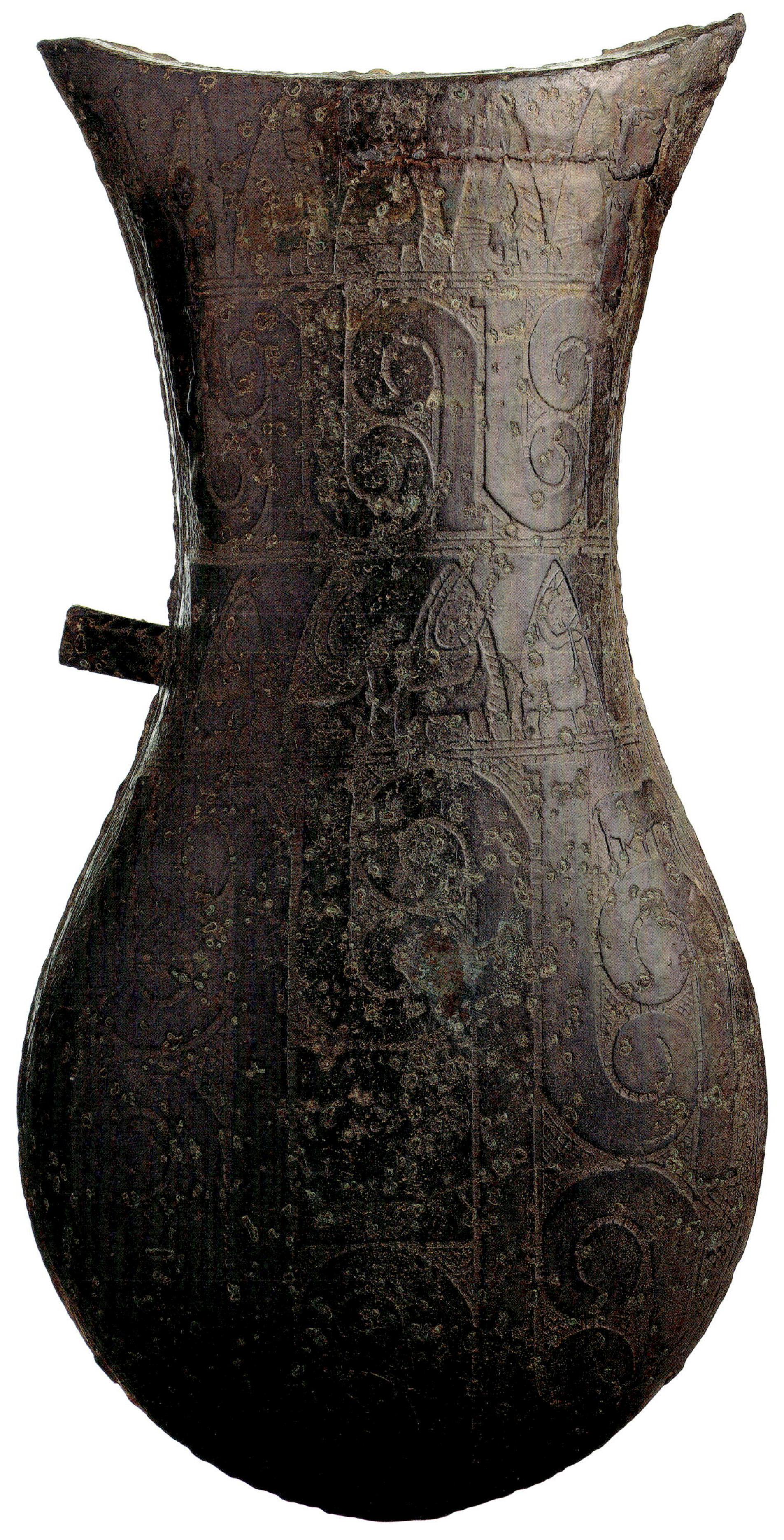

The lower half of the body below the decorative bands is virtually covered with J hooks, which surround a undecorated square in the center of the lower section. A single elephant appears in the upper right corner of the lower body. According to Malleret, near the elephant is a small boat with upturned prow driven by standing and seated paddlers; a similar boat is placed close by, on the opposite side of the urn.[14] He also mentions a small lizard in the narrow space to one end of the row of birds and what is perhaps an otter on the other end, and a horseshoe crab on either end of the row of deer.[15]

As Malleret points out, the boat design, and to some extent the animals and birds, link the Kandal urn to the pictorial elements on some of the Dong Son drums, although the form of representation is quite different. The Kandal urn, though differing in size, is so similar to the ones from Madura, in the Ortiz Collection, in the Barbier-Mueller Museum in Geneva, and in the Joel Greene collection that one can believe that they all came from the same workshop or, at least, the same local craft tradition.[16]

What are we to make of these urns, so similar in many ways, yet each with its individual character and found scattered over so broad an area of Southeast Asia? First, there is no certainty about their function.[17] Some writers refer to them as bells, pointing to the suspension loops and undecorated rectangle in the center of each side, seemingly intended for striking. Unfortunately none have survived in good enough condition for any musical qualities to be tested. Others have suggested that they might be cremation urns for prominent village chiefs.[18] On balance, though, I prefer to see them as ceremonial vessels, prestige objects, and perhaps metallic skeuomorphs from the traditional Southeast Asian fisherman's catch basket, as long ago pointed out by Bosch.

Although many collectors and dealers term the urns "Dong Son ritual vessels," it is clear that they do not belong to the Dong Son culture in any real sense. To my knowledge, none have even been found in the core area of the Dong Son culture of northern Vietnam, central Vietnam, or the Yunnan or Guangxi provinces in China—the region where by far the largest number of drums has been found. Although the distribution of the urns is notable, it so far in no way corresponds to that of the Dong Son drums. Indeed, we could almost say that the bronze urns are found in relatively "drum free" regions—Cambodia, central Thailand, and Indonesia.

The assumption is that the urns were cast somewhere in Cambodia or Thailand and some, perhaps, in Indonesia. Malleret, who gave a long and informed assessment of the three urns that were then known and realized that they did not belong to the Dong Son culture *sensu strictu* of northern Vietnam, was less sure where they were made, and most of his comparisons are to material from Indonesia.[19] He recognized that if the deer on the Kandal and Madura urns are intended to represent *Cervus eldi*, then these two at least must have been cast on the mainland since the distribution of this species does not include island Southeast Asia. The elephants, however, could have been found in Sumatra and Kalimantan as well as on the mainland.

Evidence for dating the urns is poor. None of the ones described in earlier articles has been found with burials or in prehistoric settlements that might be dated by radiometric means, nor do any appear to contain remains of a casting core that also could be dated.[20] Stylistically, they lack any of the elements of Indic art. This suggests to me that they predate the sixth century CE, when cast images of Indian deities and other elements of high Indian culture appeared in many parts of Southeast Asia and influenced the production of most other bronze objects.

Bronze Bells

The bell shown in this exhibition (figs. 4A, 4) is reported to have been found in a village in Pursat province, near Battambang in western Cambodia, and it may be one of more than seventy bronze bells said to come from one deposit in Pursat. Others have been found in Thailand and peninsular Malaysia. Although less elaborately decorated than bronze urns, the bells share elements of surface design, with swirling horizontal multiple S-curves (fig. 4A) and are rather distinct from the bells of the Dong Son culture, which usually have protruding "horns" at the top.

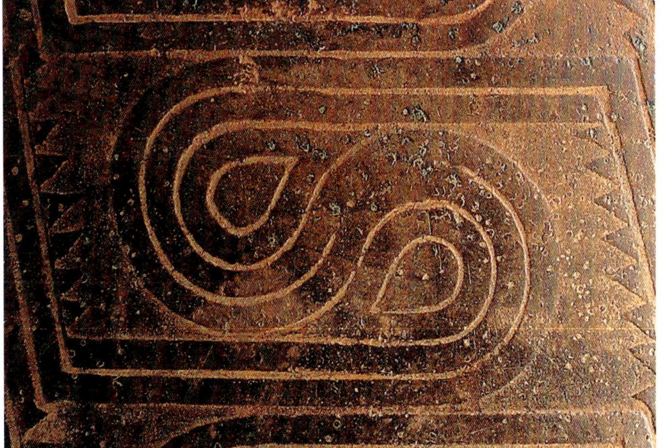

4A

The Pursat bell is very similar to the one illustrated by Malleret, who also provides a detailed description of other, generally similar bells known at the time.[21] He refers to them as "elephant bells," which makes good sense as they would have been too heavy for cattle or buffaloes. Alternatively, they might have had a religious function similar to modern temple bells.

Questions for Future Research

Bronze drums are well discussed in the literature, and many detailed studies of the decoration, composition, and manufacturing processes have been made. What is needed is more information about the archaeological context and dating of the drums. A lead in this direction has been made by the discovery and controlled excavation of a drum (among the many looted ones) and many associated finds of bronze, silver, and gold at Prohear village, Prey Veng province.[22] Likewise, we have many urns and bells, from casual finds by villagers and the systematic looting of ancient sites, but we lack good dating and a better understanding of the functions of these splendid objects for the peoples and communities that made and used them.

4 and 4A Bell detail above and pages 28–29
Probably Cambodia, prehistoric, 4th century BCE–2nd century CE
Bronze; 57.7 × 30.5 × 24 cm
National Museum of Cambodia, Ga6854

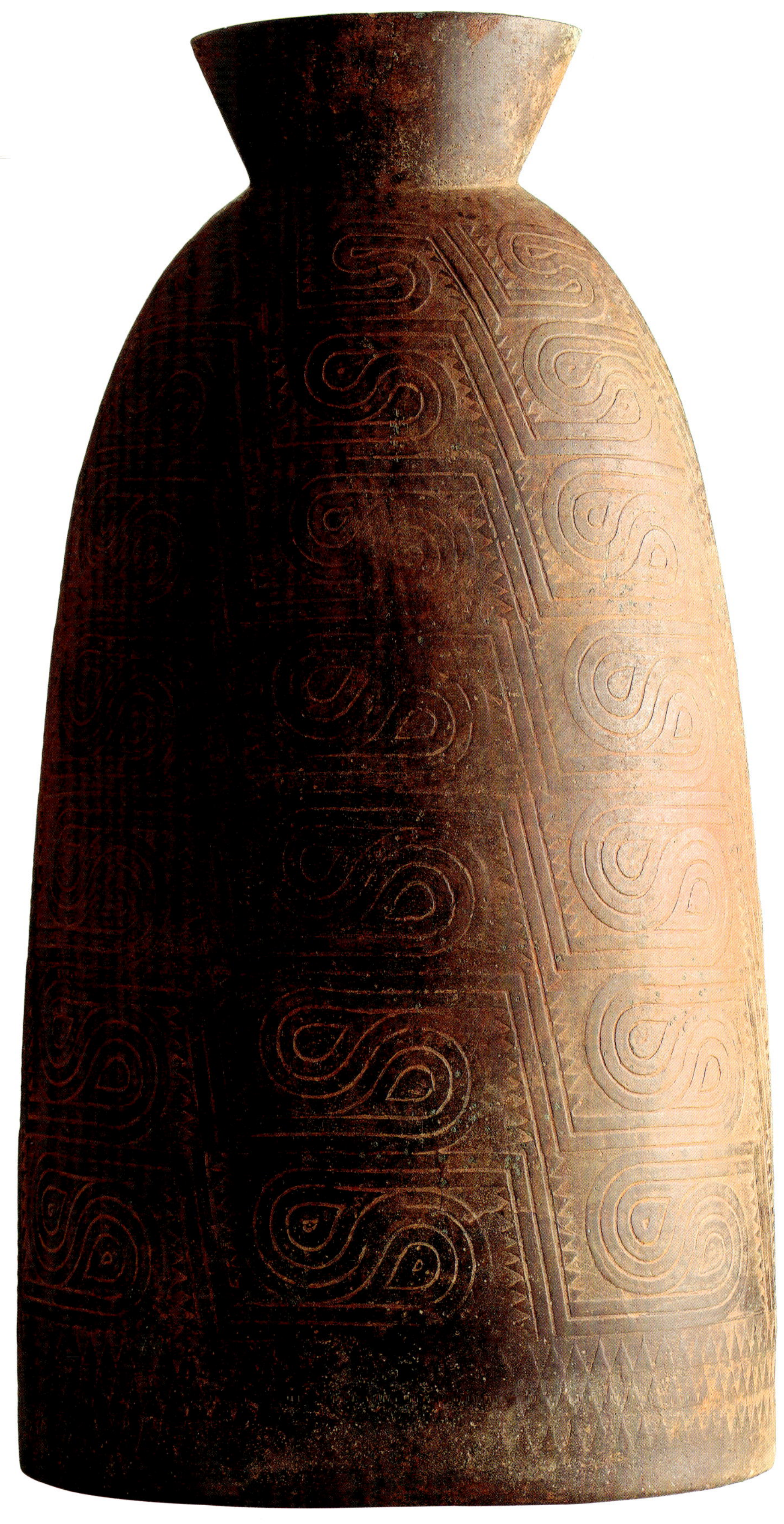

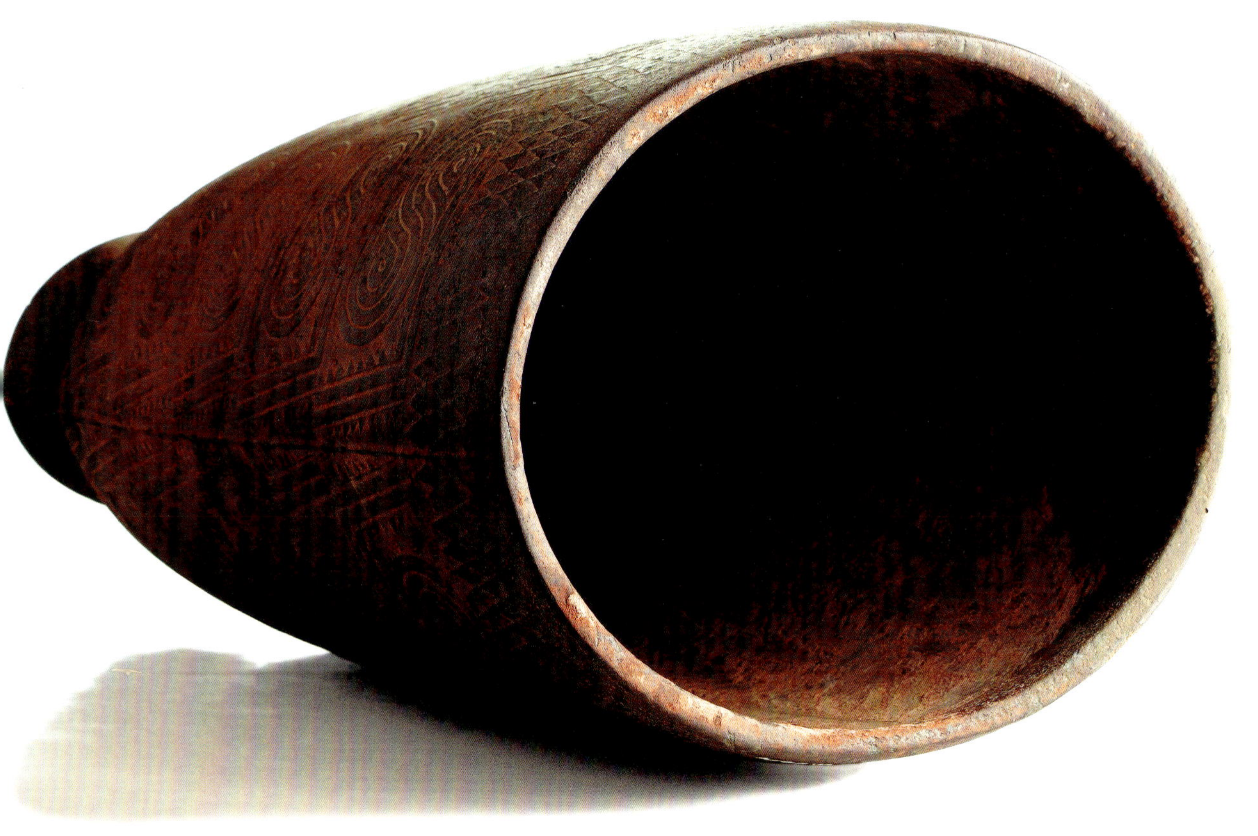

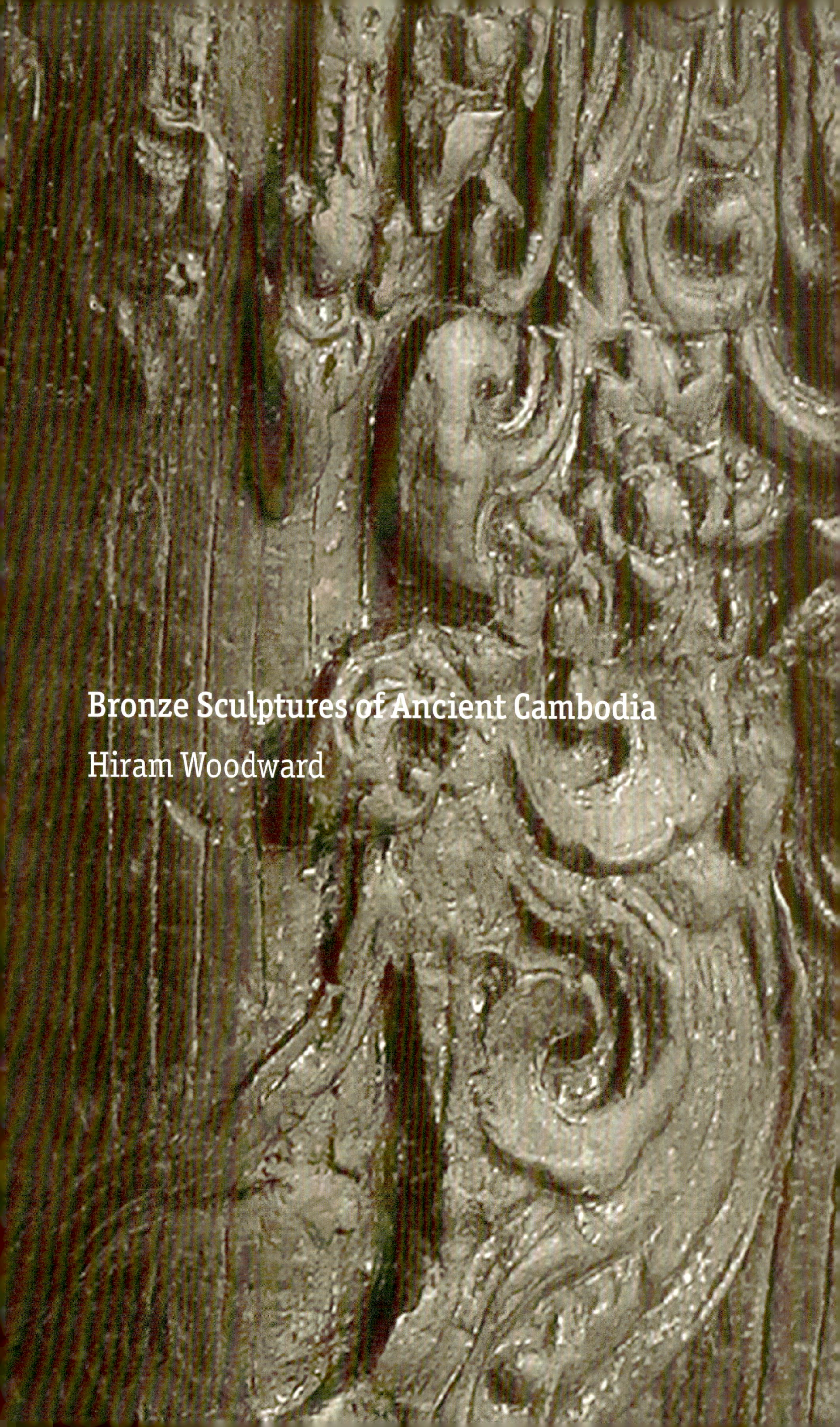

Bronze Sculptures of Ancient Cambodia

Hiram Woodward

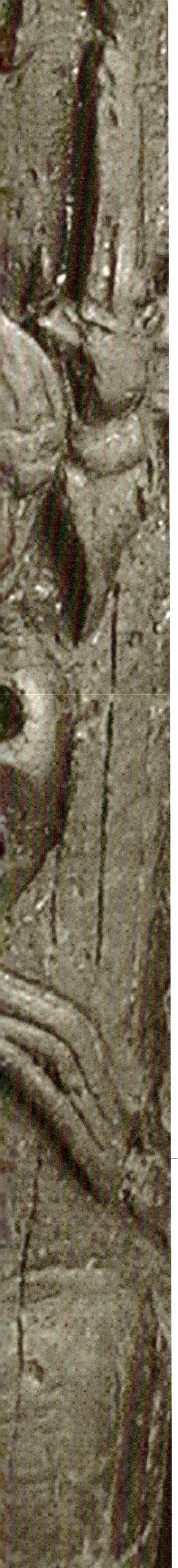

One of the most beautiful of the bronze sculptures in this exhibition represents the bodhisattva Maitreya, the future Buddha. (figs. 5, 5A) It dates from around the time, about 900, that King Yashovarman (reigned 889–circa 915) established the city of Angkor as his capital. This was not a period in which Buddhism had much importance in Cambodia. One of Yashovarman's inscriptions indicates the place he gave to the religion. A worshiper himself of the god Shiva, manifested especially in the form of the Shivalinga, Yashovarman created three lesser sanctuaries, two for the Hindu gods Vishnu and Brahma, and the third for the Buddha.[1] It was as if Buddhism could be numbered among the Brahmanical cults.

This Maitreya serves as an introduction to various themes. One is the relationship of bronze to stone. From a stylistic point of view, what is at stake is the degree to which the inherent properties of the two media are lost in the quest for ideal form. From a typological perspective, what has to be asked is whether bronzes were always reflections of stone images or whether there were established iconographic types that had no counterparts in stone. Another question is the nature of Cambodia's connections with the world outside, both its near neighbors, the kingdoms known as Dvāravatī and Champa in modern-day Thailand and Vietnam, and the more distant worlds of India and China. Yet another question is the place of Buddhism in the civilization of ancient Cambodia, and the degree to which the Buddhism recognized elsewhere—with its worship of relics and independently administered monkhood—was practiced in Cambodia prior to the thirteenth century. At the same time, in the thirteenth and fourteenth centuries, just as this sort of Buddhism was becoming established, the continued production of images consistent with long-established Hindu beliefs is a matter worth pondering.

The Relationship of Bronze and Stone

The Arthur M. Sackler Gallery is home to a stone image of a female goddess (figs. 6, 6A) that dates from about the same time as this Maitreya.[2] Many obvious differences are dictated by the subject matter. The female figure wears a crown, an element that in a way could be the most "realistic" of all the aspects of the sculpture, for it faithfully reproduces the appearance of a gold diadem. A few of these crowns have survived, most of them probably made to adorn an image, not for the use of royalty.[3] They were made from a flexible sheet of hammered gold, secured at the back by a tied cord. Despite the scarcity of evidence, it seems to be the case that stone images more faithfully rendered the appearance of gold diadems than did bronze images.

5 and 5A Maitreya pages 32–33, 34
Cambodia, Angkor period, early 10th century
Bronze; 75.5 × 50 × 23 cm
National Museum of Cambodia, Ga2024

Maitreya is the bodhisattva (future Buddha) who may be born on Earth as soon as a few thousand years from now. This depiction of him was cast in a period during which hardly any Buddhist images were commissioned, and from which few bronzes survive.

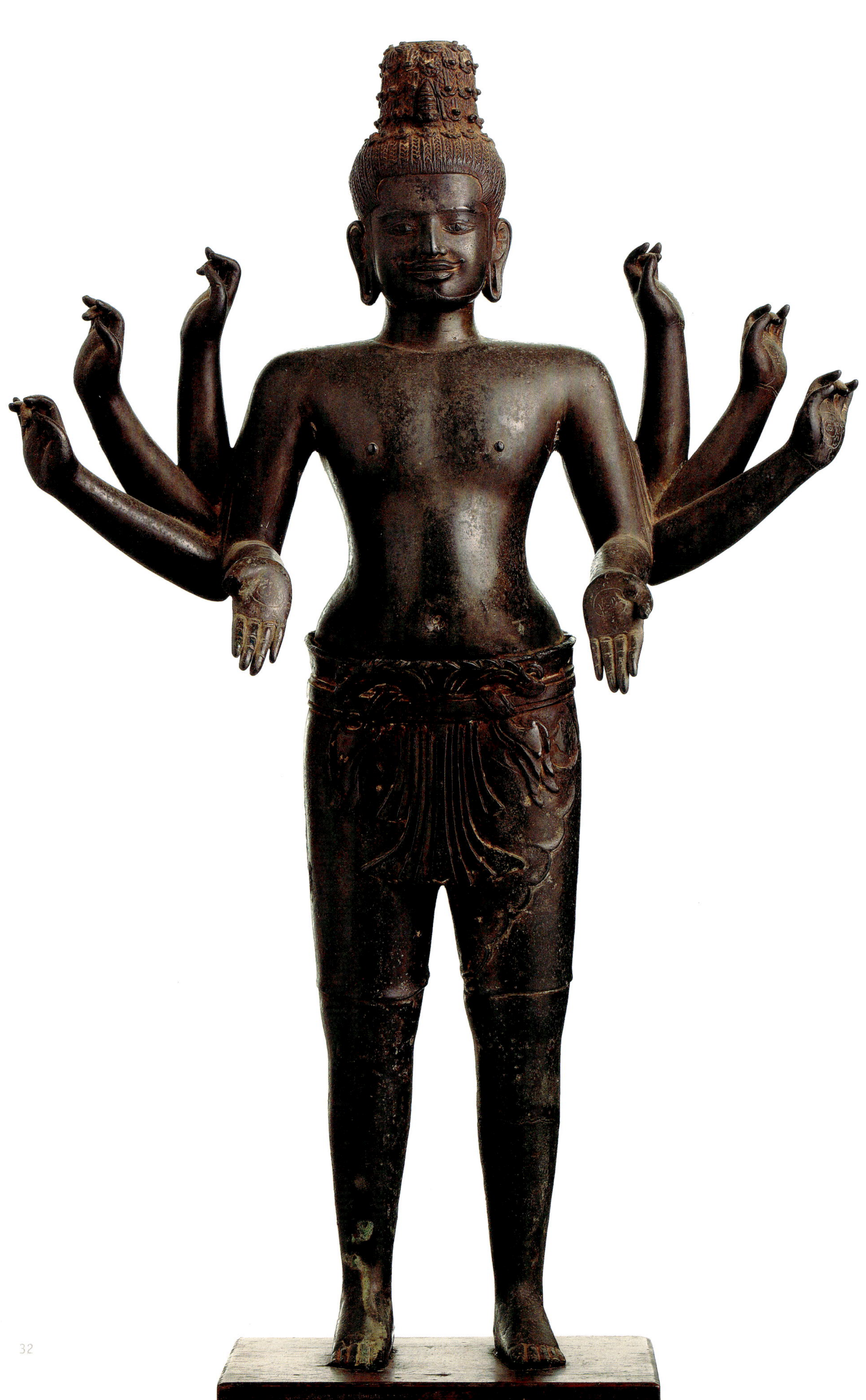

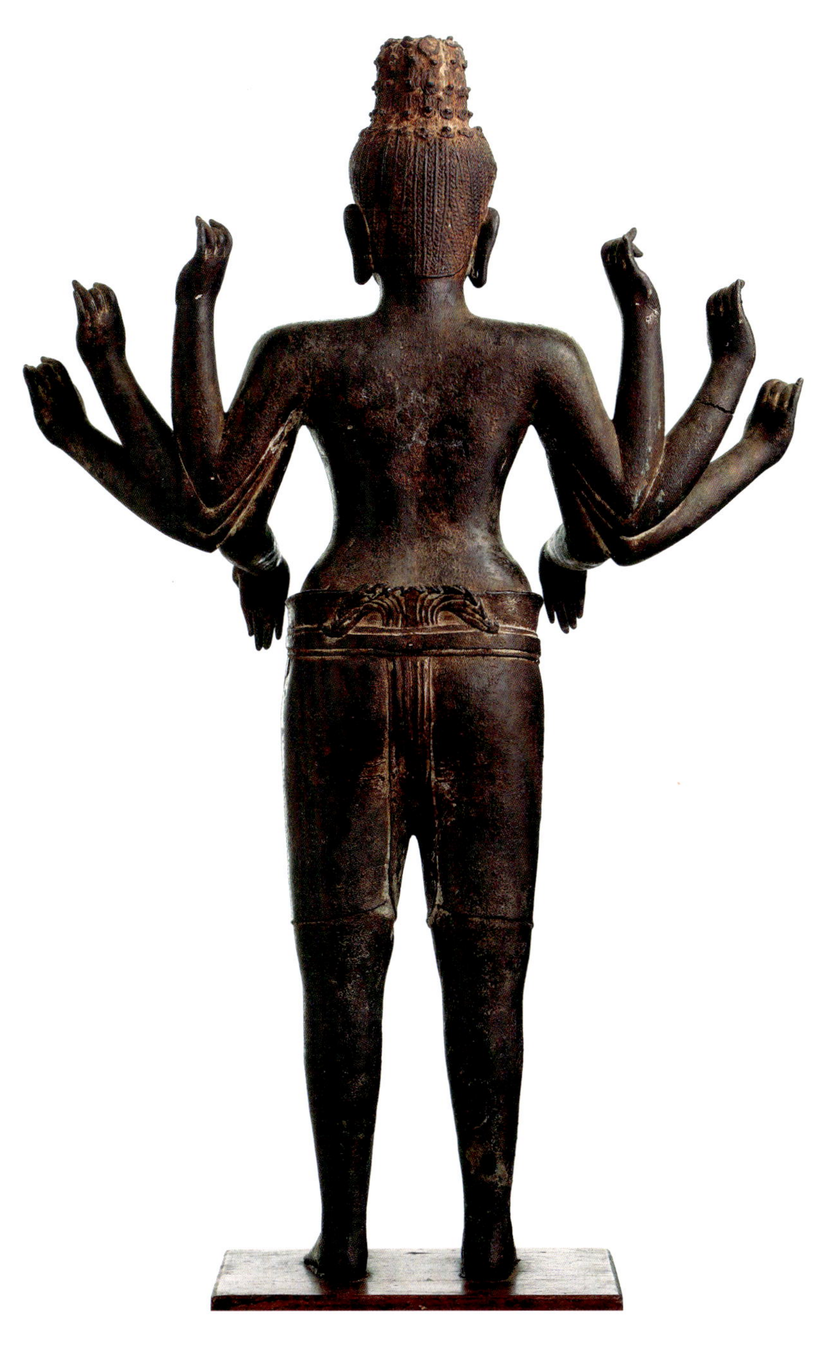

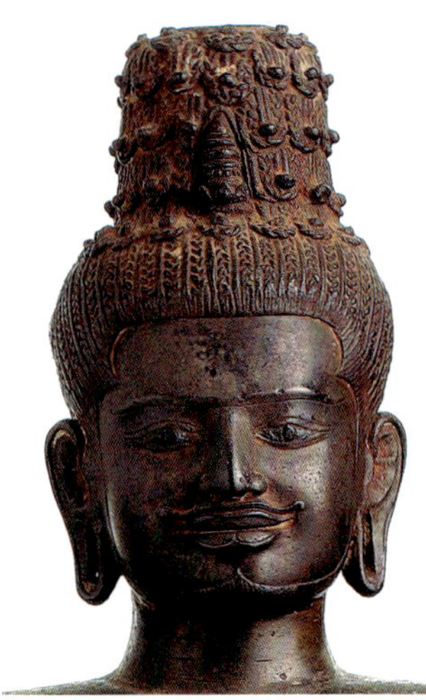

5A

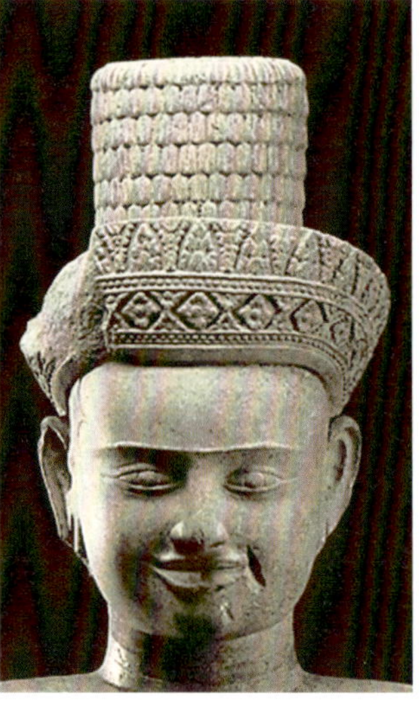

6A

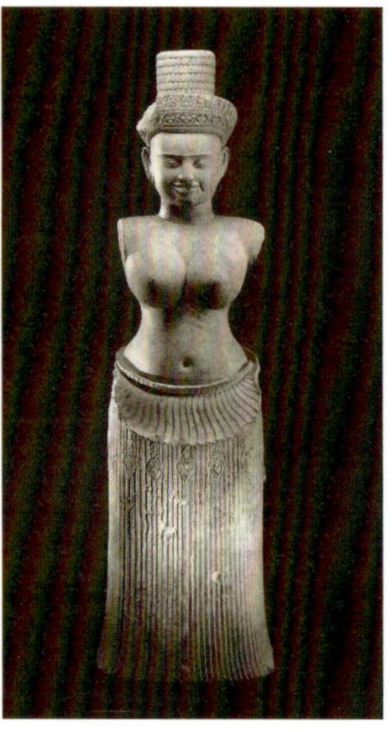

6

Even though the gender of the two figures differs, they both have coiffures of the same type, consisting of tiers of hair loops. Two specifically Buddhist features appear in the bronze. One is the presence of the miniature stupa, an emblem of Maitreya (who pays homage to the stupa-enclosed relics of his predecessor Shakyamuni, it can be said, by carrying them on his head). The other is the existence of a small pearl at the bottom of each hair loop. This feature was inherited from an earlier bronze tradition, seen in bodhisattvas belonging to the group found on Plai Bat Hill in northeastern Thailand.[4]

The faces are distinguished by gender; the Maitreya has a beard and mustache. Still, the two sets of eyebrows have nearly the same profile, although they are somewhat differently modeled; the bronze worker, shaping the brows in wax, made them thicker, and the stone carver, with his chisel, gave them a sharp edge. Despite the differences of subject matter and such nuances as the eyebrow modeling, both sculptors, working at the same time, had very similar notions of the appearance of the gods.

Cambodia and the Outside World: Influences and Inventions

In the seventh century, Chinese pilgrims visited Bodhgaya in northeastern India, the site of the Buddha's enlightenment; they found at the Mahabodhi temple an image of the Buddha flanked by two bodhisattvas, Maitreya and Avalokiteshvara.[5] Maitreya resides in Tushita Heaven, awaiting the time to descend as the future Buddha; Avalokiteshvara customarily attends the Buddha of the Western Paradise, but as an embodiment of compassion, he also has an independent existence. A key text focused on Avalokiteshvara was well known in Cambodia at the time the bronze Maitreya was cast. This was the *Kāraṇḍavyūha Sūtra*, the source of the mantra that subsequently became so popular in Tibet, *oṃ maṇi padme hūṃ*, the original meaning of which was probably, "I in the jeweled lotus," referring to lotus-propelled rebirth in the Western Paradise. A small stone image of Avalokiteshvara, which dates from this period (fig. 7), bears the text of this mantra on the reverse, and the two front arms are lowered in a gesture that alludes to the sutra's description of an act of compassion: rivers of water flow from his fingers, succoring the beings in a Buddhist purgatory, the realm of the hungry ghosts.[6] The lowered arms of the bronze Maitreya are performing a similar gesture. (The upper hands also perform a ritual gesture, thumb touching middle finger.) Among the texts of Buddhist invocations assembled in northern India in the eleventh century, none is devoted to an eight-armed Maitreya, and so quite probably he was a Cambodian invention, a counterpart to the eight-armed Avalokiteshvara. According to Mahayana Buddhists, as suffering creatures, we can be the recipients of Avalokiteshvara's compassion at any time; Maitreya's compassion, on the other hand, will be bestowed upon us in a future life, when he comes to earth.

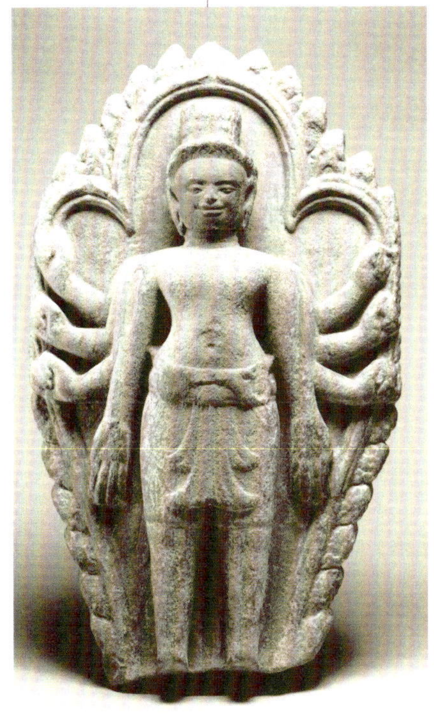

7

The garment worn by Maitreya resembles in almost every way those seen on male divinities carved from stone in this period, including the animated paired belt ends. The basic garment is a very long rectangular piece of cloth (*sampot*), wrapped around the waist, with an end folded and then pulled through the legs and tucked in at back—an adaptation of an Indian practice.[7] Sometimes, the apparently starched and pleated cloth at front represents an end of the garment; sometimes, and evidently here, it is a supplemental piece of cloth, or scarf, tucked under the belt. Variations upon this mode of dress characterize nearly all the male images of classical Angkor through the thirteenth century. The classic style, as embodied in the bronze Maitreya, had precursors in the ninth century. Anticipations of the style also can be found in the art of the sixth, seventh, and eighth centuries, in what is called the pre-Angkor period (prior not to the foundation of Angkor, circa 900, but to the establishment of the Angkor dynasty in 802). In pre-Angkorian Cambodia, the situation was more fluid, with the presence of regional styles and of a Buddhist art sometimes distinct in character. Unlike the relatively well-understood stylistic sequences of the Angkorian period, the chronology of the art of the sixth, seventh, and eighth centuries is still disputed by scholars. Seven Buddhist images in the exhibition date from this the period.

6 and 6A Lakshmi or Uma. Angkor period, early 10th century. Sandstone; 124.2 × 37.5 × 24.3 cm. Arthur M. Sackler Gallery, Smithsonian Institution, S1987.909. The sculpture is probably a product of the royal workshop during the period when Angkor first served as the capital. The bronze Maitreya (figs. 5, 5A) adheres to the same concepts of beauty.

7 Stele with Avalokiteshvara. Cambodia or Thailand, first half of the 10th century. Sandstone; 36 cm (h.). Walters Art Museum, Baltimore, gift of Yoshie Shinomoto (25.194).

This small Buddhist stele dates from approximately the same period as the sculptures in fig. 5 and fig. 6. It provides precious information about the nature of Cambodian Buddhism in the early 10th century because of an inscription on the back that quotes a famous mantra from the *Kāraṇḍavyūha Sūtra*, which is a text describing different aspects of the bodhisattva Avalokiteshvara's compassion.

The oldest images in this group are represented by two examples of the standing Buddha with his right shoulder bare. One of these (fig. 8) has been studied for decades and has been associated with stone sculpture thought to have been produced in the first half of the sixth century.[8] The stone sculptures, however, may be no older than the first quarter of the seventh century.[9] There is no question, nevertheless, that the two bronzes represent an early phase of Cambodian Buddhist art, with a graceful flexion of the legs (the right knee forward in one, the left in the other) and a forward thrust of the lower torso, akin to what can be seen in early Brahmanical stone sculpture. The right arms of both bronzes are lost, but comparison with intact examples indicates that the forearm was raised, the hand held upward, and forefinger and thumb touched in a teaching gesture (*vitarka-mudrā*). In India, the left hand would have held an end of the robe; in figure 8, the palm is just held upward, and in the second, later image (fig. 9), the hand—now freed from having to hold the robe—displays a *vitarka-mudrā*.[10]

The other five pre-Angkorian bronzes were discovered together with two Chinese Buddhist figures in Cheung Prey district, Kampong Cham province, in 2006. The group includes three images of the standing Buddha (figs. 10–12) that differ from figures 8 and 9 because of the way the robe is worn and the paired hand gestures. In the smallest of the three (fig. 11), there is an echo of the aesthetic concerns of the two oldest bronzes, in the graceful flow of the swelling contour, from chest to hips. All three images portray the Buddha standing erect, the robe covering both shoulders, the pose, including the hand gestures, rigidly symmetrical. The image type is one characteristic of the neighboring Buddhist kingdom of Dvāravatī (modern Thailand). These statues, however, are distinguished from most Dvāravatī images by the presence of diagonally slanted almond-shaped eyes (though the left eye of figure 12 reveals a hint of a Dvāravatī serpentine-outlined eye). The eyebrows are treated quite differently in the two larger bronzes—a graceful incised line crosses the bridge of the nose in figure 10, while two raised surfaces in figure 12, in keeping with the robust, very individualistic modeling of the face as a whole, suggest the hand of a sculptor with experience in working clay. Despite the differences, the sculptors' interest in the interplay between eye and eyebrow suggests that the two works were the product of the same stylistic milieu.

In addition to the three Buddhas, there are an Avalokiteshvara (generally called Lokeshvara, "the lord of the world," in Cambodian inscriptions) and a Maitreya. (figs. 13 and 14) Since they differ in size, these two bodhisattvas can be only conceptually considered a pair, like the pair at the Mahabodhi temple. In the case of the Avalokiteshvara, a comparison with a seventh-century

8 Buddha
Cambodia, pre-Angkor period, 7th century
Bronze; 27 × 11.8 × 7.7 cm
National Museum of Cambodia, Ga5412

Despite the many losses and the poor condition of the surface, it is easy to appreciate the subtlety and grace with which each part of the body flows into another. In subsequent images of the Buddha, a more rigid posture was in general preferred.

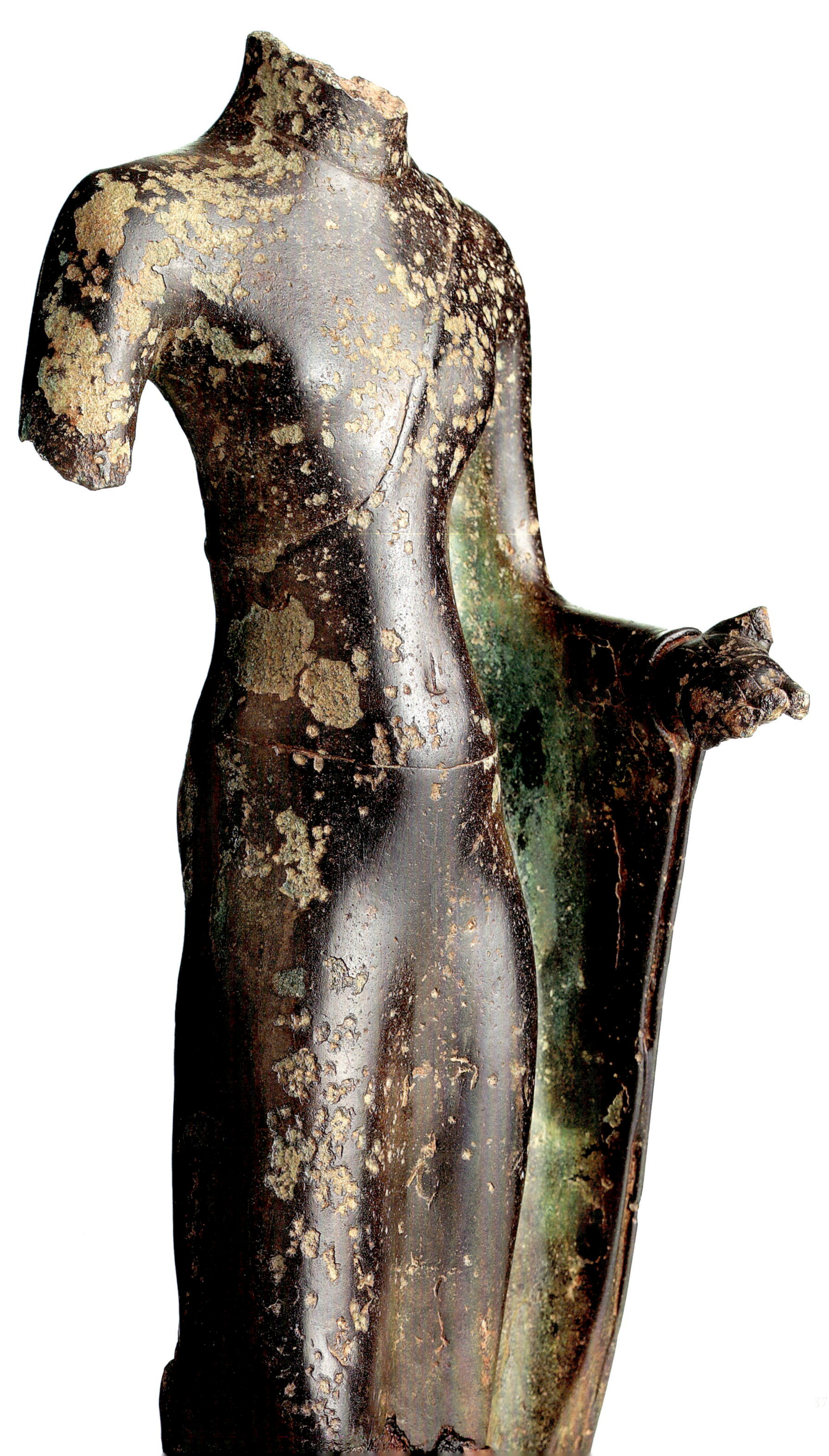

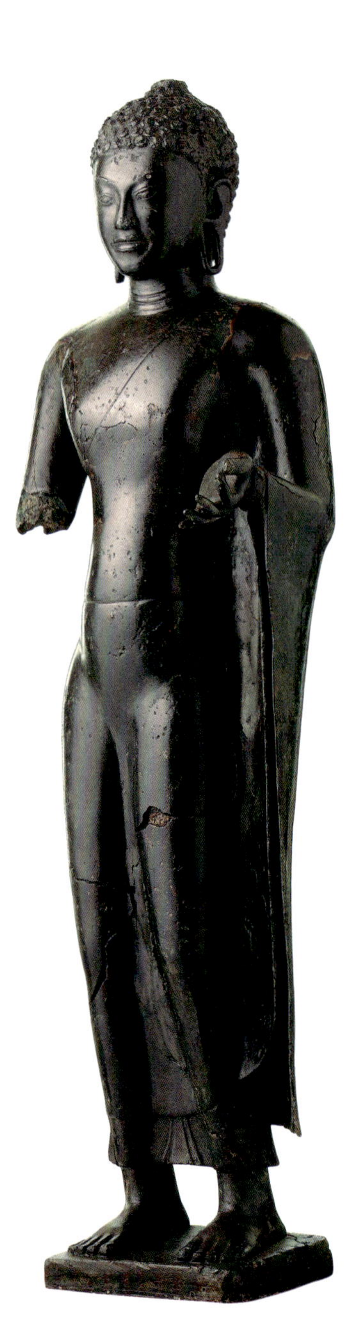

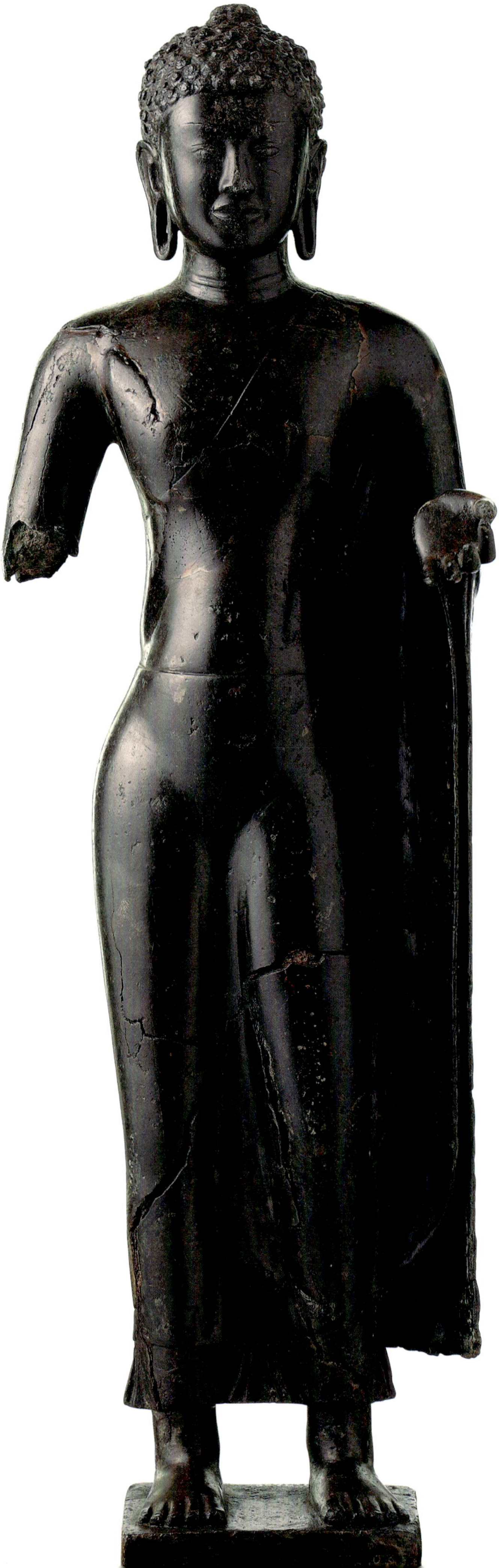

9 Buddha page 38
Cambodia, pre-Angkor period, 7th century
Bronze; 49 × 16 × 10 cm
National Museum of Cambodia, Ga5406

This image is of the same type as fig. 8, except that the left hand is shown in a teaching gesture. (The lost right hand also was held in a gesture of instruction, but with palm raised, not lowered.) No true counterparts in stone are known, suggesting the existence of an independent bronze tradition.

10 Buddha page 40; see also figs. 33 and 33A
Cambodia, pre-Angkor period, second half of the 7th century
Bronze; 39 × 11.5 × 10.5 cm (figure and base)
National Museum of Cambodia, Ga6937

11 Buddha page 41 (left); see also figs. 34 and 34A
Cambodia, pre-Angkor period, second half of the 7th century
Bronze; 14 × 5 × 3 cm
National Museum of Cambodia, Ga6938

12 Buddha page 41 (right); see also fig. 35
Cambodia, pre-Angkor period, second half of the 7th century
Bronze; 25 × 8 × 5 cm (figure and base)
National Museum of Cambodia, Ga6939

These three images of the Buddha, from a cache discovered in 2006, are of the same type: the robe is treated symmetrically, left and right (though on the wearer, the robe corners are not distributed symmetrically), and the hand gestures are identical. The type is one that developed in the Dvāravatī kingdom of neighboring Thailand. Among the three images, however, there are considerable differences of detail: in fig. 10, the eyebrows are an incised line, joining across the bridge of the nose; in fig. 12, broad eyebrows appear in low relief, and the face of the Buddha has a pronounced ethnic cast.

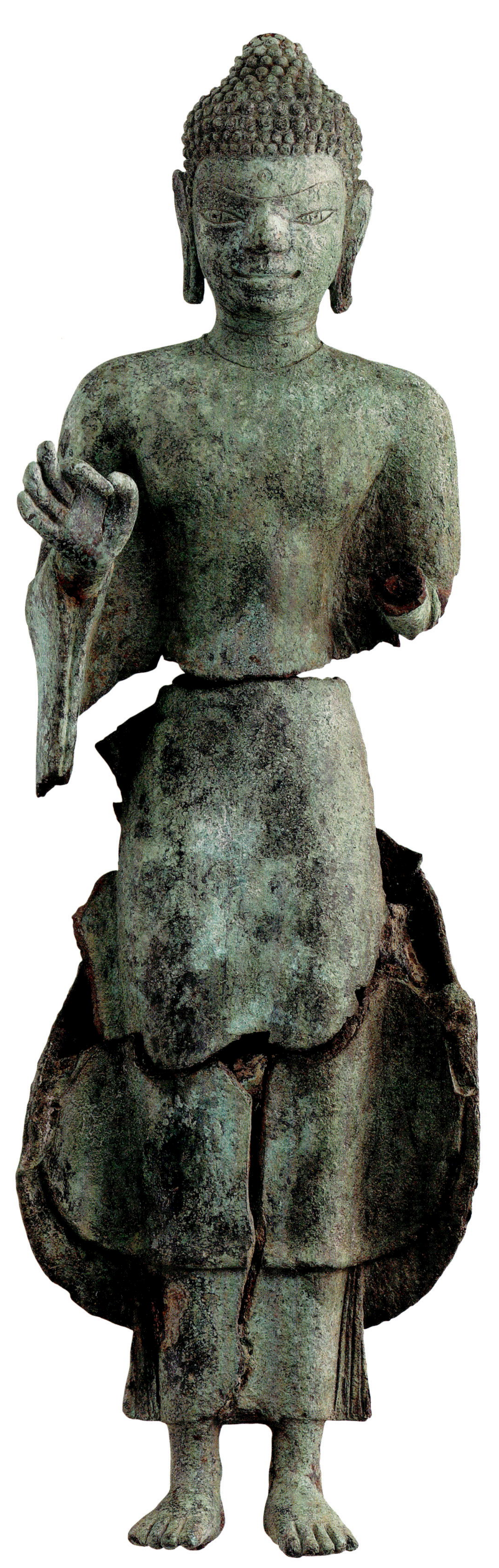

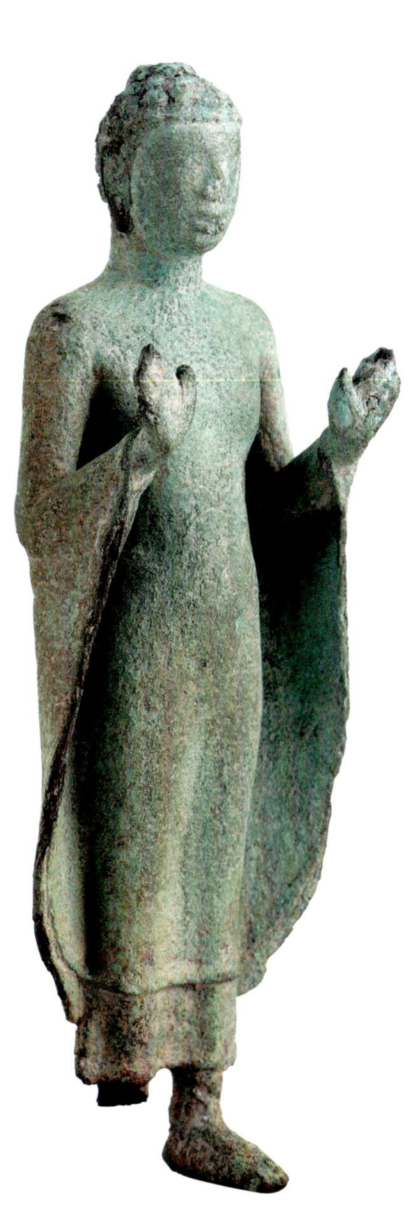

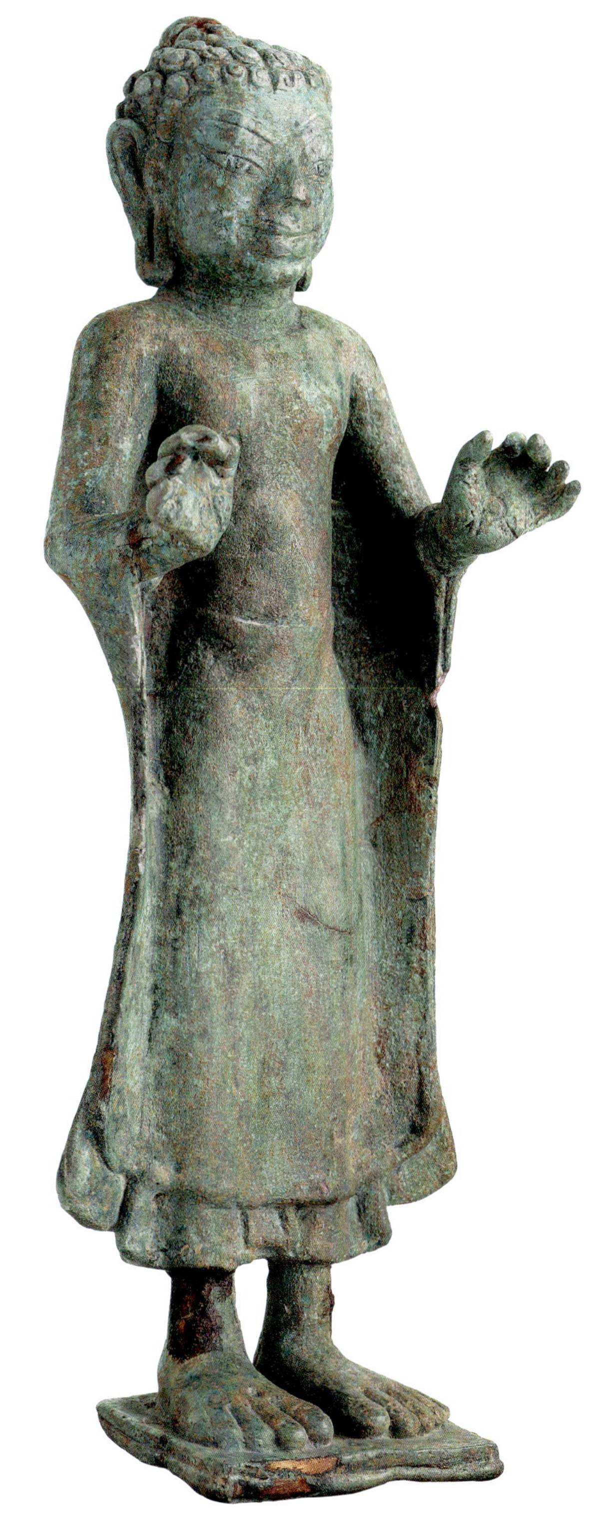

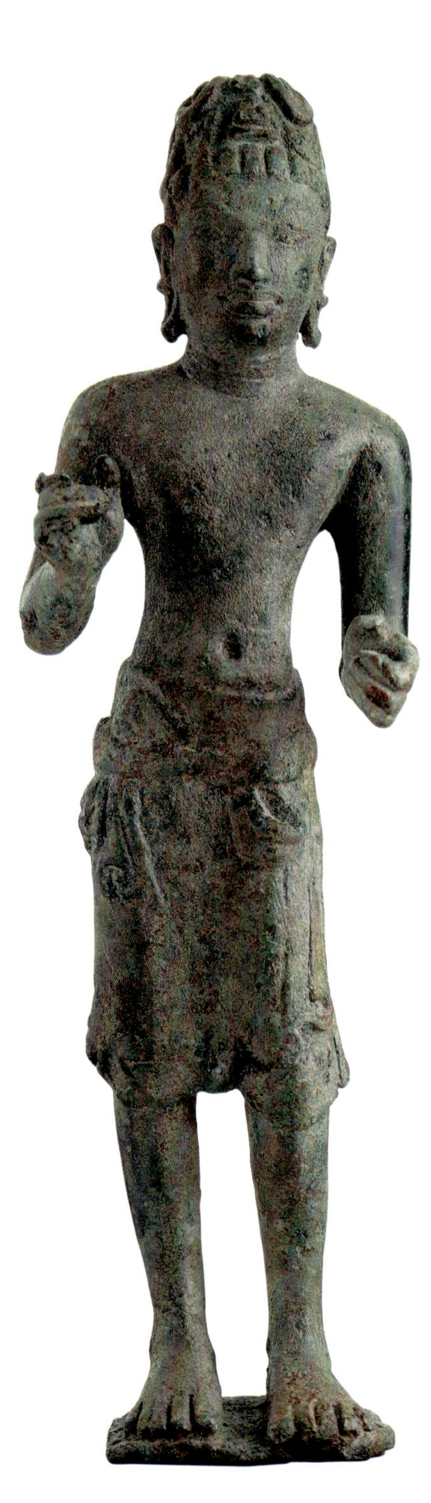

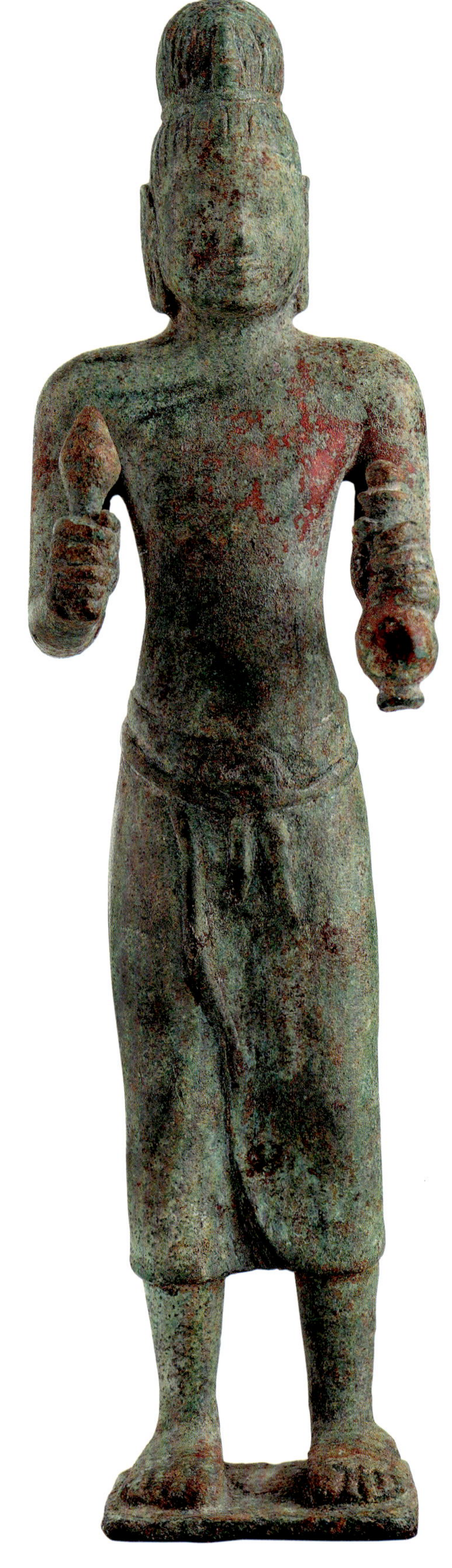

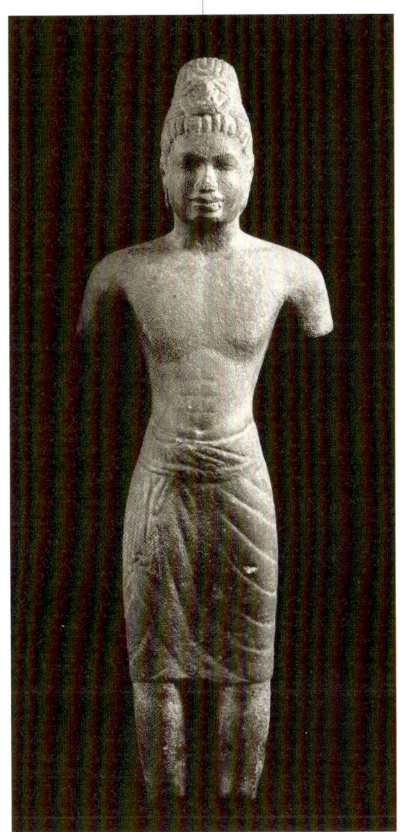

stone image can be made. The findspot of an Avalokiteshvara in the Musée Guimet (fig. 15) is not known, but the anatomical rendering of the lower part of the torso indicates origins in the workshop tradition responsible for a stone sculpture known as the Harihara of Sambor Prei Kuk, sanctuary N10, probably dating from the second quarter of the seventh century.[11] Sambor was the site of a great assembly of Brahmanical shrines, associated with King Isanavarman (reigned circa 616–after 627). The bronze Avalokiteshvara has hair loops of exactly the same type as the sculpture in Paris, as well as facial modeling characterized by rounded cheeks and by eyebrow and mouth profiles that reinforce the sense of spherical volumes. On it, too, there is a simple loincloth (not as long as the classic *sampot*), secured by a cloth belt. There is a slight sway to the torso, a feature shared with another bronze Avalokiteshvara of this period, one adorned with a diadem.[12] The greater amount of evidence for the presence of Buddhist art in the second half of the seventh century, as compared to the first half, is attested by two inscriptions, one dating from 664, the other from perhaps the last quarter of the century.[13] The latter, at the temple of Ampil Rolum (like Sambor, in Kampong Thom province), records gifts to images of the Buddha, Maitreya, and Avalokiteshvara, which probably stood in the three sanctuaries of the temple. The invocation of this triad suggests awareness of the Mahabodhi Temple images

15

13 Avalokiteshvara page 42 (left); see also fig. 37
Cambodia, pre-Angkor period, second half of the 7th century
Bronze; 13 × 3 × 2 cm
National Museum of Cambodia, Ga6941

The bodhisattva Avalokiteshvara (the lord who looks down [upon the world's suffering beings]), generally called Lokeshvara (the lord of the world) in Cambodian inscriptions, is recognizable by the presence of a small image of the Buddha in his coiffure. The simple loin cloth and the piled-up hair are those of a mountain hermit. He leans slightly to one side, and perhaps in his original setting he stood on a platform beside the Buddha, flanked on the other side by a figure of the bodhisattva Maitreya, leaning in the opposite direction.

14 Maitreya page 42 (right); see also fig. 36
Cambodia, pre-Angkor period, second half of the 7th century
Brass; 17 × 4.5 × 4 cm
National Museum of Cambodia, Ga6940

The bodhisattva Maitreya's long hair is gathered and cinched by a cord, adorned by a miniature stupa (a solid building holding, ideally, a relic of the Buddha), and he holds a lotus bud and a metal flask with a low, flaring foot. Both corrosion and plainer modeling prevent his face from possessing the liveliness of the Avalokiteshvara (fig. 13).

15 Avalokiteshvara. Cambodia, pre-Angkor period, late 7th century–early 8th century. Sandstone; 80 cm (h.), Musée Guimet, Paris (MG14885).

and, further, the presence and influence of Chinese pilgrims, who in the seventh century were visiting India and traversing the Southeast Asian sea routes in considerable numbers. There is a relatively large amount of evidence about one eminent well-traveled monk: Puṇyodaya, who was born in central India, arrived in China in 655 but, at the emperor's request, went to Southeast Asia the following year. He returned to China, but in 663 he left again (he espoused doctrines that were somewhat more esoteric than those currently in favor), this time moving to Cambodia (Zhenla).[14]

The two Chinese bronzes in the Kampong Cham discovery included a standing bodhisattva dating from the sixth century (fig. 16) and a late sixth- or seventh-century figure whose left hand holds an elongated *vajra*, a weapon (sometimes translated as "thunderbolt") carried by the bodhisattva Vajrapani in his role as protector of the Buddha. (fig. 17) Over the course of the seventh and eighth centuries, it became a ritual instrument that was used in ceremonies by advanced Buddhist practitioners. In Chinese Buddhist art, the primary function of the *vajra*-bearer was as a guardian; a pair of them appears at the edges of depictions of Buddhist assemblies and at the front corners on gilt-bronze altarpieces.[15] Only rarely might such a figure be placed on his own pedestal.[16] Does this mean that the sculpture found in Cambodia came from a multi-figure altarpiece? How did it become detached? It is tempting to assume that the bronzes were once the personal property of a religious personage, even someone like Puṇyodaya. In fact, however, almost nothing is known about what kinds of images might have been carried by individual monks journeying from one spot to another.

At any rate, the presence of these Chinese sculptures provides an occasion for thinking about the nature of "Indianized" Southeast Asia. In this very period, the second half of the seventh century, at least one learned Brahman from Chidambaram in southern India was residing in Cambodia.[17] But such

---

16 Bodhisattva page 45 (left); see also figs. 38, 38A, and 38B
China, 6th century
Bronze with traces of gilding; 9.5 × 3 × 3 cm
National Museum of Cambodia, Ga6942

In China, the standing bodhisattva with one hand raised and one lowered (a posture also assumed by the Buddha in China) sometimes can be identified as Maitreya. Chinese Buddhist pilgrims passed through Southeast Asia on their way to and from India, and Tang-dynasty potsherds found at port sites on the Malay Peninsula indicate the presence of flourishing trade. It is not surprising that Chinese religious objects made their way to Cambodia.

17 Vajra-bearing Guardian page 45 (right); see also fig. 39
China, Sui or Tang dynasty, late 6th–7th century
Bronze with traces of gilding; 15 × 6 × 3 cm
National Museum of Cambodia, Ga6943

This lively figure makes a calming gesture with his right hand and holds a cudgel (*vajra*) in his left. He originally might have been one of a pair of such figures, at the front corners of an altarpiece with a larger-scale image of the Buddha in the central position.

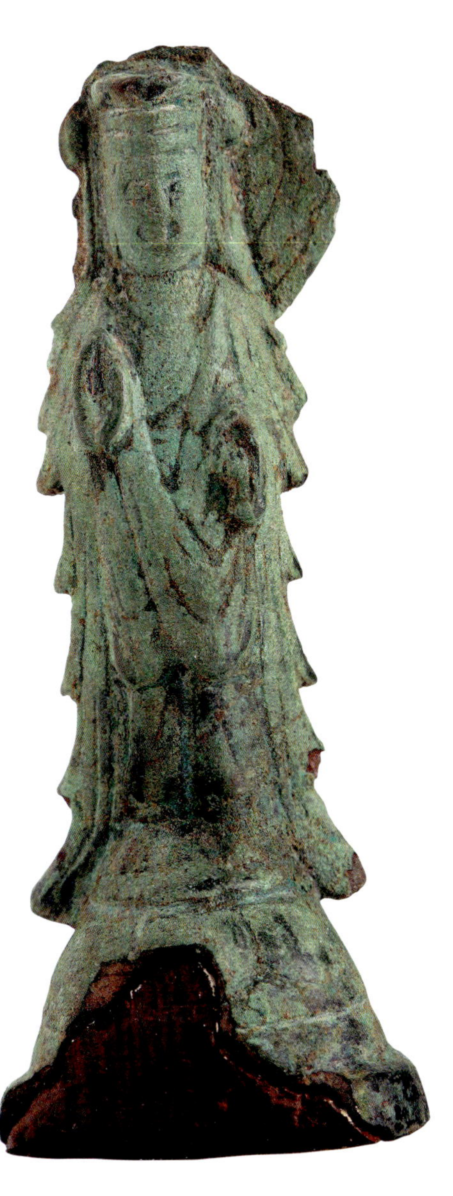

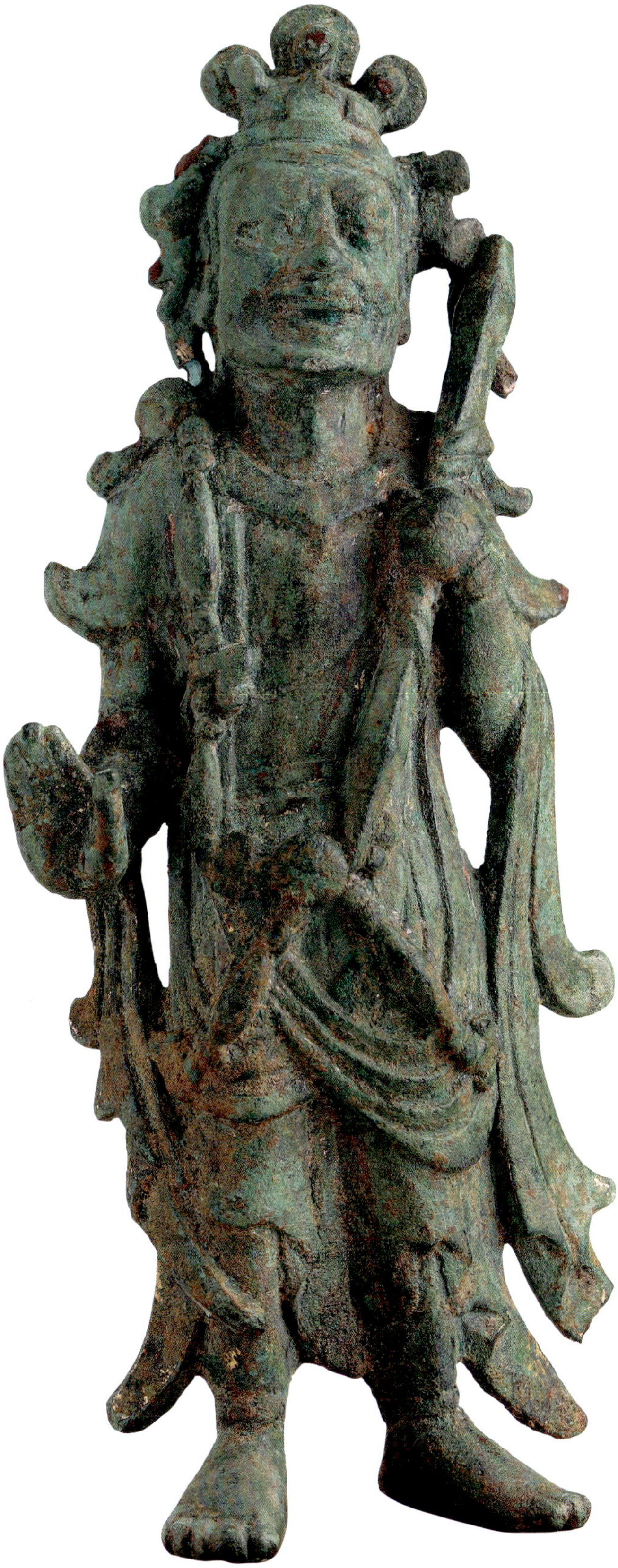

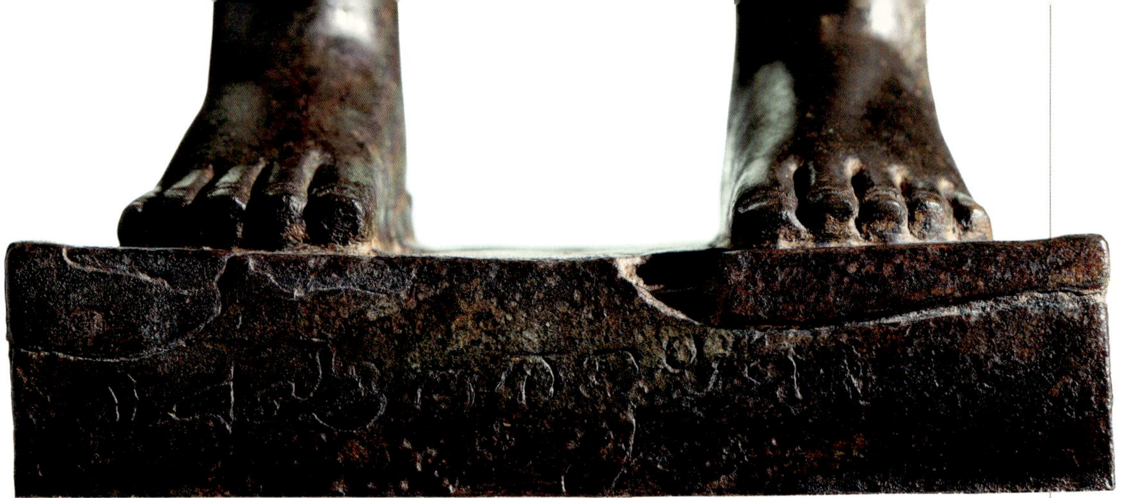

18

Brahmans—who by composing Sanskrit texts engraved in stone and sanctifying temples dedicated to the Hindu gods played an essential part in court culture—did not necessarily occupy the same niche as Buddhist monks, whose spiritual position owed nothing to a bloodline and who might have been equally revered, whether ethnically Indian, Cambodian, or Chinese. Moving back in time, the prehistoric objects in this exhibition provide evidence that the connections with the north (China) were deeper than those with the west (India). Some scholars, despairing of the tendency to overemphasize outside connections, hope to define a true Khmer identity. One of the difficulties with that approach, however, is that cultures are not fixed entities but in constant flux; their character is always the product of interactions of one sort or another, and no "true identity" is discoverable.[18]

In such a light, there should be no hesitation in making the case, for instance, that the shift in Cambodia (and Thailand) from Buddha images in which only the right hand performs a significant gesture to those in which the two hands are of equal importance was directly due to the penetration of Chinese concepts. Similarly, actual historical events might have contributed to the development of the Cambodian temple-pyramid. The earliest such pyramid is that of Ak Yom, near Angkor, which appears to date from a period in the first few decades of the eighth century.[19] One lintel there is unimaginable without the presumption of a Chinese model, with the theme of inward-facing dragons flanking a central flaming pearl.[20] Furthermore, if there is a Chinese element in the lintel, it is quite possible that there is one in the design of the monument itself. Prasat Ak Yom could have been directly inspired by the earth and heaven altars at Mount Tai, Shandong, where Emperor Xuanzong (reigned 712–56) carried out *feng* and *shan* sacrifices in 725, in a sequence of ceremonies whose participants included not only high officials but ambassadors from Asian nations, apparently including Southeast Asians. In an inscription engraved in 726, the emperor declared that he had carried out the sacrifices in order to conform with custom, and that if his sincerity touched heaven, heaven would bestow prosperity upon his people.[21] Ak Yom, situated on the plain, would have corresponded to the earth altar. Prasat Rong Chen on Mount Kulen—a plain but even larger pyramid (one hundred meters, each face of the extant base), which is considered to be later but is more-or-less impossible to date—would have been a kind of heaven altar.

The Bakheng, the pyramid temple built on a hill at the new city of Angkor around 900, housed a Shivalinga (see fig. 56), emblem of the god Shiva. Still, like the Mount Tai altar, the Bakheng was intended to bestow prosperity.

Furthermore, this may not have been the end of a relationship between Cambodian monumental pyramid temples and Chinese architecture. Jacques Dumarçay has proposed that by the time of the construction of Angkor Wat in the first half of the twelfth century, the Cambodian architects had in their heads a new model or schema, a different conceptual ideal, one that was influenced by Chinese palace architecture, with its sequences of enclosed spaces.[22] Angkor Wat's long galleries are reflections of these enclosures.

Hindu and Buddhist Images from the Tenth to Early Thirteenth Century

The second major Angkorian bronze image in this exhibition is another male divinity, also large in size. (figs. 18 and 50) Most probably it represents the bodhisattva Avalokiteshvara. The two upper arms perform the same gesture (thumb and touching middle finger) seen on the Maitreya (fig. 5) and never held attributes. It is one of the very few bronzes that is inscribed with a date, one equivalent to 970 CE.[23] This was, in fact, a period in which Buddhism had a following, and some of the evidence, like this image, comes from western Cambodia. The garment is basically similar to that of the Maitreya; the odd feature is the absence of the "pocket fold," the edge along the left thigh where the cloth has been folded over against itself.[24] Yet the character is different. While the Maitreya's sash ends have curvilinear pleats that convey something of the quality of rippling cloth, here the belt and supplementary panel ends have a degree of thickness and solidity. It is not possible to determine to what extent fashions changed (in the direction of a preference for stiffened, heavily starched fabrics) or whether the change was the product of shifts in aesthetic outlook within the stone-carving workshops (a newfound desire to make cloth seem as solid as the stone from which it is carved). Still, if about seventy years separate the two sculptures, we are looking at a conservative society.

18 Male divinity, probably Avalokiteshvara or Shiva
detail of base on page 46; see also fig. 50
Cambodia, Angkor period, 892 *śaka* (970 CE)
Bronze; 72.5 × 36 × 23 cm
National Museum of Cambodia, Ga5166

The base of this sculpture is inscribed with three numbers and three words, "In *śaka* 892, founded." In Cambodia, the standard dating system was always the Indian *śaka* era that began in 78 CE. In India, this was just one of the eras used.

19 Rishi pages 48–49
Cambodia, Angkor period, 11th century or later
Bronze with traces of leaf gilding; 18.5 × 8 × 6 cm
National Museum of Cambodia, Ga5288

The god Shiva can appear as a *rishi*, an ascetic hermit seer, and his followers in his mountain paradise include *rishi*. The figures of squatting *rishi* that occupy secondary positions in the temples at Angkor, in niches at the base of pillars, are both allusions to the hermits of Shiva's paradise and counterparts of the real-life hermits who were a part of Cambodian religious life.

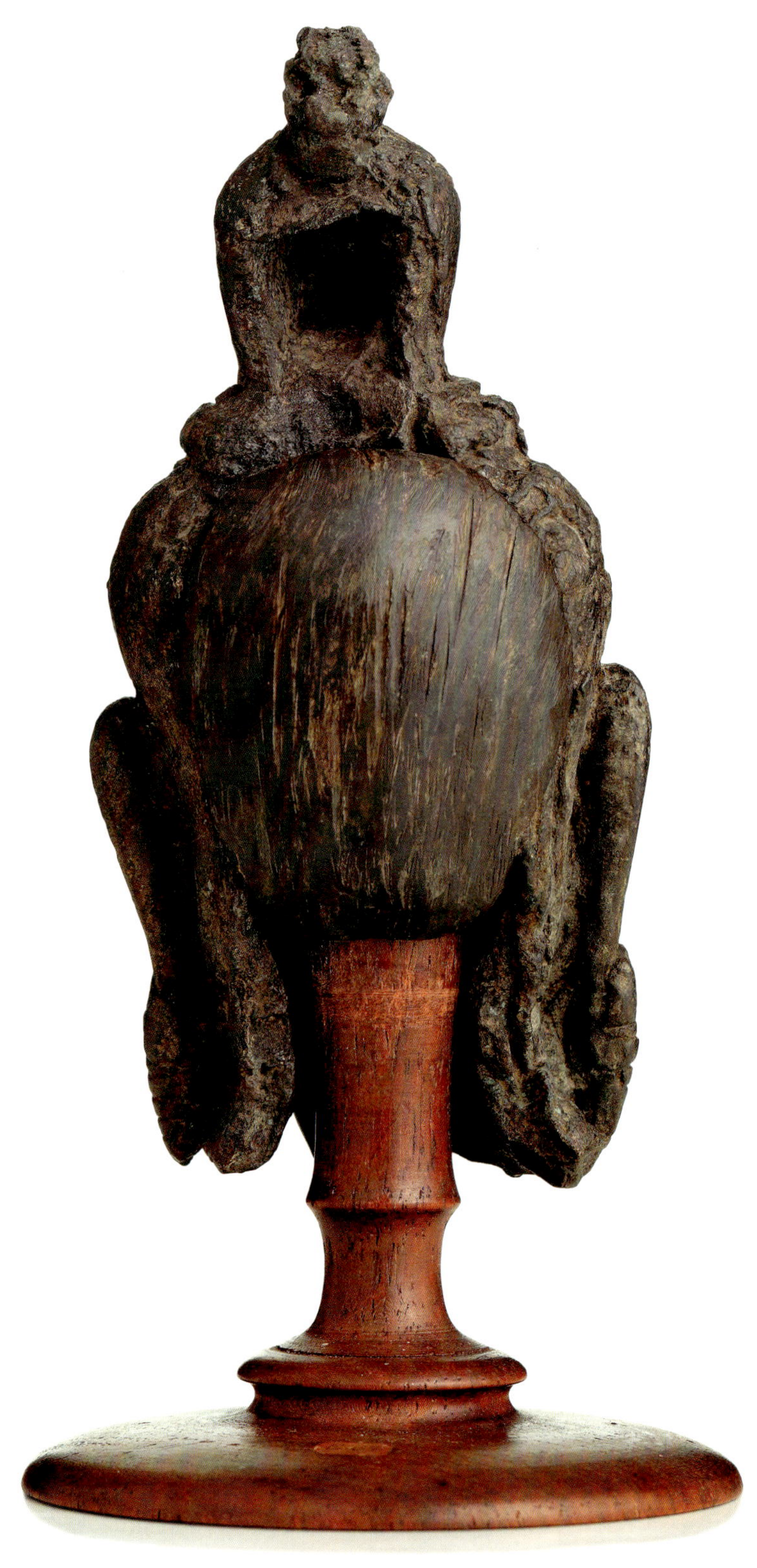

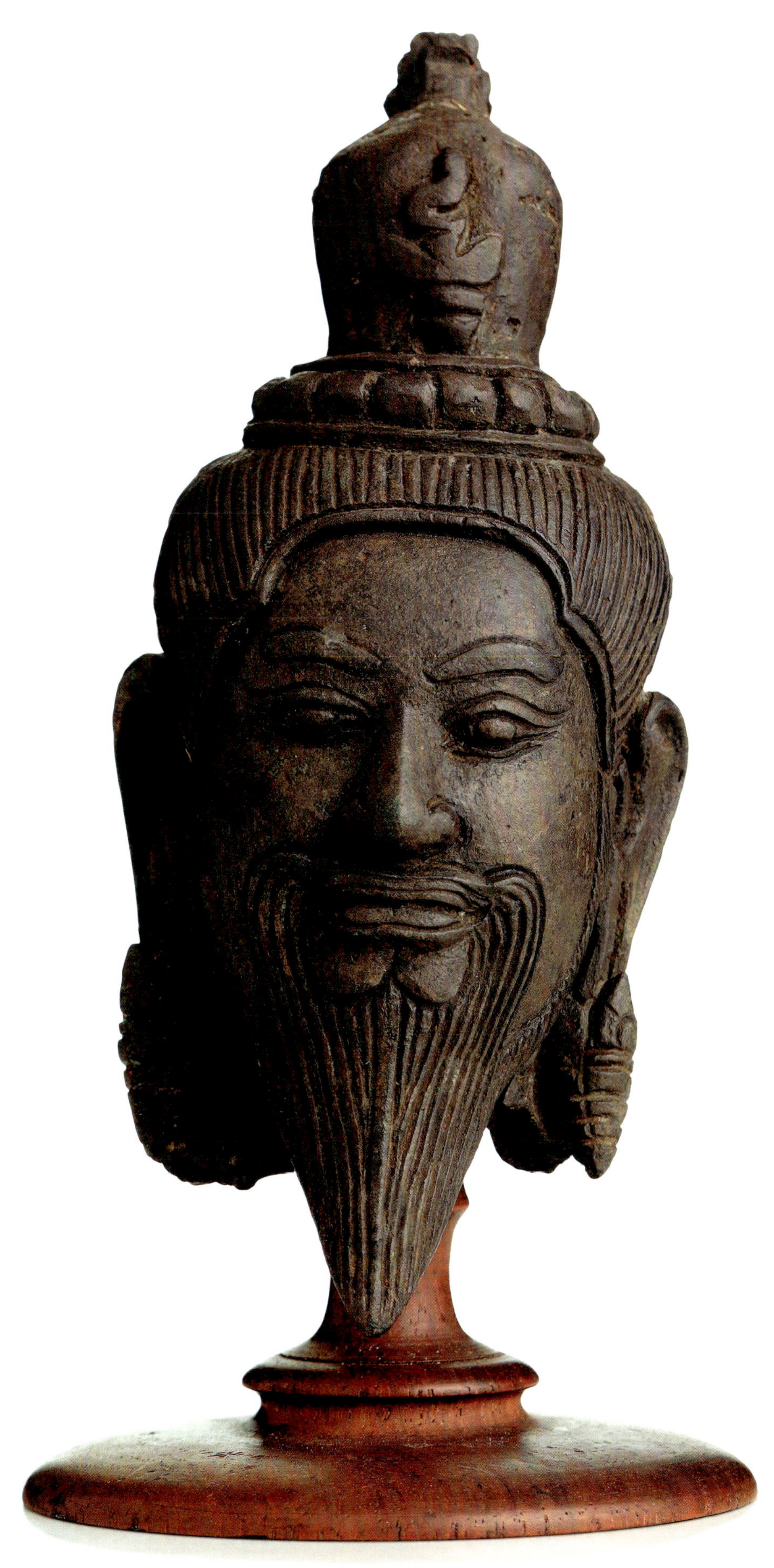

Images of the tenth century came to have something of a classic quality for Cambodians in subsequent centuries. (As the royal genealogies in the inscriptions suggest, Cambodians were well aware of history.) In the eleventh century, however, there was a reaction against the severity of the tenth-century style, and a predilection for smoother curvilinear outlines arose. One possible example (fig. 19) is the head of the seer (*rishi*). (The relative lack of finesse suggests that it could also be a work from circa 1200, imitating the earlier style.[25]) It is an interesting work because it is unfinished at the back, suggesting it was once attached to something else. In temples, cross-legged meditating *rishi* appear in high relief on antefixes or at the base of pilasters, and so perhaps this head was once part of an architectural construction like that seen in the miniature shrine (see fig. 27) but on a larger scale. Emblazoned on his gathered ascetic's hair is the syllable *oṃ*, an indication of his oneness with ultimate truth.

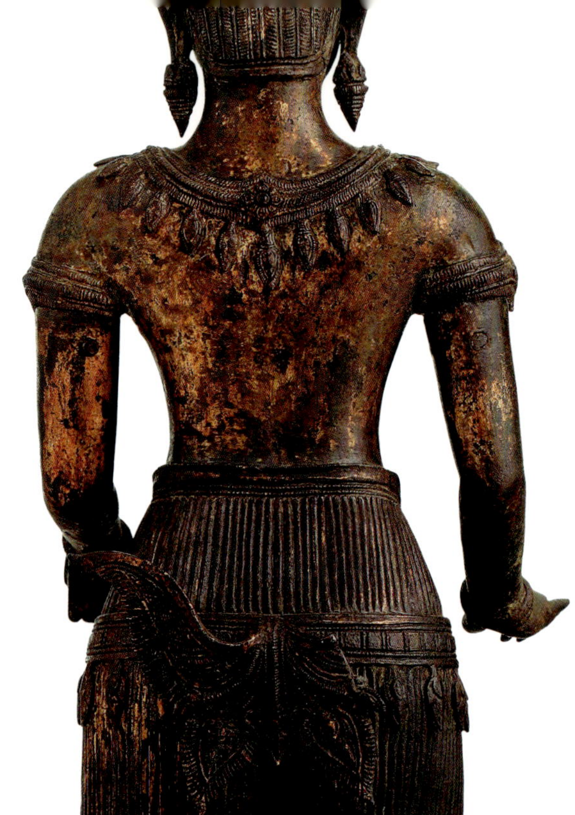

20

In the male divinity (figs. 20, 20A, and 51), instead of the severely horizontal eyebrow line of the Maitreya (see fig. 5), there are separated, curved eyebrows, and many features have a similar character, typical of the eleventh century. The garment hugs the hips (fig. 20), and its upper edge curves upward at the sides. This image belongs to a group of figures, most of which were produced in the shadow or aftermath of the most extraordinary of all the bronze sculptures of Angkor—the "Baphuon-style" reclining Vishnu (see fig. 47). Thought to have extended six meters (the head, shoulders, and right arms survive intact), the Vishnu had been established on an island in Angkor's western reservoir by King Udayadityavarman II (reigned 1050–66).[26]

Although the male divinity holds no attributes (fig. 51), identification as Shiva can be proposed on the basis of its connection to a group of related images.[27] The right hand evidently once held a removable attribute, perhaps a lotus.[28] The left hand is performing a gesture. The bronze was found at Phnom Bayang, a seventh-century hilltop temple in Takeo province, in the delta region of southern Cambodia, a site so associated with the god Shiva it was known as "Shivapura," the palace of Shiva. It could have been locally made; the Baphuon style spread to the area to the east. On the other hand, related bronzes have been found in northeastern Thailand and can be associated with the upstart Mahidharapura dynasty, which came to power in 1080, following the death of King Udayadityavarman's brother. An interest in Phnom Bayang on the part of the Mahidharapura monarch Dharanindravarman is attested by an inscription of 1107, recording the establishment of an image of Shiva at the temple.[29] That date may be a little late for the male divinity, however.

The magical syllable *oṃ*, seen on the head of the ascetic (fig. 19) and frequently associated with the god Shiva, also appears on the headdress of the Vishnu image. (fig. 21) In this case, justification is provided by a tenth-century inscription that follows the doctrines of the Pāñcarātra sect, which was present in Cambodia as early as the fifth century.[30] Different aspects of Vishnu are called by different names; for instance, the name "Vishnu" is associated

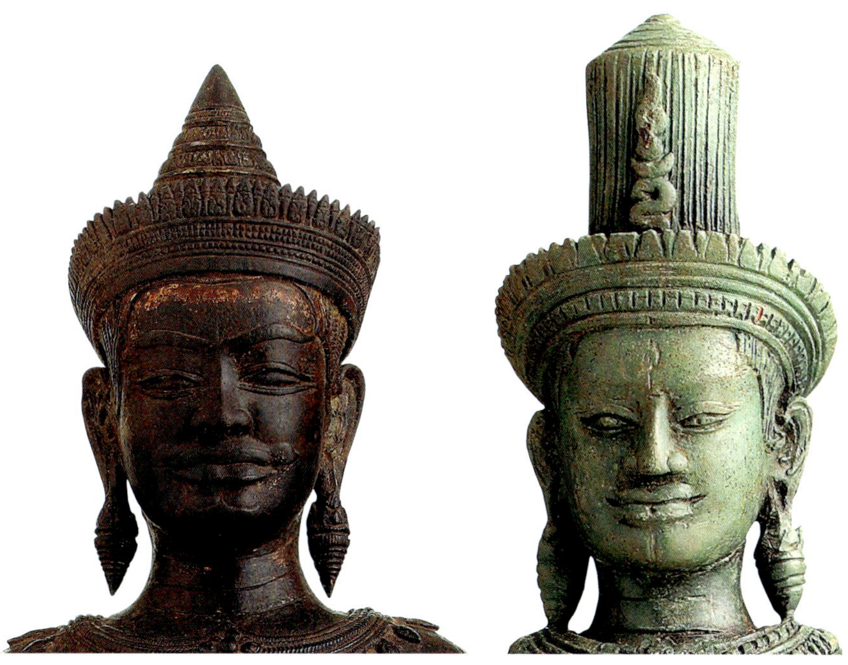

20A 21

with the god's regency over the directions of space, symbolized by the four arms bearing the discus, the earth (a small ball in the lower right palm), the conch, and the mace. The name Nārāyaṇa refers to the god as efficient cause of the evolution of not only matter but, as the syllable *oṃ*, of all the sounds of the alphabet. It has been proposed that the temple of Angkor Wat, built by Suryavarman II (reigned 1113–circa 1150) to honor the god Vishnu, embodied Pāñcarātra beliefs.[31]

20 and 20A Male divinity, probably Shiva details above; see also fig. 51
Cambodia, Angkor period, late 11th century
Gilt bronze; 57 × 16 × 17 cm
National Museum of Cambodia, Ga2993

This is one of a number of small bronze images produced in the 11th-century style epitomized by the giant reclining Vishnu installed at Angkor (fig. 47) and characterized by a graceful flow, one body part to another. Found at a center for Shiva worship in the Mekong Delta region, it may have been commissioned by a monarch of the Mahidharapura dynasty and cast elsewhere.

21 Vishnu-Vasudeva-Nārāyaṇa detail above and pages 52–53
Cambodia, Angkor period, late 11th–first half of 12th century
Bronze; 40 × 18 × 11 cm
National Museum of Cambodia, Ga5291

At Angkor, Shiva was generally considered the chief god until the reign of Suryavarman II (1113–circa 1150), builder of the temple Angkor Wat. This image may precede his reign. The arrangement of cloth at the back—presumably a separate panel, starched into the shape of what Western scholars have called a butterfly—became especially elaborate in the 11th century. The earlier example (fig. 20) was cast separately and was reattached upside down. The later example (fig. 21, pages 52–53) was cast integrally, and the sprues that made possible the flow of bronze into the furthest extensions were never removed. Very likely elaborate butterflies were reflections of the very latest in palace fashion.

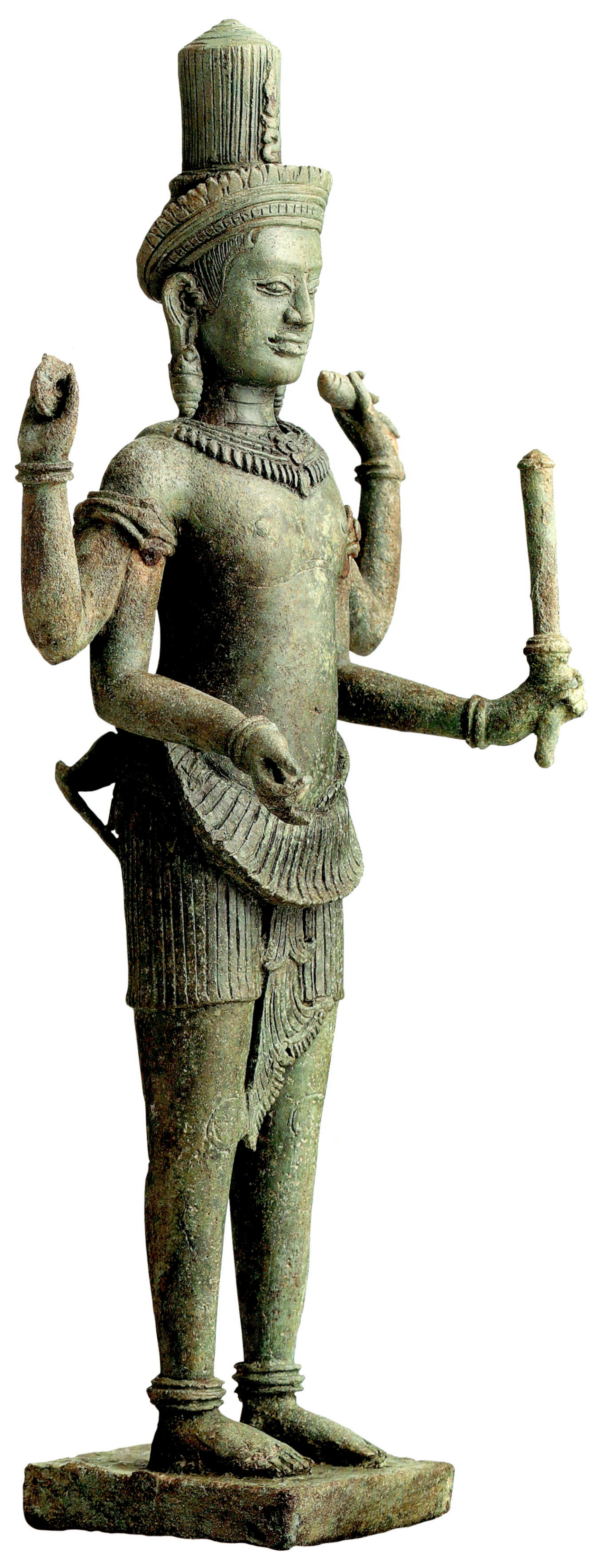

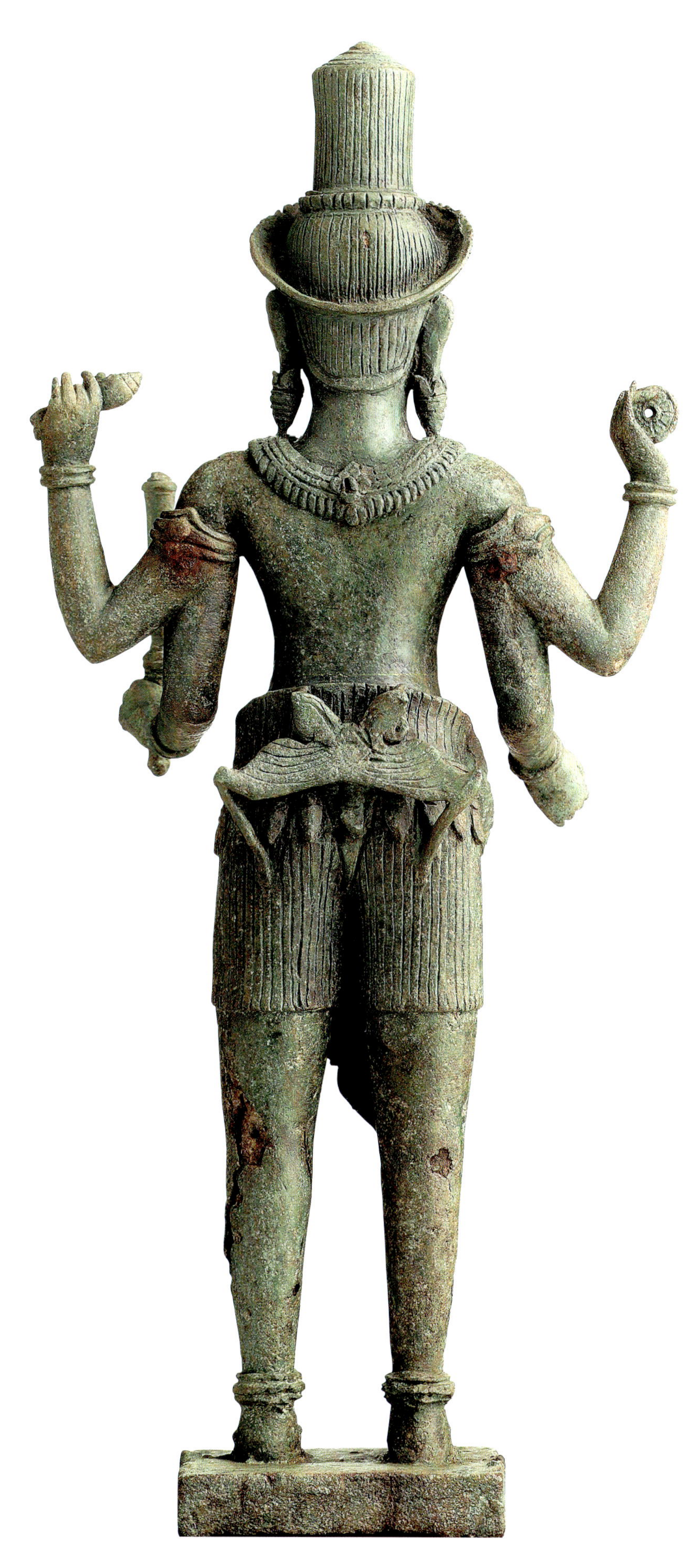

This sculpture might date from the early twelfth century, a moment when sculptors were turning away from eleventh-century ideals and back to the tenth century for inspiration. The kneeling female (fig. 44) is probably somewhat later. This exquisitely graceful and much-admired figure originally held something aloft; because of a slot in the hair that sticks up behind the crown, it probably was a thin plate of some sort, possibly a mirror. Two rather different sorts of explanation can be proposed. A group of older but comparable crouching and kneeling figures, both male and female, appear to have supported offerings.[32] Incense-burner bearers are also known.[33] Very probably all these figures served as attendants to the much larger image of a god and were stand-ins for individual donors. On the other hand, a glance at a later group of figures suggests another sort of explanation altogether. (fig. 22) In this ensemble, dancing Shivas are flanked by a pair of females who hold disks aloft. Their primary identification has not been determined, but their secret meaning may be guessed at: the disks are the sun and the moon, and the female figures stand for the side channels in the yogic anatomy, as practiced in what is called Kundalini yoga. If that is how this famous beauty is to be understood, she was originally one of a pair.

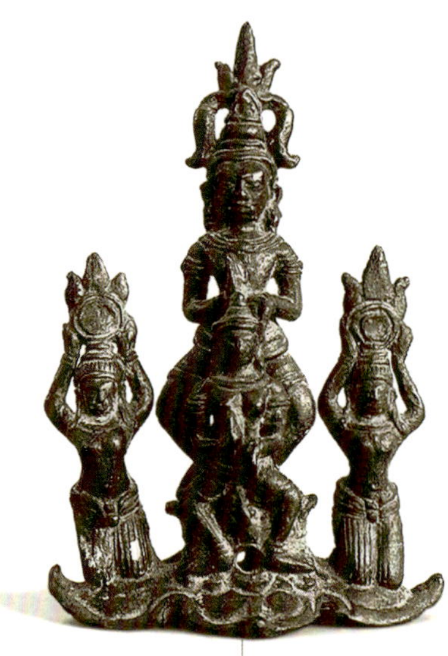

22

The Tantric Buddhist temple of Phimai, under construction in the early 1100s, presumably was overseen by adepts who professed secret doctrines passed on from master to pupil. Somewhere in the background were Buddhists of the tenth century, responsible for the bronze Maitreya (fig. 5) and knowledgeable about the *Kāraṇḍavyūha Sūtra*, a proto-Tantric text. At the temple of Bat Cum in Angkor, inscriptions from 953–60 reveal the presence of Tantric doctrines but describe a peculiar relationship between the monks and the court Brahmans: one of the responsibilities of the shaven-head monks in residence was to prevent elephants from entering the temple pond, where only high-ranking Brahmans were allowed to bathe.[34] Whether practicing monks, as we understand them, were much in evidence at Phimai is not known.

A standing crowned Buddha appears on an inner lintel at Phimai. Context suggests that he stands for victory over death.[35] During the course of the twelfth and thirteenth centuries, the standing crowned Buddha—usually in bronze, almost never stone, and so a case of an exclusive iconographic type—became a common icon, especially in the western territories (today, central Thailand) that had become part of an expanded Cambodian empire. The distribution of the type (fig. 23) indicates that it was appropriated by the followers of Theravada (or Theravada-like) Buddhism, which in the thirteenth and fourteenth centuries would become dominant at Angkor and throughout Cambodia. It was a still-not-entirely understood brand of Mahayana Buddhism, with strong Tantric elements, however, that became the state religion in the last decades of the twelfth century.[36]

Jayavarman VII came to power in 1181, and the chief religious icon became not just the Buddha but a Buddha protected by a serpent, the *nāga*. (fig. 24) This subject had entered the repertory of Cambodian art in the tenth century, and no text survives that gives it a name or explains its significance. Biographies of the Buddha state that following his enlightenment, he was protected for a week from a storm by the *nāga* Mucalinda; but even in southern India, where the *nāga*-protected Buddha first appears, there is little indication that the subject is specifically biographical. Instead, especially in Cambodia, the broadest significance possible should be awarded to the serpent, as the spirit of the irrigating waters. But more specific interpretations have been made: perhaps the *nāga*, as in the *nāga* railings of the Angkor temples, and like the Chinese dragon, is a rainbow-like means of conveyance to heaven; or perhaps there is a secret meaning, and the *nāga* lies inside the body of the Tantric adept, who achieves enlightenment by focusing on a serpent-like energy that flows through psychic centers within

22 Ensemble with images of the dancing Shiva, flanked by a pair of kneeling females holding disks over their heads. Cambodia, Angkor period, second half of the 12th century. Metal alloy; 15.3 cm (h.). Bangkok National Museum. The flanking figures hold disks or mirrors over their heads, but their meaning is enigmatic.

23 Crowned Buddha pages 56–57
Cambodia, Angkor period, 12th century
Bronze; 79.5 × 25 × 16.5 cm
National Museum of Cambodia, Ga2081

Regardless of where this image of the Buddha was made, the somewhat elongated face indicates a connection with the styles of Cambodia's far-western territories and the city of Lopburi, in modern Thailand, which was actually independent for a period between the death of Suryavarman II in the 1150s and the accession of Jayavarman VII in 1181. Above the forehead is a hair line, a bit of striated hair, and then the lower edge of the crown—an uncommon configuration seen in the depiction of Suryavarman II in the bas-reliefs of the southern gallery at the temple of Angkor Wat.

24 Crowned nāga-protected Buddha pages 58–59
Cambodia, Angkor period, second half of 12th century
Bronze; 71 × 31.5 × 18 cm
National Museum of Cambodia, Ga5986

Perhaps as early as the 10th century, the Buddha protected by the *nāga* (serpent) had become for the Khmer the way the supreme cosmic Buddha manifested himself. This image is in the stylistic tradition of the Angkor Wat style (first half of the 12th century), but the scale of the jewelry, the presence of rosette-like elements on the crown, and the animated outlines of the facial features suggest a date in the third quarter of the 12th century or in the early years of the reign of Jayavarman VII (1181–circa 1218).

25 Nāga-protected Buddha with Avalokiteshvara and Prajñāpāramitā
pages 60–61
Cambodia, Angkor period, late 12th–early 13th century
Bronze with mercury gilding; 54.5 × 40 × 15 cm
National Museum of Cambodia, Ga5470 and Ga2424

No later than the 1180s, it seems, a stylistic revolution occurred at Angkor. The new facial types were fleshier and more naturalistic, as if the king saw divinity in his own physiognomy. In precisely the same time period, interestingly, there was a revival of naturalistic Buddhist portrait sculpture in Japan, and painted portraits of monks became increasingly popular in Tibet.

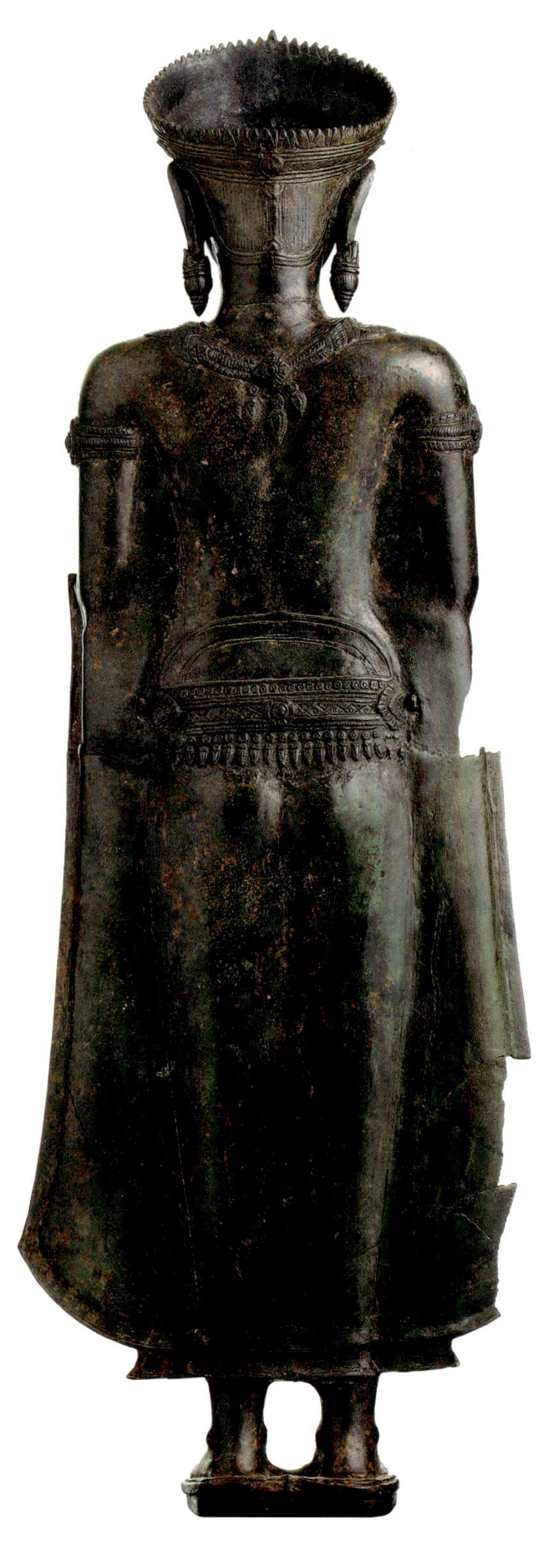

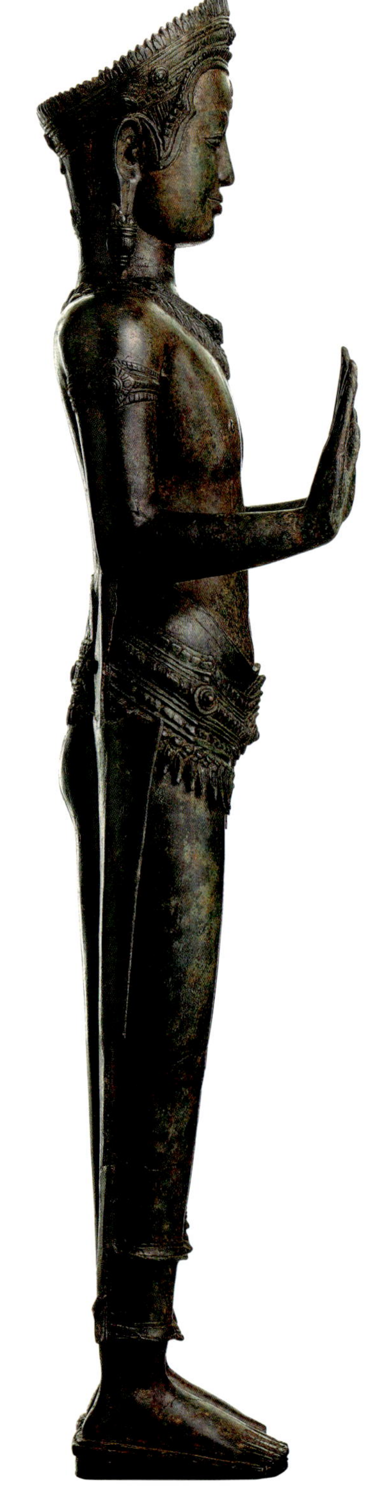

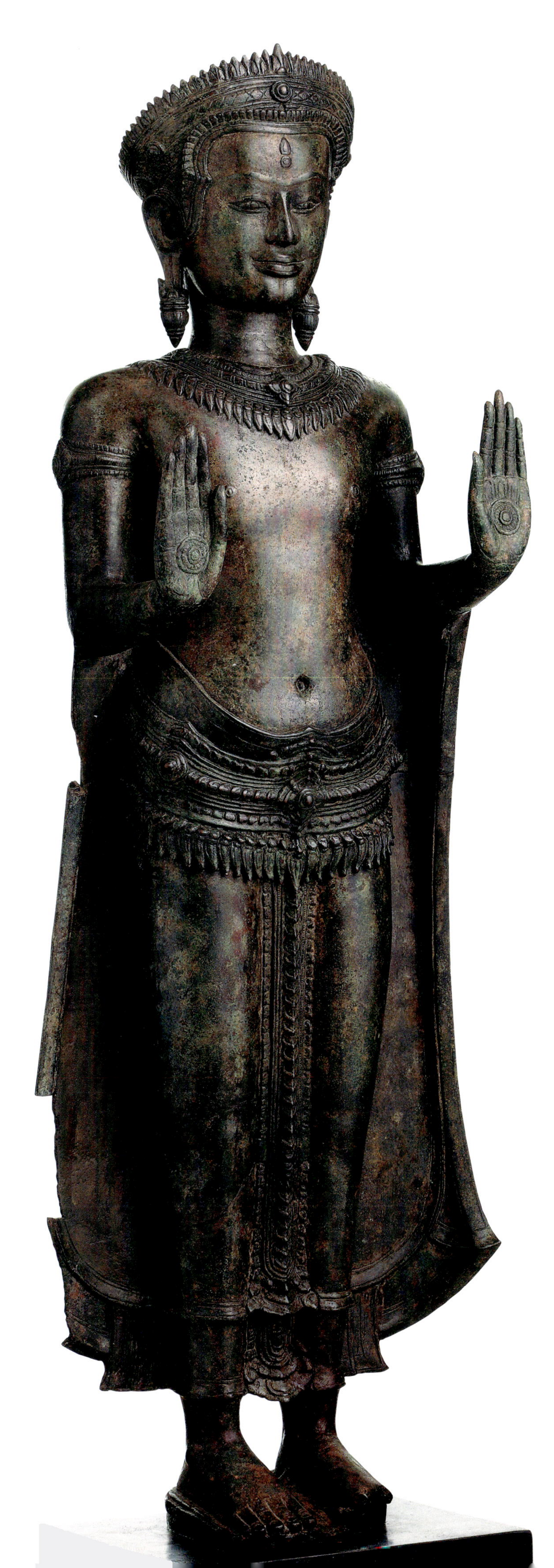

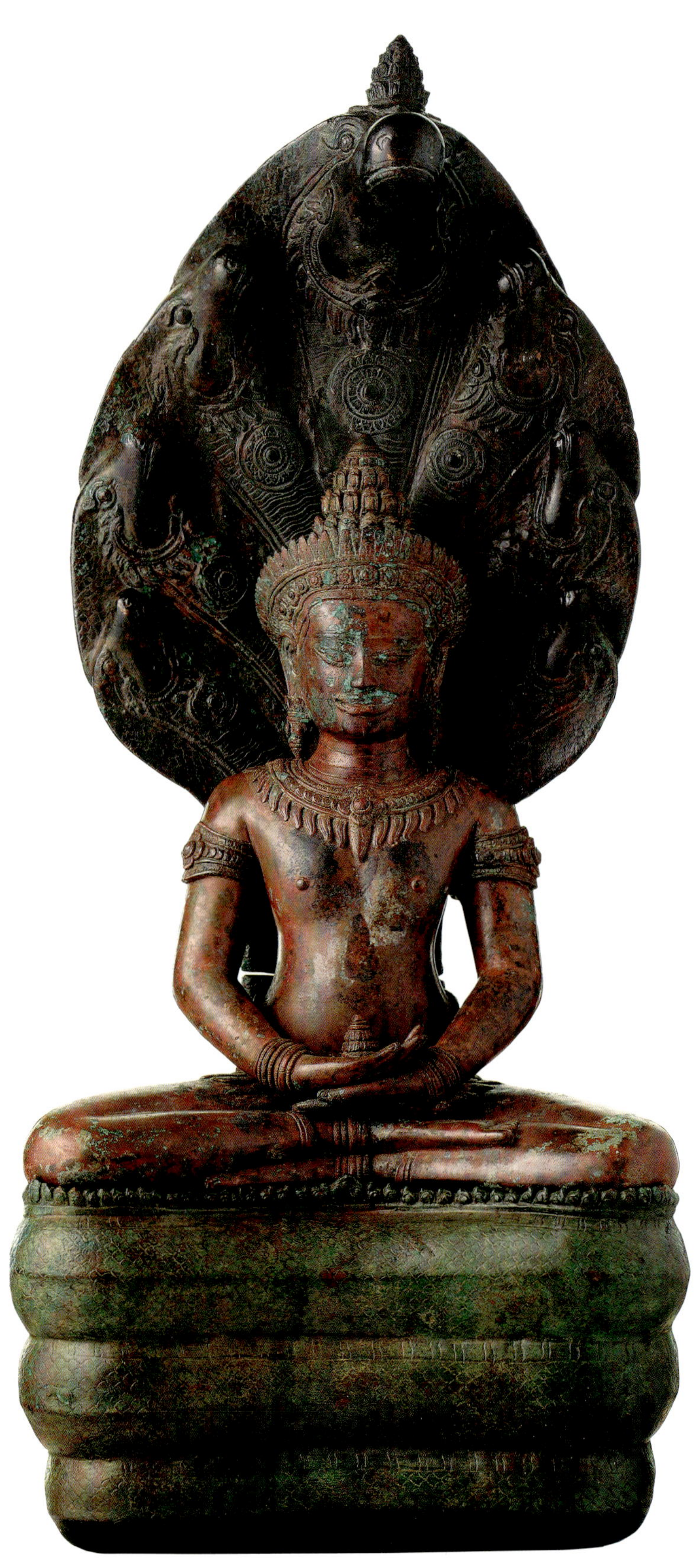

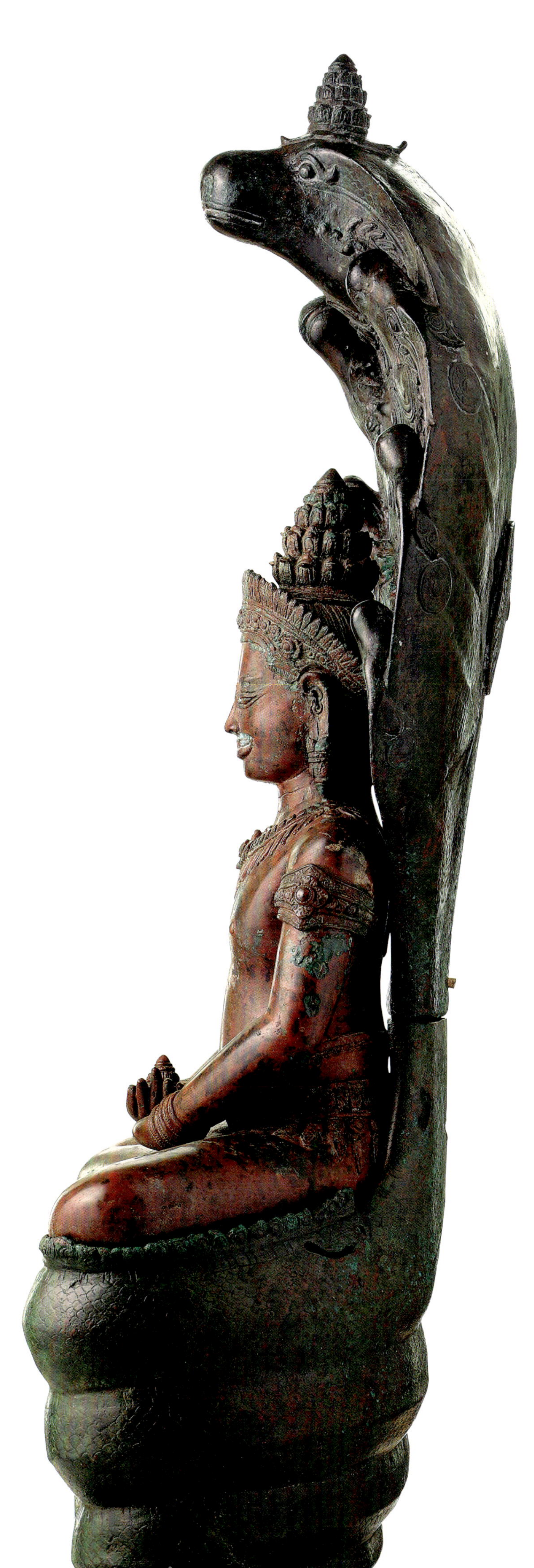

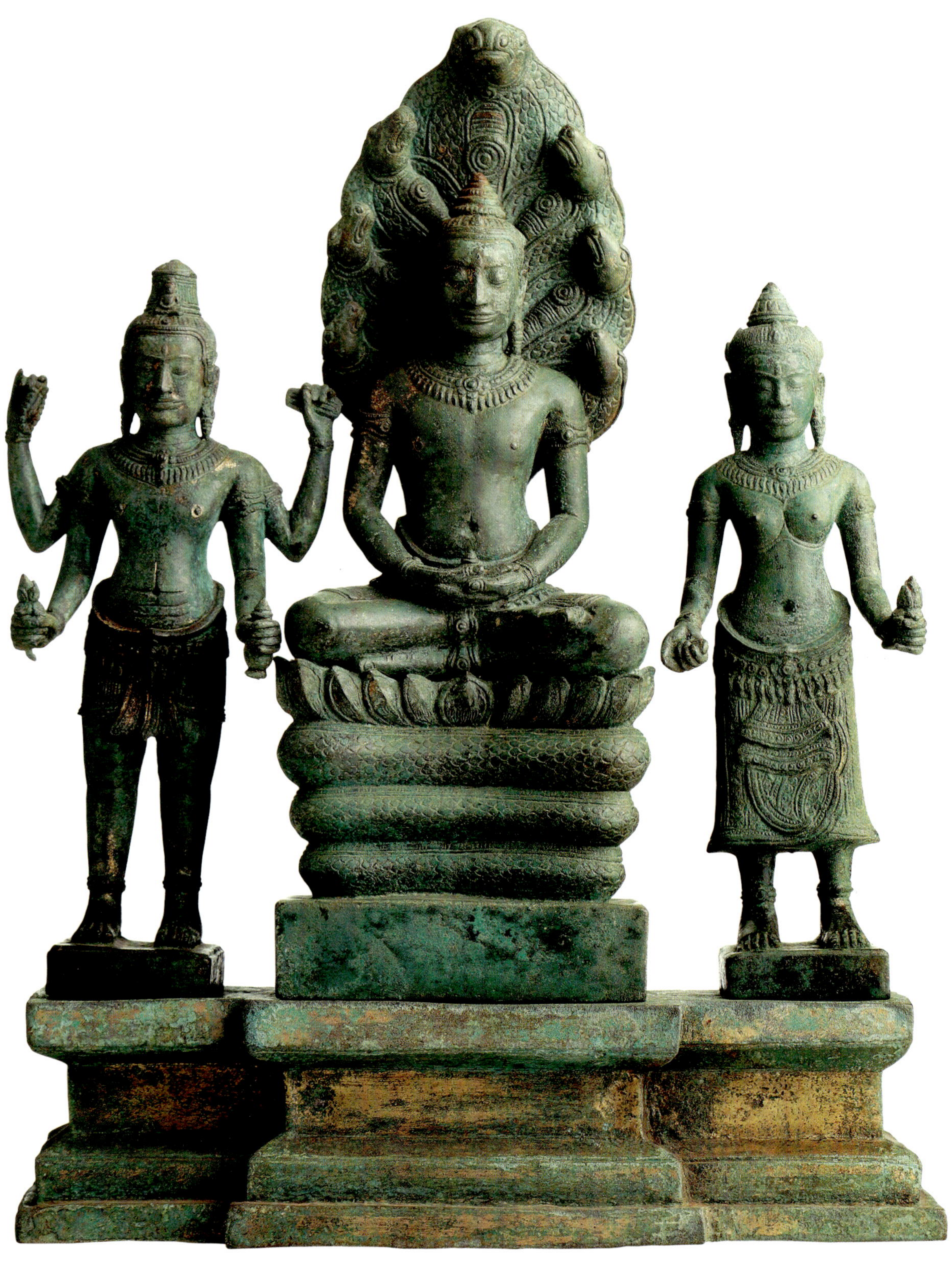

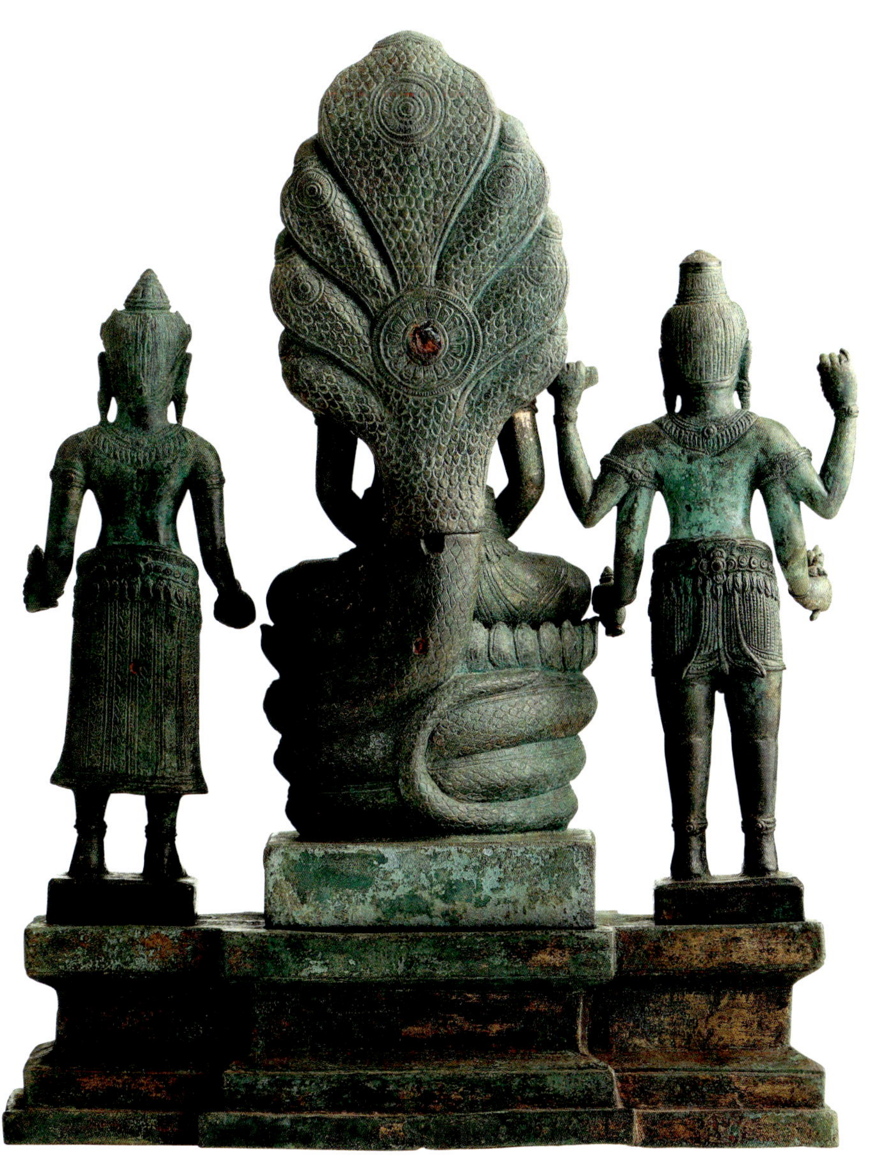

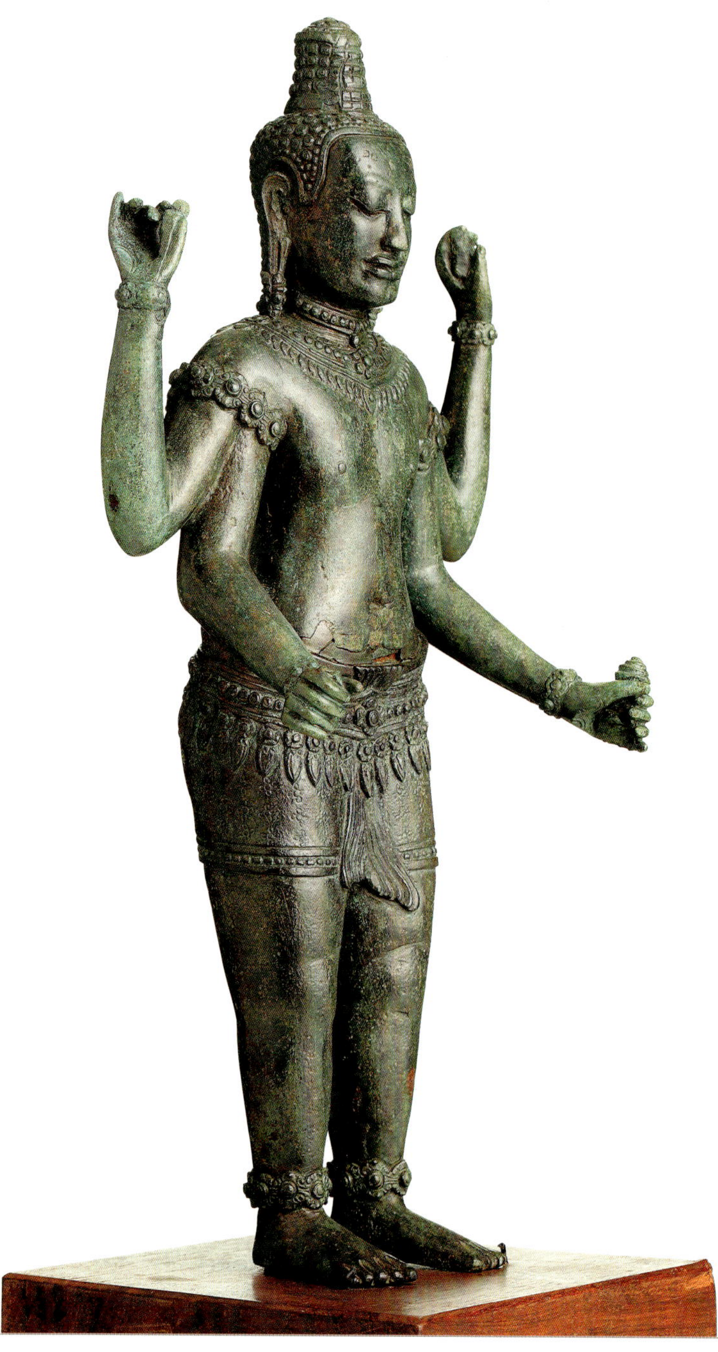

26

the trunk.[37] In addition, this Buddha wears a crown, in accordance with the belief that true enlightenment did not occur under the *bodhi* tree at Bodhgaya but in heaven, in a coronation by cosmic Buddhas. He also holds an object in his lap, perhaps a jeweled container that alludes to the supreme Buddha's role as Medicine Buddha (Bhaisajyaguru), a cult that inspired Jayavarman's creation of hospitals throughout his kingdom in 1186.

In Jayavarman's religious system, this *nāga*-protected Buddha was flanked by two Buddhist deities, Avalokiteshvara and Prajñāpāramitā (the Perfection of Wisdom)—one standing for the great compassion, the other for the understanding of the nature of reality, which together engender Buddhahood. (figs. 25, 26) Furthermore, Jayavarman commemorated his father with an image of Avalokiteshvara and his mother with one of Prajñāpāramitā, putting himself, by implication, in the position of the Buddha. There are differences between the three figures of this triad and the crowned *nāga*-protected Buddha. (fig. 24) The facial modeling of the crowned Buddha is very much in the tradition of earlier works like the Vishnu (fig. 21) and the kneeling figure (fig. 44); indeed, some scholars place it in this earlier period. But in the triad, the faces are no longer animated by such elements as the curve of an eyelid; instead, the lids are lowered, and the faces are modeled in such a way as to suggest an element of portraiture. In fact, the appearance of the king is known both from the reliefs of his main state temple, the Bayon, and from portrait sculptures, and he had features that are reflected in the physiognomy of the Buddha and the Avalokiteshvara of the triad. The absence of a crown also should be noted. Either these developments were entirely internal, and can be credited to the overbearing personality of the monarch, or else new doctrines were introduced that encouraged both the king to stress a newfound humanity and the sculptors to create a new style.

Meanwhile, specifically esoteric elements, such as those present at Phimai, were also a part of the religious system of Jayavarman VII. In this exhibition, a votive tablet mold (fig. 28) featuring the Tantric deity Hevajra provides

26 Avalokiteshvara pages 62, 64–65
Cambodia, Angkor period, late 12th–early 13th century
Bronze; 42 × 20 × 13 cm
National Museum of Cambodia, Ga5340

Although Avalokiteshvara—in his role as savior—was the subject of an independent cult, it is also possible that this image stood on a platform, like that in fig. 25, and was one member of a triad.

27 Miniature shrine with Hevajra in a circle of yoginīs
pages 66–67; see also fig. 58
Cambodia, Angkor period, late 12th–early 13th century
Gilded bronze; 20 × 16 × 16 cm
National Museum of Cambodia, Ga2494

This exhibition brings together three different manifestations of the Tantric Buddhist deity Hevajra in his circle of eight *yoginīs*, dancing female partners—in a small shrine, in a votive tablet mold (fig. 28), and on a ritual conch shell (see fig. 56). In Nepal and Tibet, Hevajra is also shown embracing a female goddess—a feature almost never encountered in Cambodia. Philosophically, Hevajra and his partners stand for the same qualities embodied in the triads: male "means" (benevolent magical projection) coupled with female "wisdom" (correct understanding). But the techniques of the Hevajra path were passed down in secret from master to pupil.

28 Votive tablet mold with Hevajra shrine and feline handle pages 68–69
Cambodia, Angkor period, late 12th–early 13th century
Bronze; 22 × 12 × 9 cm
National Museum of Cambodia, Ga5653

Votive tablets were made all over the Buddhist world; they were a way to produce multiple images and to pile up a fund of merit for the donor. "Stamped images" might be a better term (they need not have been made to fulfill a vow, and, although portable, they had no direct connection with pilgrimage).

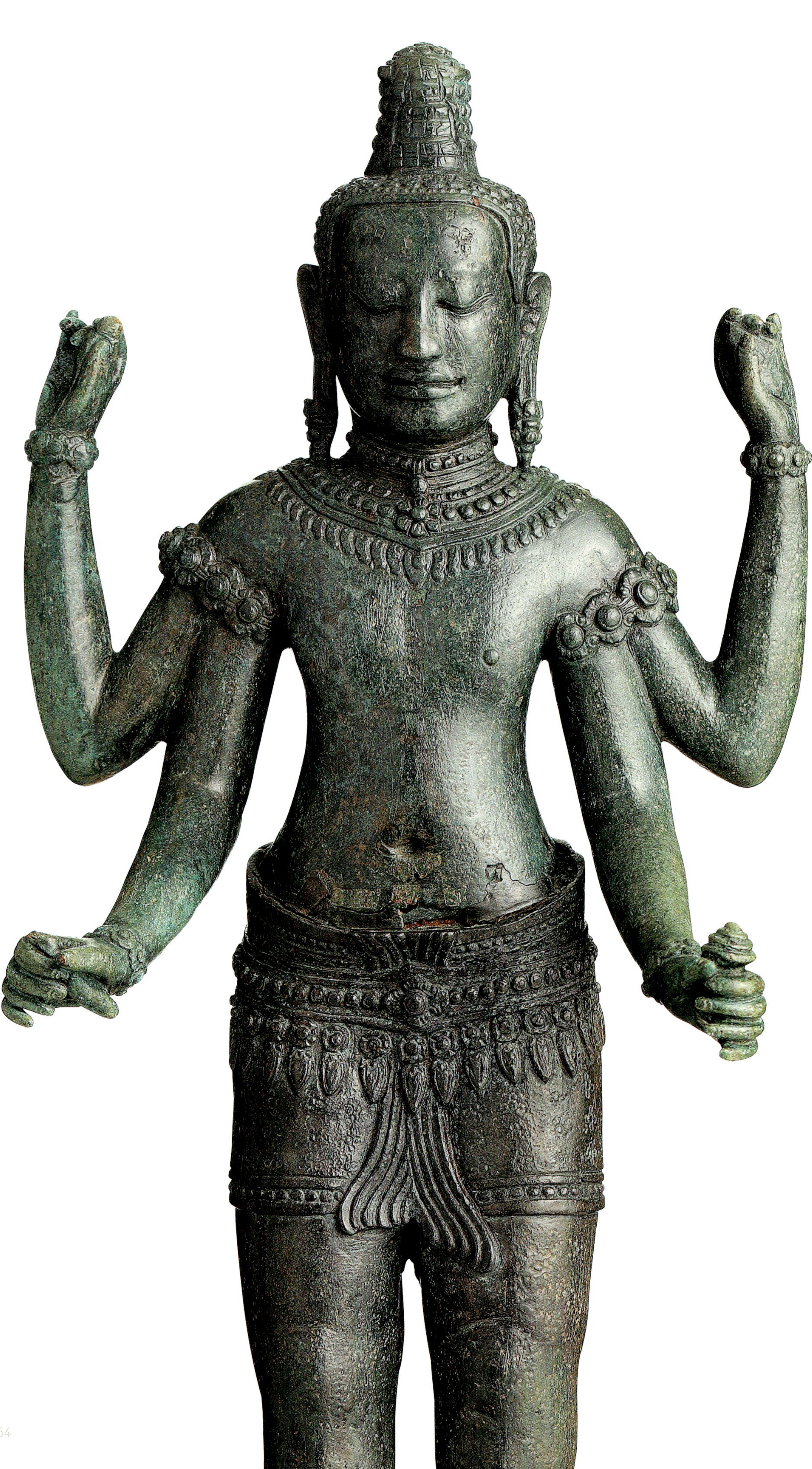

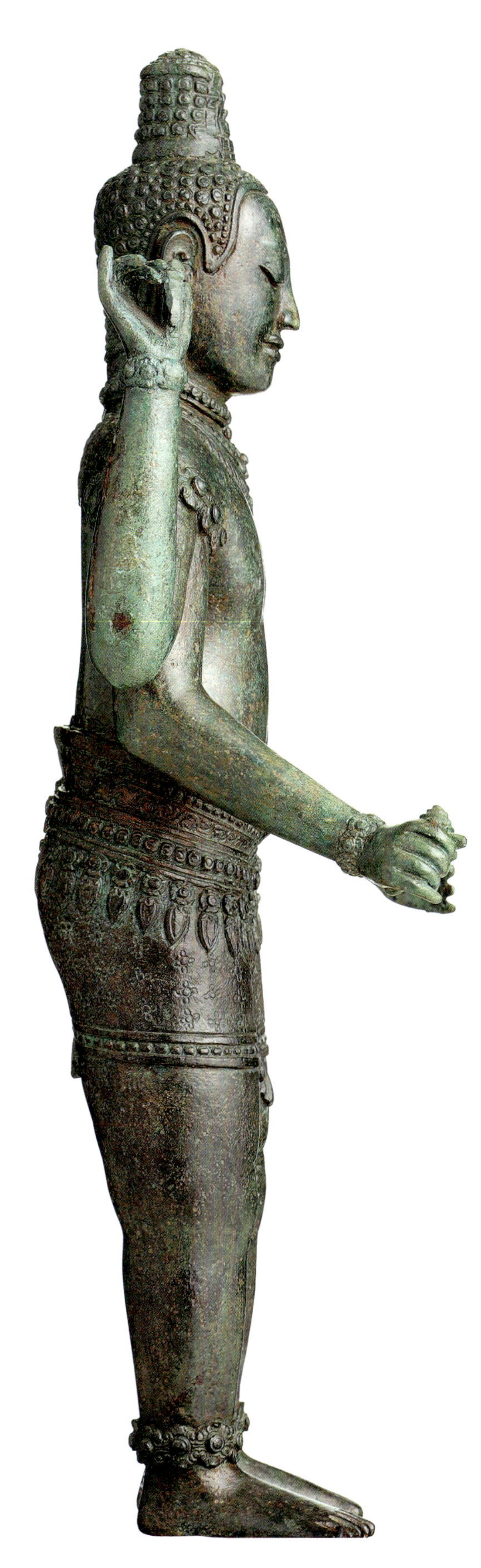

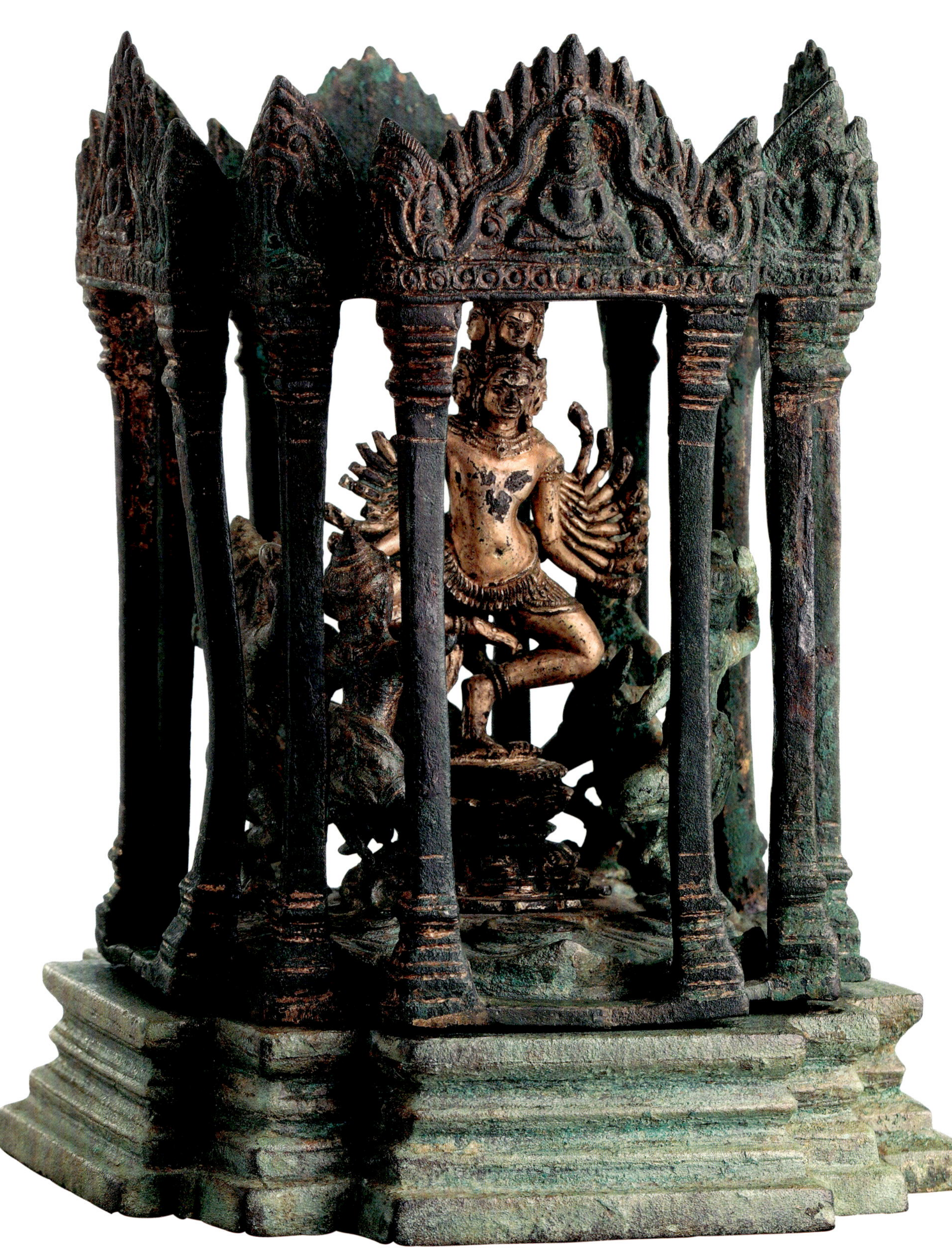

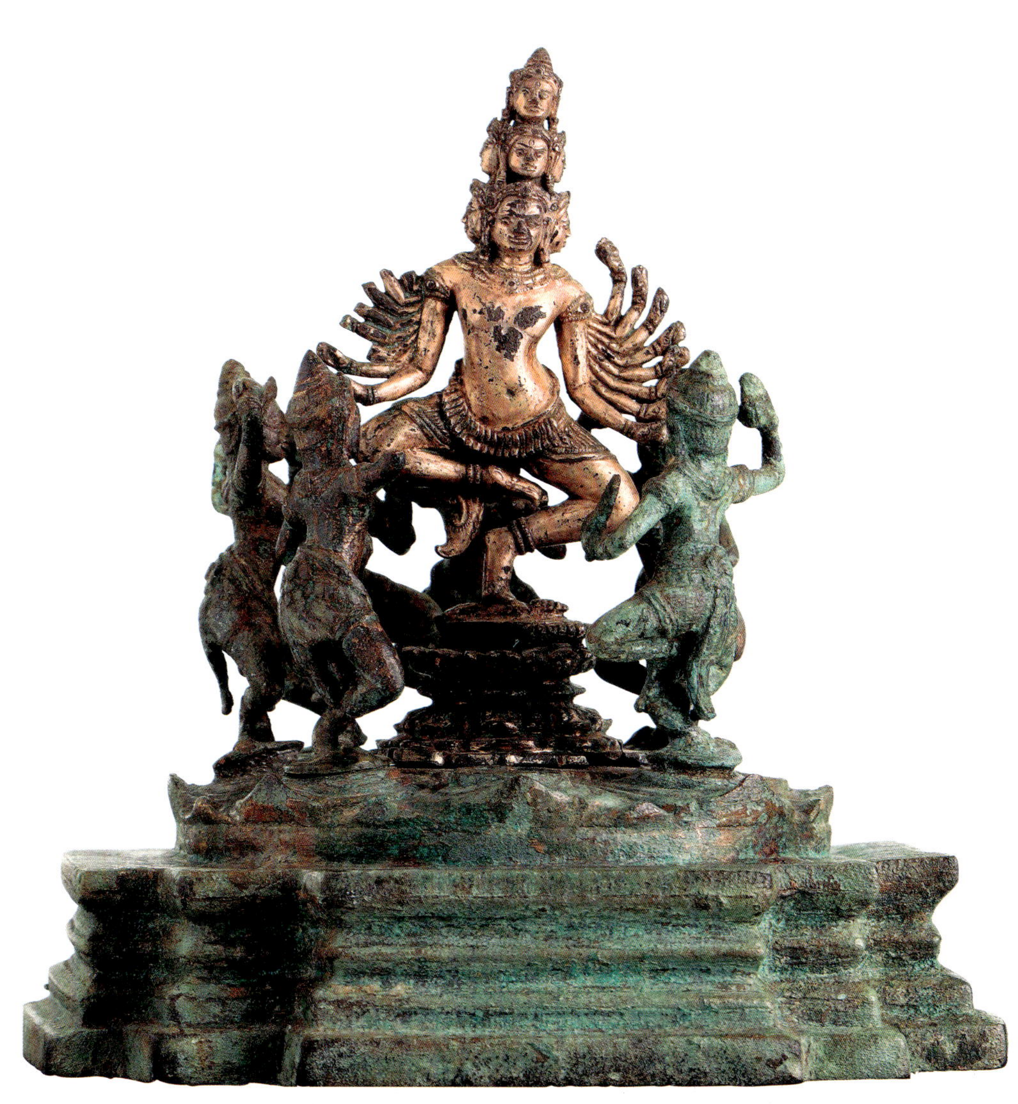

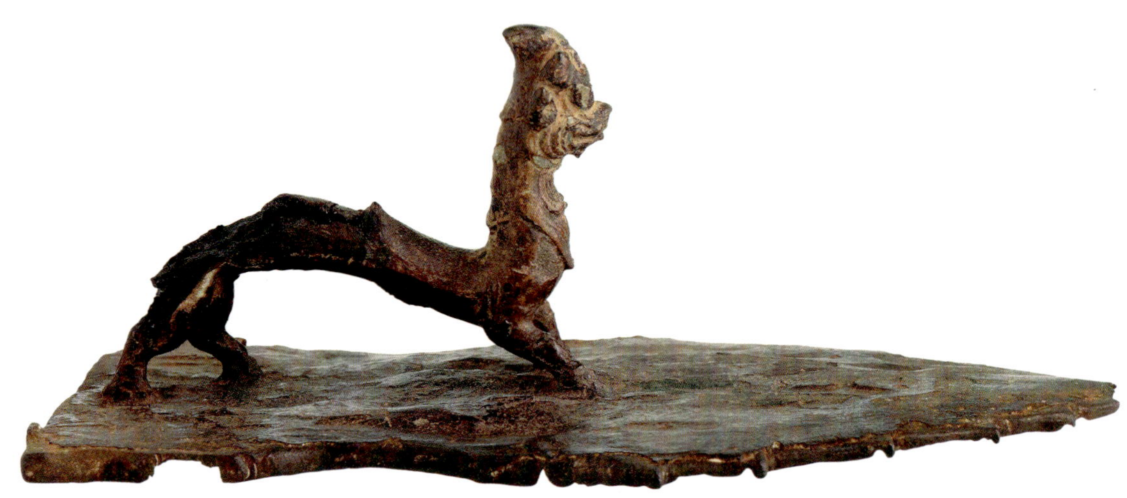

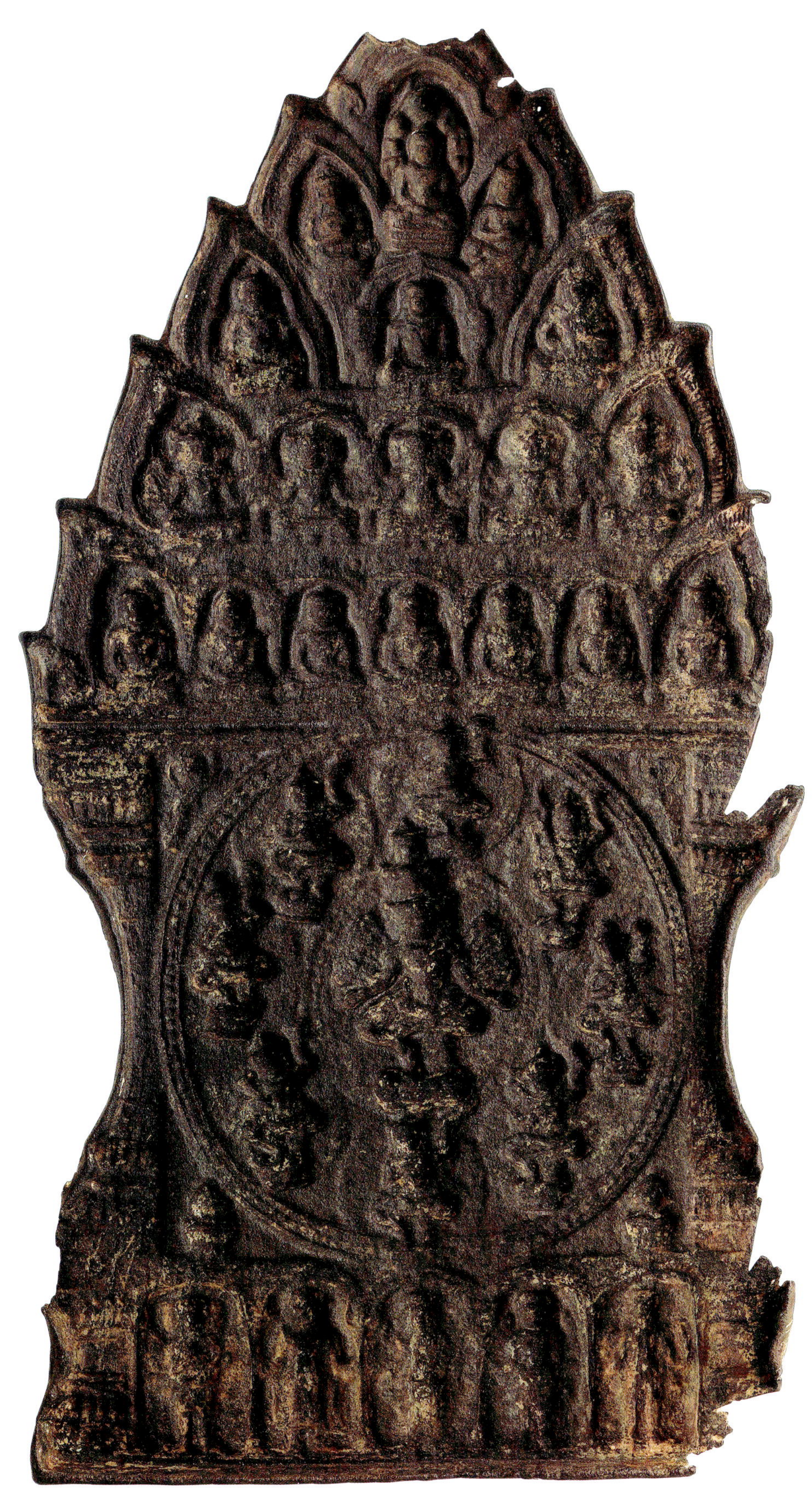

significant if inconclusive evidence for understanding his place in the hierarchy of Buddhist deities. Hevajra is the central deity of the well-known ninth- to tenth-century *Hevajra Tantra*, which probably was brought to Cambodia at some point in the eleventh century. Through a combination of ritual and meditative practices involving identification with Hevajra, enlightenment can be achieved. Hevajra is surrounded by a circle of eight dancing female figures, of whom six can be seen in three dimensions in the Hevajra shrine. (fig. 27) On the votive tablet mold, the *nāga*-protected Buddha, as might be expected, appears at the apex. The other figures, however, are less easy to identify, and it is not clear whether ritual initiation into the Hevajra mandala brings mastery of all the levels of the temple-like structure, or whether additional procedures are necessary. At any rate, the five figures at the bottom might be Avalokiteshvara; the first row of seven in the superstructure, seven Buddhas of the past or the seven Medicine Buddhas; followed by five Vajrasattva Buddhas; then three Prajñāpāramitā, two adorants, and finally the supreme *nāga*-protected Buddha.

That priests who had undergone Hevajra initiation frequently carried out ceremonies of lustration is indicated by the number of surviving bronze conch shells and conch holders bearing images of Hevajra. (see fig. 57) If provided with a hole at the bottom, both actual conch shells and shells cast in bronze also could be blown.[38] An important element in Tantric practices in Cambodia, as elsewhere, was presumably what has been called state protection, and rituals involving conch shells no doubt helped ensure the king's invulnerability.

Hindu Gods in the Closing Centuries of the Angkor Period

The paucity of inscriptional evidence from the decades following the death of Jayavarman VII (perhaps in 1218) means that the political and religious history of Cambodia in the thirteenth century is not well understood; in fact, it is the subject of some controversy.[39] It is clear that at some point there was a turn to the worship of the Hindu gods. Buddha images associated with Jayavarman were carefully chipped away at temple sites in Angkor and in some cases were transformed into Shivalingas.

Tracing Brahmanical art is complicated by the fact that during Jayavarman's reign, Hindu gods were worshiped and were considered one aspect of a total system that had the Buddha at the apex. A work like the sculpture of Nandin, Shiva's mount (fig. 49), provides too few clues to assign it to a secure position over the course of the twelfth and thirteenth centuries.[40] Two other works, however, probably were made in the thirteenth century, and a third may belong to the first half of the fourteenth century. (figs. 30, 31) These three display subtle stylistic connections, specifically the tendency to turn panels of cloth into decorative scrollwork. This tendency can be seen at the back of the Ganesha (fig. 29; see also fig. 55), a sculpture discovered with others of apparent post-Bayon date at the former airfield, Siem Reap,[41] and on the front of the Sadāshiva. (fig. 30)

The term "Sadā-" (eternal) Shiva, found in Indian texts, has come to refer to the five-headed Shiva. The heads were given different names and associated with the five elements—earth, water, wind, heat, and, when it came to the fifth, topmost head (sometimes considered invisible to ordinary people), space.[42] Unlike the case of Vishnu described above, there appears

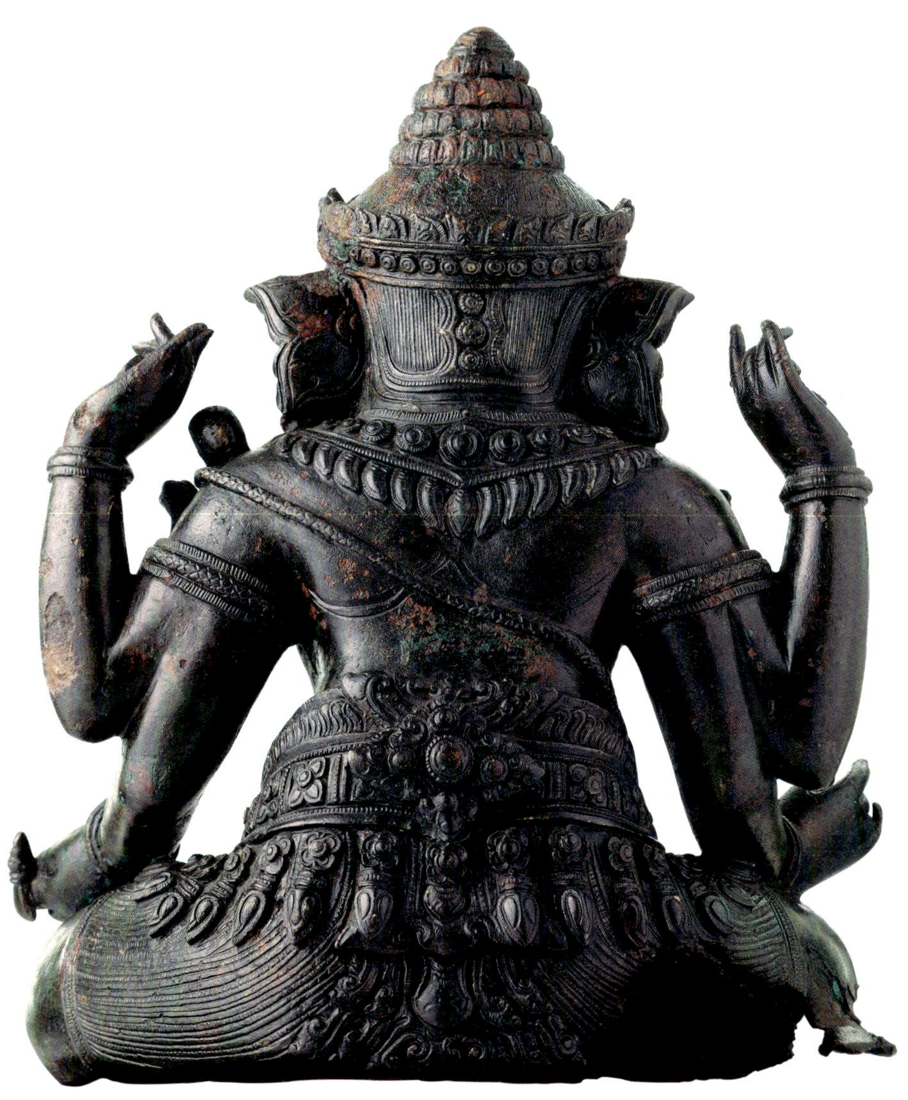

29

29 Back of Ganesha see also fig. 55
A son of Shiva, Ganesha, with his elephant head on the body of a boy, is in India the lord of Shiva's troops and the lord of beginnings. Although specific evidence is lacking, Tantric Buddhists probably made a place for Ganesha in the Jayavarman VII period. The elaboration of the garment and the inclusion of scrolling elements on Ganesha's back suggests a stylistic connection with figs. 30 and 31.

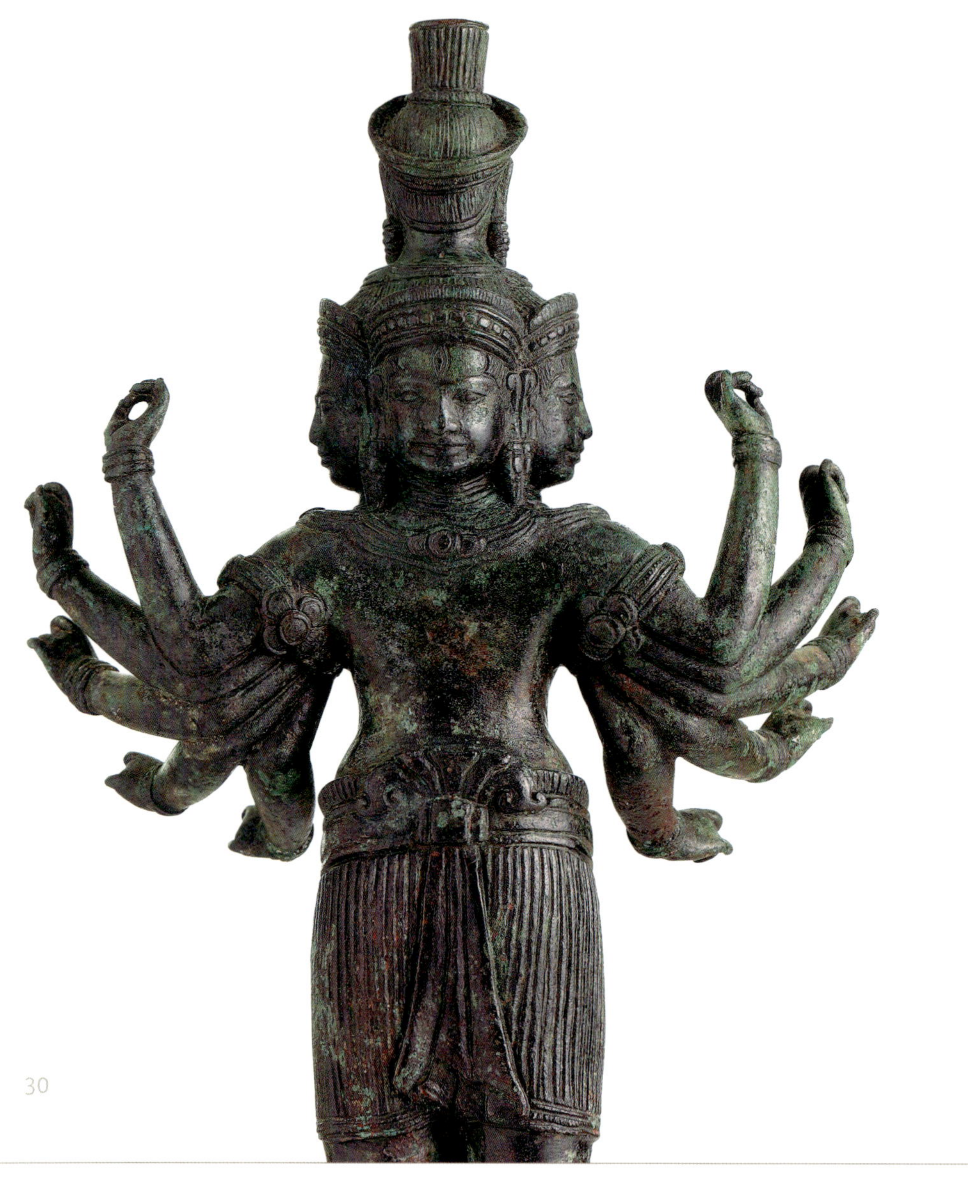

30

30 Five-headed Shiva (Sadāshiva) detail above and pages 74–75
Cambodia, Angkor period, 13th century
Bronze; 34 × 18 × 8.5 cm
National Museum of Cambodia, Ga2682

The state Buddhism of Jayavarman VII did not bring an end to the worship of Shiva and Vishnu; indeed, it was accommodated. Nevertheless, the facial types and the treatment of the garment suggest a date sometime in the decades after Jayavarman's death (circa 1218).

31 Vishnu-Vasudeva-Nārāyaṇa pages 76–77
Cambodia, Angkor period, first half of the 14th century or later
Bronze; 67 × 22 × 16 cm
National Museum of Cambodia, Ga5457

Although the Chinese traveler Zhou Daguan described a flourishing Angkor at the time of his visit in 1296–97, the production of stone inscriptions and ambitious temples had already diminished. The stylistic sequences are as hard to discern as the relationship between the Brahmanical cults and the newly established Theravada Buddhism. This sculpture could date from the reign of a king who ruled in the first half of the 14th century and apparently favored Hinduism.

to be no iconographic account of Sadāshiva in a Cambodian inscription, but the name was known because a record dating from the first half of the eleventh century states that a member of a high-ranking priestly family was named Sadāshiva, "a Sadāshiva come to earth."[43] One stone ten-armed, five-headed Shiva dates from the tenth century.[44] The small bronze (fig. 30) has an extremely unusual cloth panel hanging from the waist. The interest in scrolling tips can be understood as an outgrowth of certain decorative tendencies of the Angkor Wat style, but whether the depiction was prompted by a development in the realm of fashion (a piece of cloth terminated by shaped segments of fringe?) or by predilections within the bronze-casting workshop cannot be determined.

Integrating the meager epigraphic evidence with surviving works of art and monuments in this period is not so simple. A cache of hundreds of Buddha images buried at the temple of Banteay Kdei reveals two historic moments: one is the damaging of the images (perhaps contemporary with the iconoclastic movement); the other is their subsequent burial (possibly around the third quarter of the thirteenth century).[45] An inscription of 1267 mentions the dedication of a Buddha called "Sugata Māravijita"—that is, no longer the supreme *nāga*-protected Buddha of Jayavarman VII but a depiction of the historical Buddha at the time of his victory over the devil Māra at Bodhgaya.[46] At least some of the Preah Pithu complex, a group of Brahmanical shrines, must date from the same time as Prasat Top East (formerly known as the Mangalartha), a small temple dedicated in 1295. The oldest inscription using the Pali language of the Theravada Buddhist scriptures was set up in 1309, suggesting a possible date for sections of the Buddhist temple of Preah Palilay, near Preah Pithu at Angkor. But this did not mean a definitive turn to Theravada Buddhism: in 1327, the year of his accession, King Jayavarmaparameshvara dedicated a Shivalinga in the Bayon, the state temple of Jayavarman VII.[47]

There are reasons to think that figure 31 might belong to Jayavarmaparameshvara's reign: the coiffure consists of cascading clumps of hair, as can be seen in sculptures of Shiva dating from the second half of the thirteenth century; and the swirling ornament on the surface of the garment recalls decoration at some of the Preah Pithu monuments.[48] This Vishnu appears to predate a pair of Brahmanical images cast in Sukhothai, in neighboring Thailand, in 1349 or 1361.[49] Still, the shape of the face suggests some knowledge of stylistic developments in Siam in the fourteenth century—a harbinger of challenges for Cambodia in the following centuries.

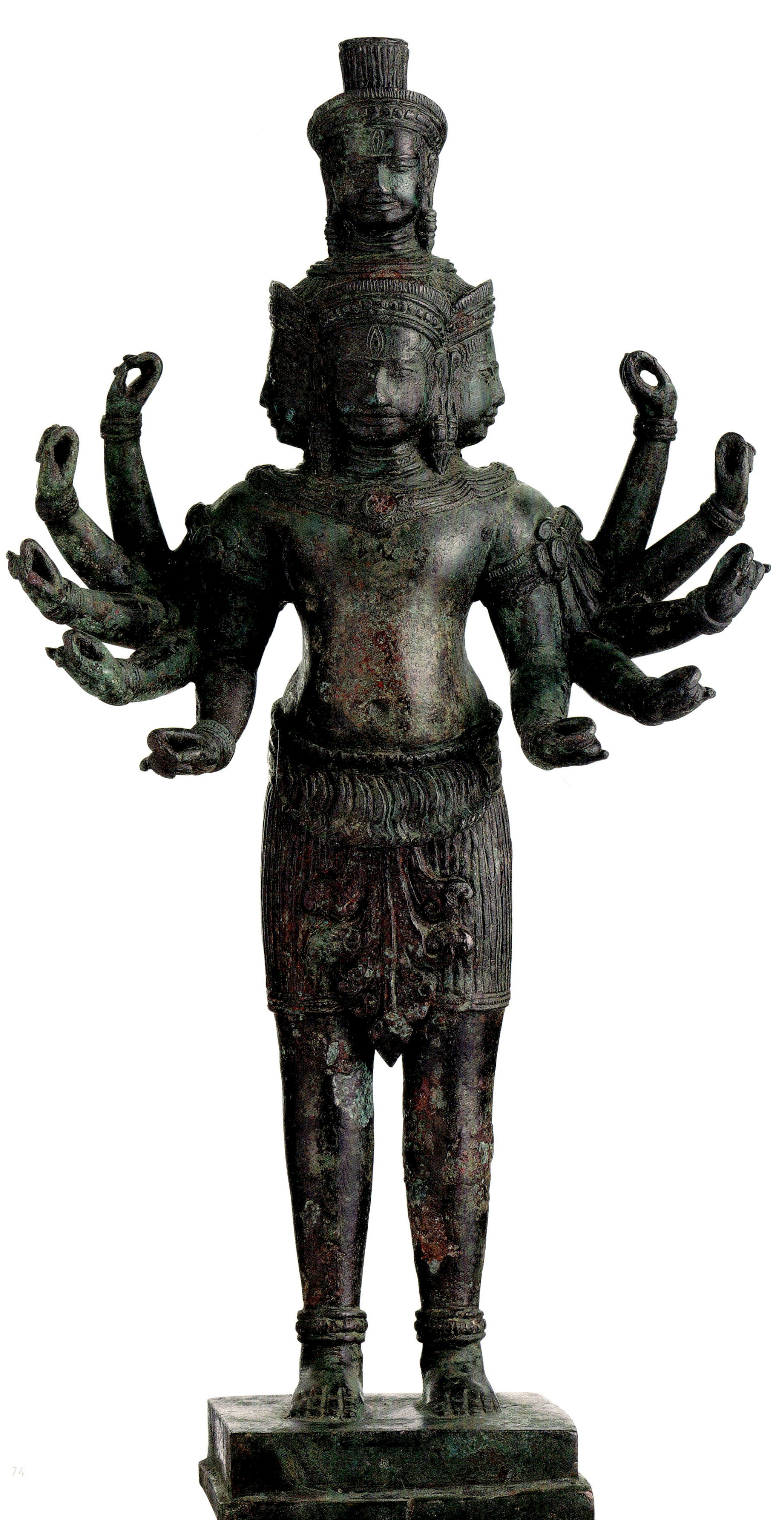

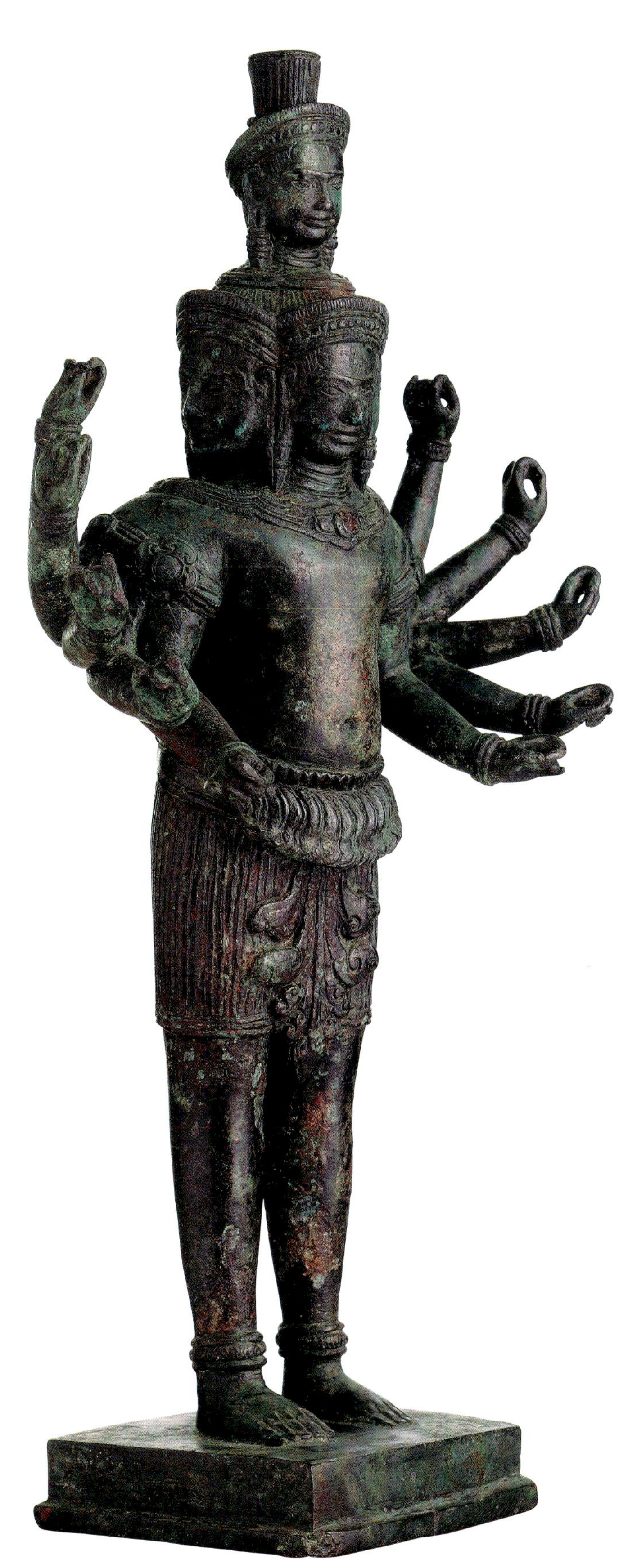

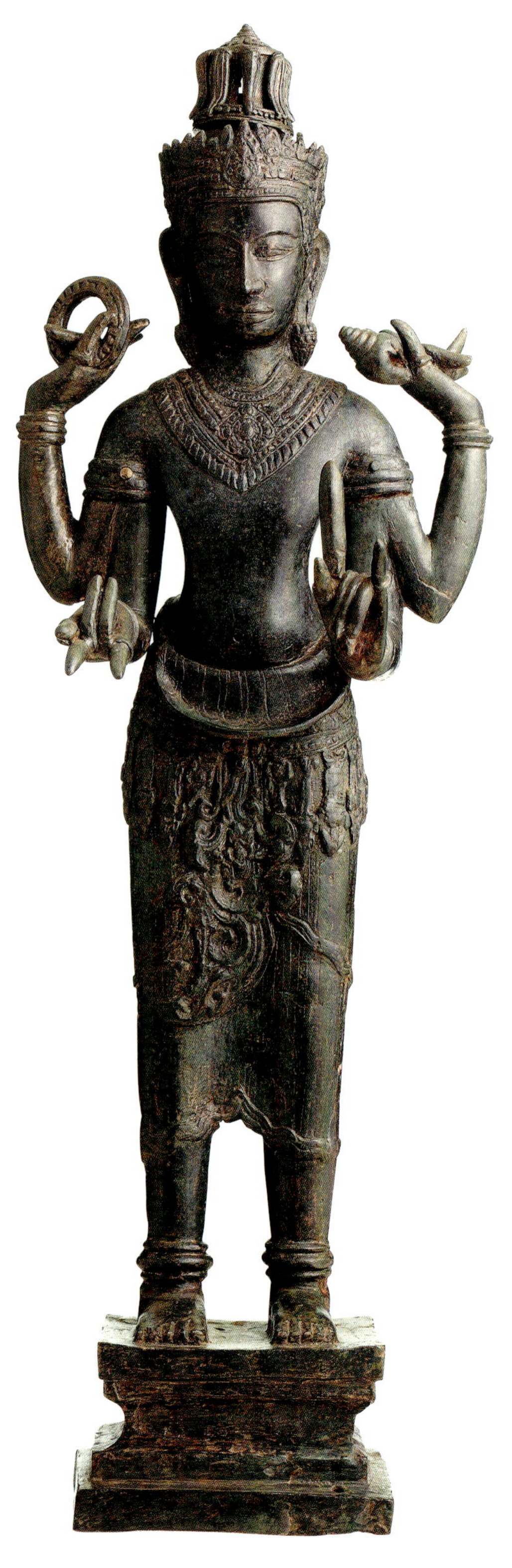

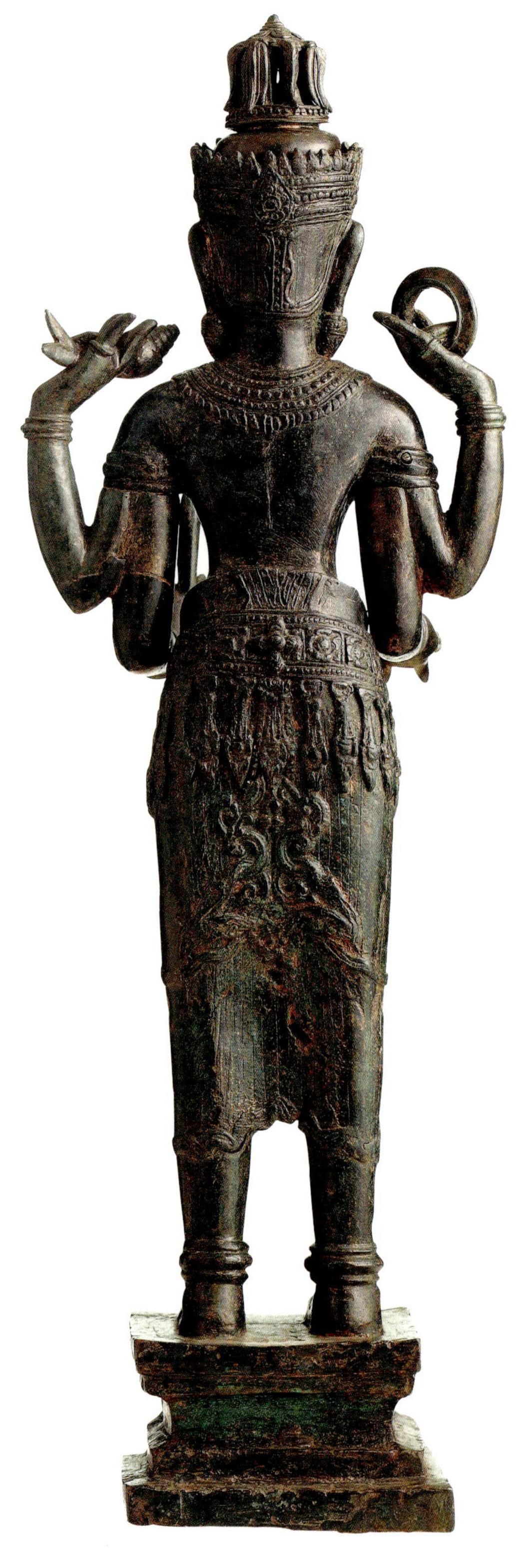

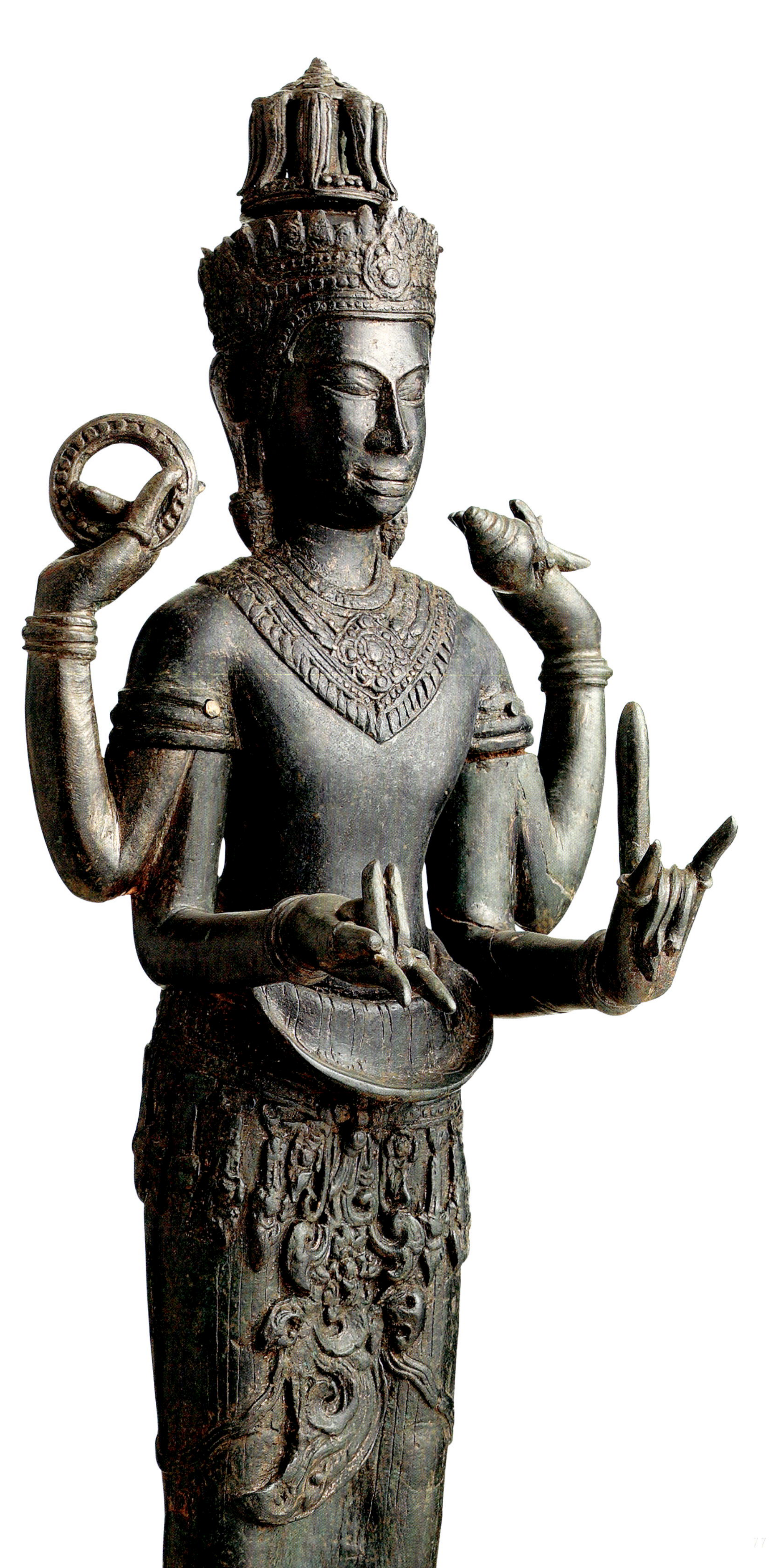

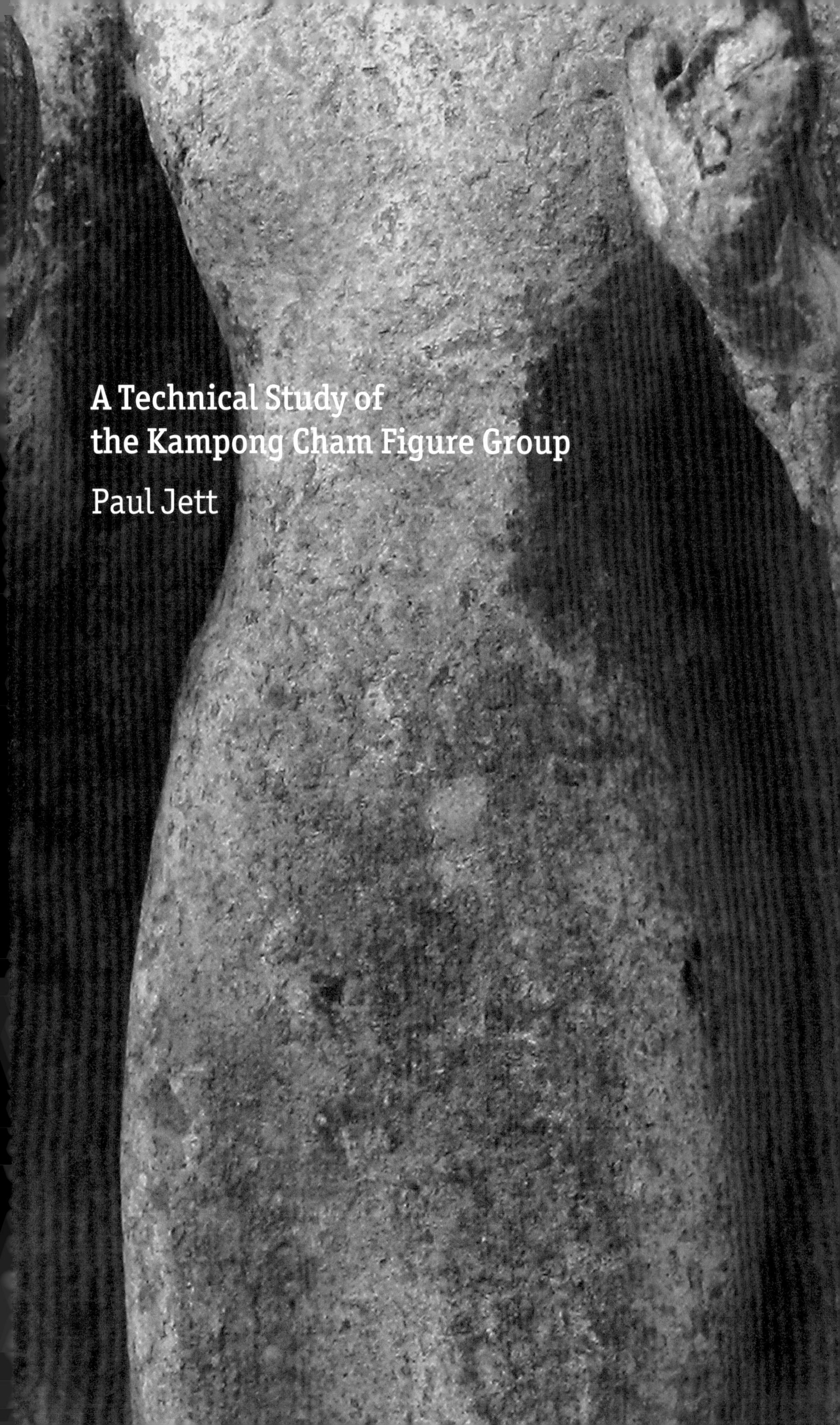

A Technical Study of the Kampong Cham Figure Group

Paul Jett

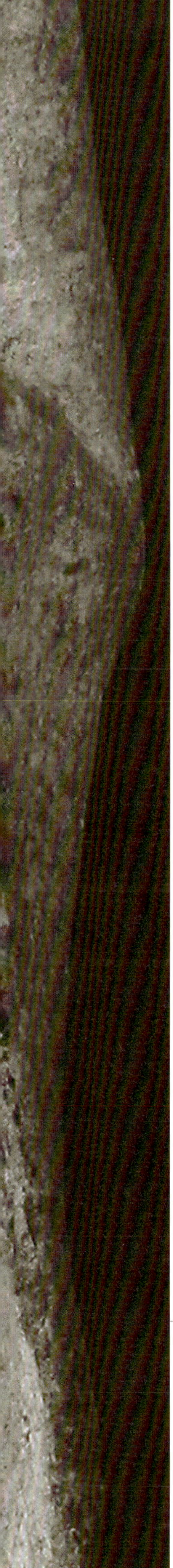

While digging a hole to plant a tree on the grounds of her house in the spring of 2006, a woman in Sdaeung Chey village, Cheung Prey district, Kampong Cham province, unearthed a remarkable group of seven bronze figures. She informed the authorities of her find, and in the fall of that year, the sculptures became part of the collection of the National Museum of Cambodia, Phnom Penh. The figures are related by their Buddhist subject matter and, while it is clear that they are the products of several different artistic traditions, all appear to be of a similar age, dating within the late sixth to late seventh centuries. The sculptures are discussed from an art historical point of view elsewhere in this publication; this essay presents the results of a technical examination.

The seven bronze sculptures, which range in height between ten and forty centimeters, display features typical of bronzes created by the technique of lost-wax casting. This technique begins with the creation of a wax model of the intended image, over which layers of clay are built up to create a mold. After the clay dries, the mold is heated, the wax melts and runs out (i.e., is lost), and what remains is a clay vessel with an internal cavity in the form of the wax model. Molten metal then is poured into the clay mold. After the metal solidifies, the clay mold is broken away to reveal the metal sculpture. When a solid wax model is used, the resulting casting is solid metal, and it is termed a solid-cast piece. Frequently, however, the wax model is built up over a clay core to produce a relatively thin layer of wax and, subsequently, a thin layer of cast metal; this type of figure is said to be hollow-cast. Clay cores often were built up over an iron-wire armature to give the core greater strength. Enclosed in metal after casting, clay cores and iron armatures may remain inside the bronze, providing evidence of how the sculptures were made. In some cases, samples can be removed from the clay cores and used for a test known as thermoluminescence (or TL) dating. Because TL reveals the last time the clay core was heated to a high temperature, it sometimes indicates when a bronze was cast, although it frequently gives only a rough estimate of the date.

The consistent state of preservation for the seven sculptures supports the report of their having been found together as a cache or, at least, a group that spent considerable time together in the same environment or under the same burial conditions. While minor losses appear on some of the figures, the bodies, with the exception of the largest figure, are complete. The extent of corrosion and the surface appearance are similar for all the figures. The corrosion layer is fairly heavy, relatively even, and pale green in color. While all of the pieces have been lightly cleaned since entering the museum, the cleaning did not alter their basic coloration or appearance.

Differences in the lost-wax casting features and other elements of the Kampong Cham figures appear to relate to their different origins. This discussion of the physical features of the figures separates them into three groups according to their supposed cultural origins and notes their individual traits. A discussion of the results of chemical analyses follows.

32 **The seven bronze sculptures after conservation treatment** pages 80–81

Their pre-conservation state is presented on pages 84, 85, and 87.

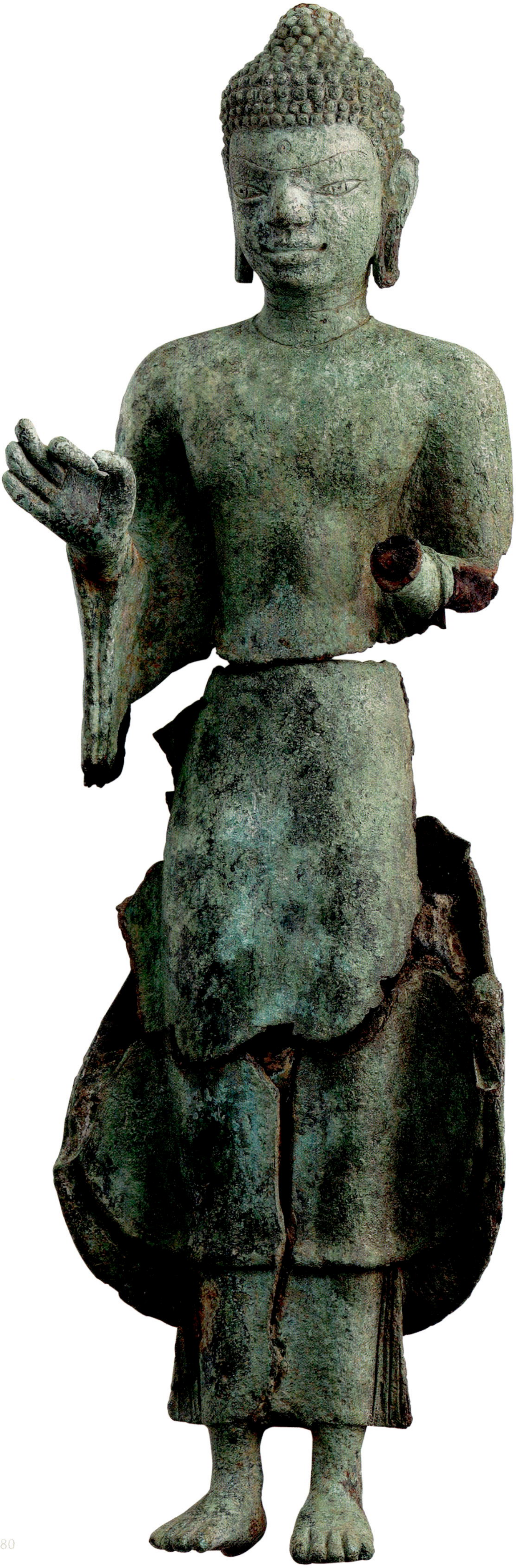

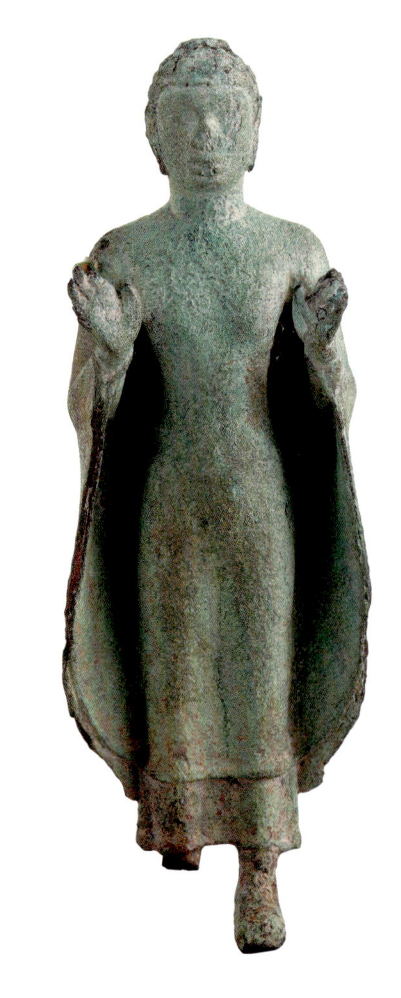

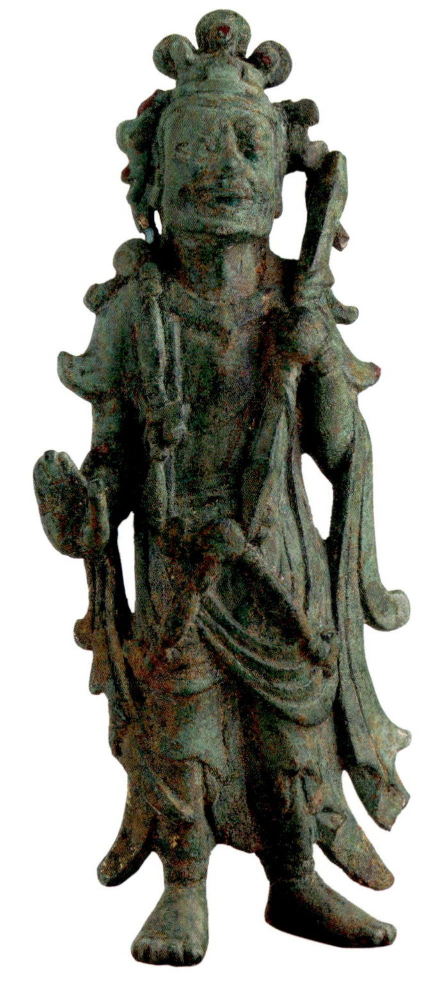

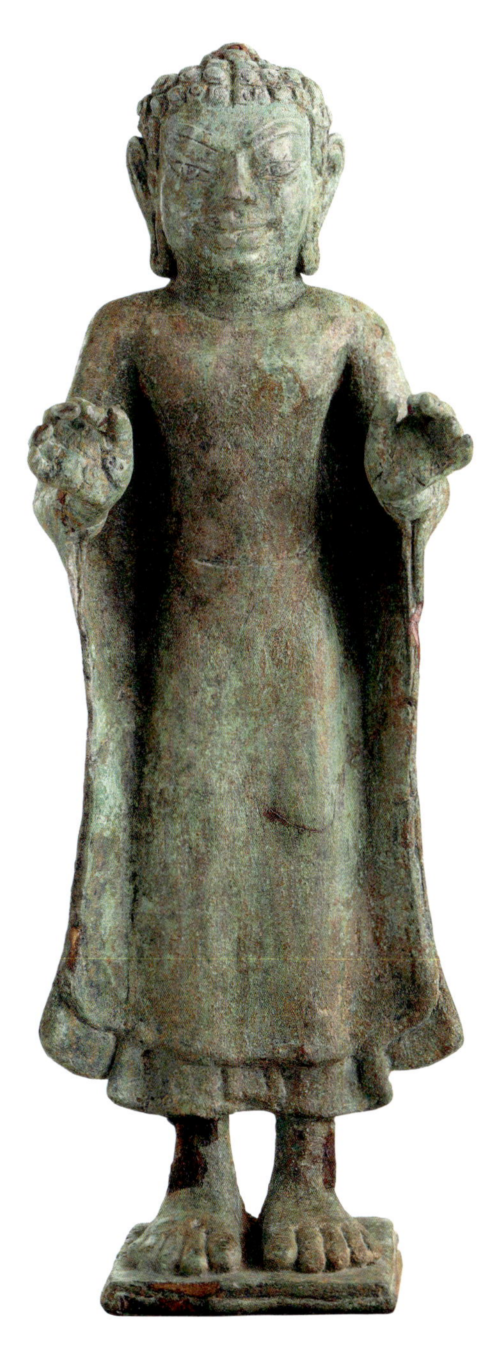

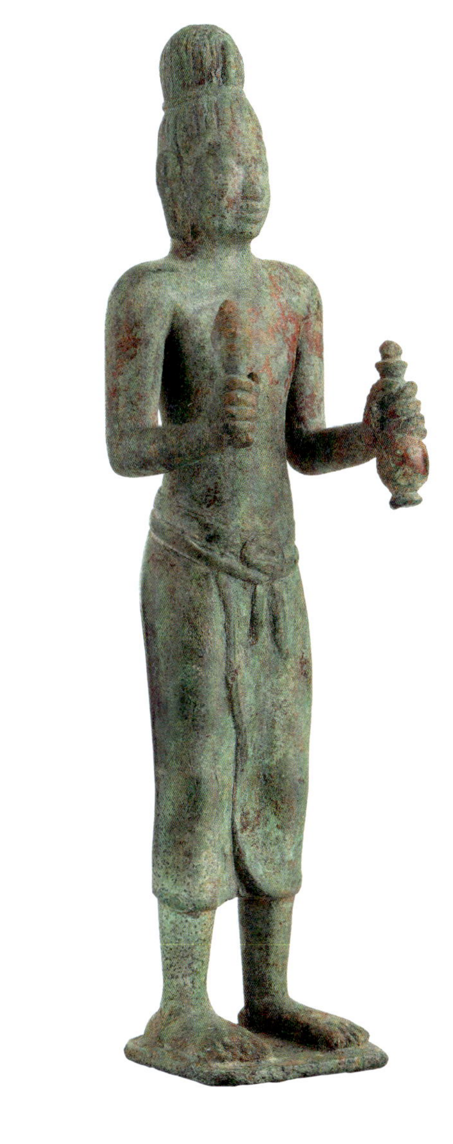

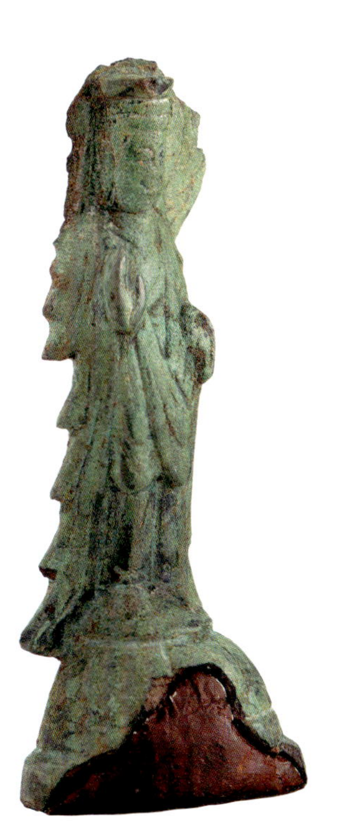

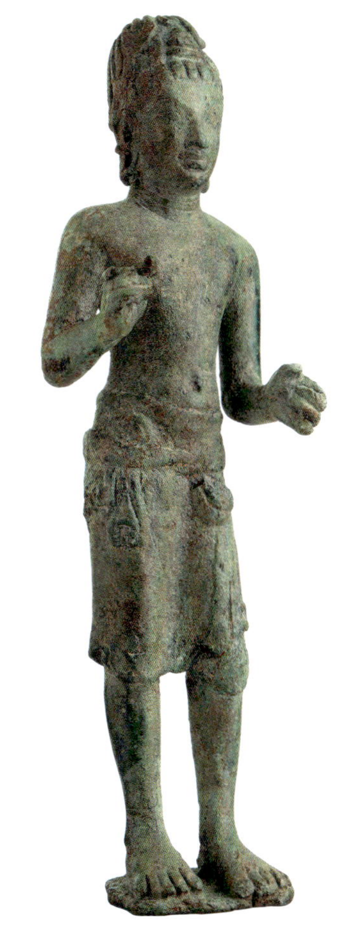

Dvāravatī-style Figures

Three of the figures are standing images of the Buddha, executed in the style associated with the Dvāravatī kingdom in what is now central Thailand. (figs. 33–35) All three figures have quite similar alloy compositions.

Figure 33 was hollow cast and still contains core material. Within the core is an iron armature. TL testing of the core did not yield a useful date because of the great range of the results—indicating the sculpture was made 1,100 to 1,800 years ago—but it does confirm the antiquity of the piece.[1] The eyes are depicted by sharp, recessed lines that appear to have been engraved rather than cast. (fig. 33A) Of the seven sculptures, this one has suffered the greatest losses. It now exists in three pieces, and is missing a large area from the back and the left hand and forearm. Neither the remains of a base nor tangs (used to secure the figure in a base) are present, and the original means of support for the figure is not apparent.

Figure 34 is of a small size that usually would have been cast solid, but this work appears to have been cast hollow. What seem to be rust stains are found on the bottoms of the left leg and right foot, suggesting the presence of a core with an iron armature inside the sculpture. Four stubs on the back, in a rectangular pattern, further suggest that the figure once had some attached element, perhaps an aureole. (fig. 34A) No tang or base is present.

Figure 35 is nearly complete, with the exception of a small hole in the back of the right arm; this hole indicates that the piece was hollow cast. The details of the eyes have the same incised look found on figure 33. Unlike the other two Buddha figures, figure 35 has a base—small, square, and low in shape—and a round tang.

Khmer-style Figures

Two figures are Khmer in style. Figure 36 represents Maitreya; its atypical alloy composition makes it perhaps the most enigmatic of the group. The other, figure 37, depicts Avalokiteshvara.

The Maitreya, like the last Buddha figure described above, has a small, square base and a round tang. (fig. 36) It appears to have been cast solid and stands out due to the alloy used, which is unusual for its period and provenance. The metal is a mixture of copper, tin, lead, and zinc; as zinc makes up nine percent of the metal alloy and is the most abundant element after copper, the alloy is a brass. The use of brass was rare in Southeast Asia at this time, though some occurrences have been noted in sculpture of a similar age. A standing Buddha from Thailand dating to the ninth century was found to have more than fifteen percent zinc, and in that case, it is speculated that the metal came from northern India, where the use of brass was common.[2] Later in date, but of Cambodian origin, are three figures in the Bayon style (late twelfth–early thirteenth century) that also were found to be made of brass.[3] The alloys for those figures probably resulted from the use of imported raw materials—either brass metal, zinc metal, or zinc ore—or from the recycling of a brass object or figure that was melted and employed to create a new casting.

The Avalokiteshvara, like the two previous figures, stands on a small, square base with a tang. The base differs from those of the other two figures in being somewhat trapezoidal in shape, with the front edge wider than the

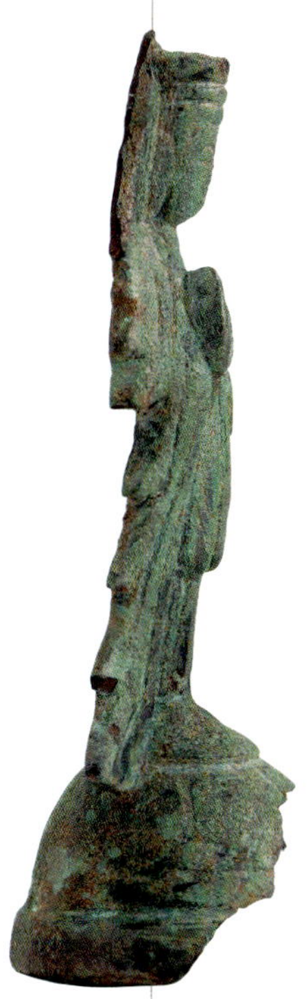

38

back edge; moreover, the tang for this figure is more square than round. (fig. 37) The figure appears to have been cast solid. Its alloy also distinguishes it from the others; it has the lowest copper content and highest combined content of tin and lead of the group.

Chinese Figures

The two Chinese figures stand out because they are gilded, a trait typical of Buddhist bronzes in China from as early as the second century CE onward. (figs. 38, 39) The scientific means for determining the type of gilding were unavailable at the time the figures were examined, but the surfaces do not suggest anything other than fire gilding (also known as mercury gilding or amalgam gilding), which is to be expected for figures of this type.[4]

Figure 38 (see left and page 87) is a bodhisattva, possibly Avalokiteshvara. Small in size, the figure is cast solid except for its base, which forms an inverted cup shape; the back is featureless and concave. (fig. 38B) The shallow and indistinct details of the face and robe suggest that the figure has suffered a fair degree of wear.

Figure 39 depicts a guardian figure. Like its Chinese partner, it was solid cast and bears a layer of gilding. It has no base, but it does have tangs—each one pierced with a hole—that extend down from the bottoms of the feet. The pierced tangs suggest that the figure once may have been part of a larger group and attached to a base that supported multiple figures. Such tangs are commonly seen on figures from altar groups.

Alloy Composition

Analysis of the metal was performed using energy-dispersive x-ray fluorescence analysis of drilled samples. The results give the basic alloy compositions.[5]

Figure	Copper	Tin	Lead	Zinc	Iron
33	81%	14%	4%	—	—
34	82%	15%	3%	—	—
35	85%	10%	4%	—	—
36	82%	2%	6%	9%	—
37	77%	10%	13%	—	—
38	82%	9%	8%	—	1%
39	80%	11%	9%	—	—

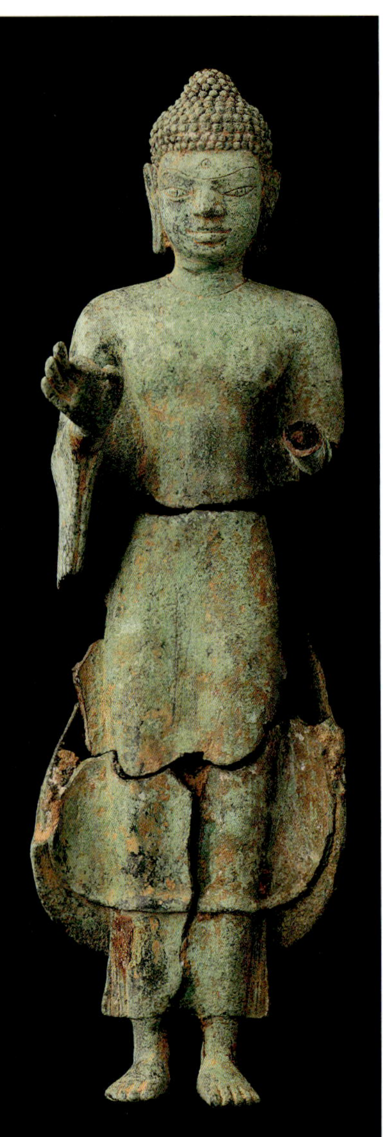

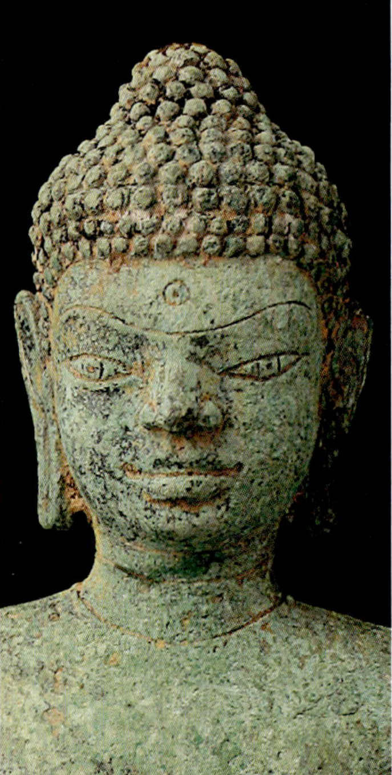

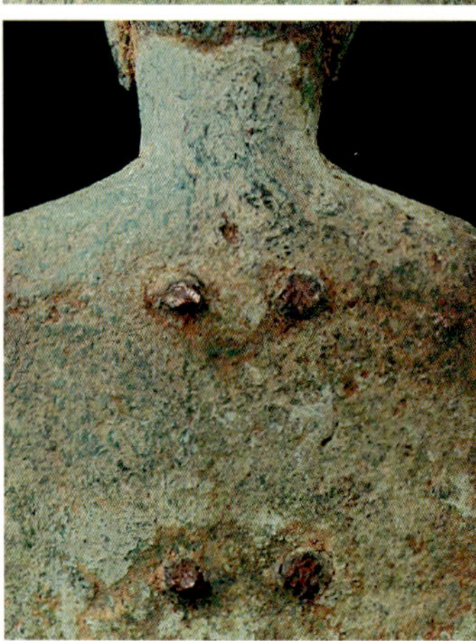

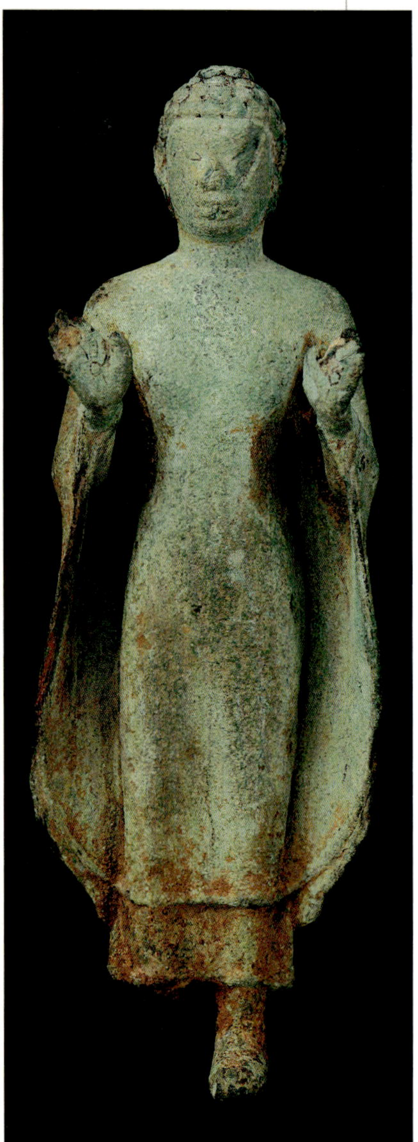

33 33A, 34A 34

33 and 33A Buddha (before conservation); see also fig. 10
Cambodia, pre-Angkor period, second half of the 7th century
Bronze; 39 × 11.5 × 10.5 cm
National Museum of Cambodia, Ga6937

Before cleaning (left).
Detail of eyes showing incised detail (center, top).

34 and 34A Buddha (before conservation); see also fig. 11
Cambodia, pre-Angkor period, second half of the 7th century
Bronze; 14 × 5 × 3 cm
National Museum of Cambodia, Ga6938

Before cleaning (right).
Back of figure showing four stubs on back (center, bottom).

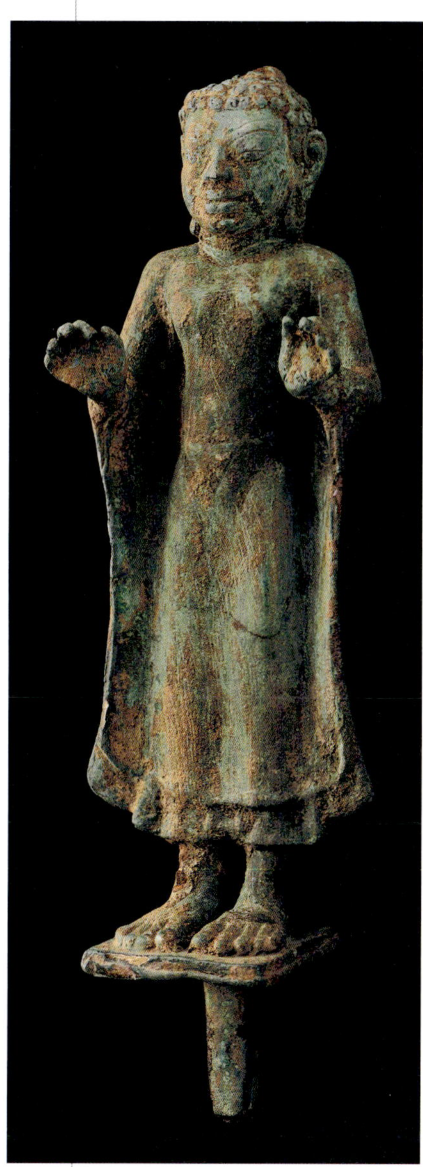

35

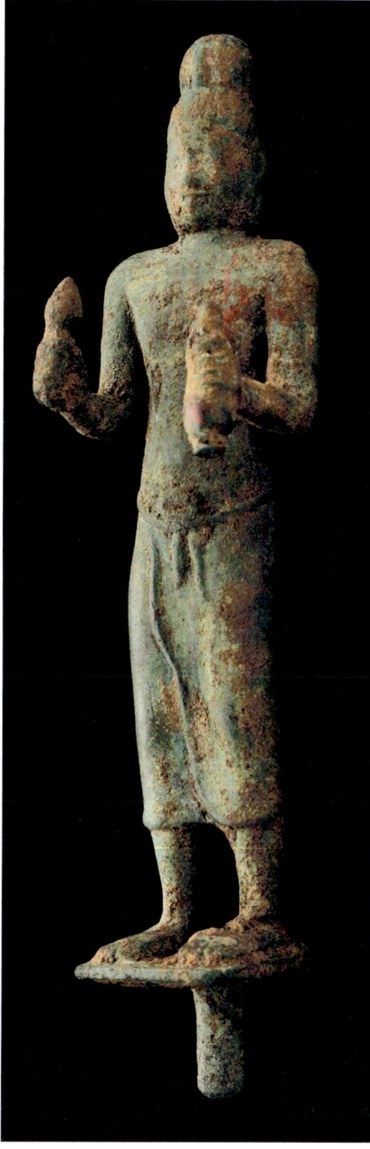

36

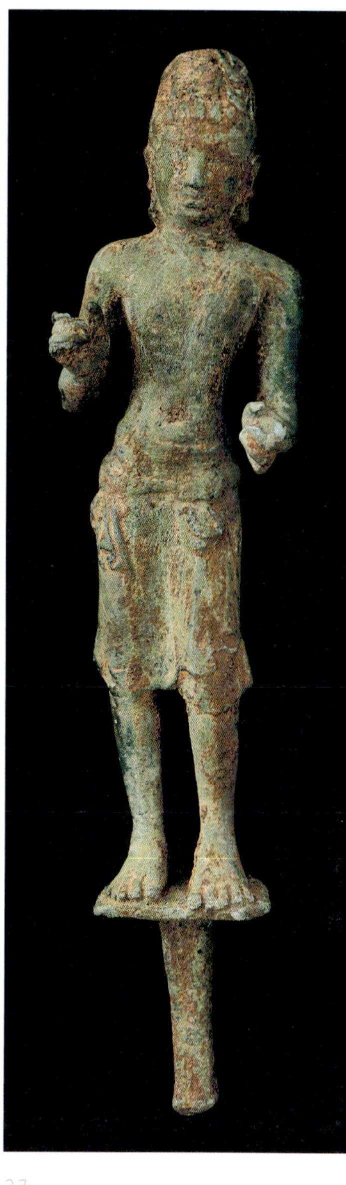

37

35 Buddha (before conservation); see also fig. 12
Cambodia, pre-Angkor period, second half of the 7th century
Bronze; 29 × 8 × 5 cm (including tang)
National Museum of Cambodia, Ga6939

Before cleaning and showing tang.

36 Maitreya (before conservation); see also fig. 14
Cambodia, pre-Angkor period, second half of the 7th century
Brass; 19 × 4.5 × 4 cm (including tang)
National Museum of Cambodia, Ga6940

Before cleaning and showing tang.

37 Avalokiteshvara (before conservation); see also fig. 13
Cambodia, pre-Angkor period, second half of the 7th century
Bronze; 16 × 3 × 2 cm (including tang)
National Museum of Cambodia, Ga6941

Before cleaning and showing tang.

Conclusion

There appear to be three sources for the Kampong Cham figures, and their technical features seem to reflect those different origins. The three Dvāravatī-style Buddha figures are hollow cast. An iron armature is obvious in the largest one, and what seem to be iron stains on the other two figures strongly suggest that they, too, enclose iron armatures. These three figures also have similar alloy compositions; each contains a small percentage of lead and ten to fifteen percent of tin, with the rest (except for some trace element contents) made up of copper. Two of the figures (figs. 33 and 35) share similarity in the delineation of their eyes and eyebrows: sharp, narrow lines that appear to have been created by engraving. (The facial features of the third figure are worn, but the details of the eyes and eyebrows do not appear to have been engraved.) Figure 35 differs from the other two in that it has an integral base and a fairly long tang, like the two Khmer figures.

The two small, slight figures attributed to the Khmer culture are physically similar in a number of ways. Both are solid cast and have integral, small, square bases and tangs. Their eyes are not sharply delineated like those of the three Dvāravatī-style figures. The alloys of the Khmer figures not only are unlike the Dvāravatī-style figures, they also are quite unlike one another. The highly unusual use of a brass alloy for figure 36 suggests imported materials or, perhaps, the reuse of metal from another figure of foreign origin. While it is possible that an inadvertent use of ores containing zinc resulted in production of an accidental brass alloy, this chance occurrence seems less likely than the reuse of metal that happened to be a brass alloy.

The two Chinese figures share a number of similarities. They are solid cast. Their alloy compositions are similar and also somewhat distinct from the Dvāravatī-style figures, in the greater amount of lead and smaller amount of tin present. The compositions fit comfortably within the range found for Chinese bronzes of a similar age (sixth–seventh century).[6] The material feature that most distinguishes these two from the rest of the group is the presence of gilding. The use of gilding appeared in China many centuries before it did in Cambodia, where the earliest gilt bronzes are believed to have been produced in about the seventh century. The dating of the two Kampong Cham Chinese figures to that era is thought-provoking.[7] Could the influence or inspiration of Chinese gilded bronzes have led to the use of gilding in Cambodia?

While the technical and material features of the Kampong Cham figures appear to bear associations to three cultures—Dvāravatī, Khmer, Chinese—only Chinese Buddhist bronzes of this era have undergone detailed technical study. Similar research on Thai and Cambodian bronzes from this period has been limited,[8] and too little has been done to say that the bronze sculptures of Southeast Asia in the mid to late first millennium possess technical attributes that can determine their cultures of origin.

The interrelationships across cultures in and around Southeast Asia have a long history that has been the subject of extensive study and discussion. The Kampong Cham cache nicely illustrates some of those interconnections in the seventh century. Chinese figures and Dvāravatī-inspired works were recovered in combination with Khmer images, and what appears to be a Khmer figure was made from an alloy that possibly originated in India. The Kampong Cham group of sculptures exemplifies the complexity and diversity of the cross-cultural milieu in the region at that time.

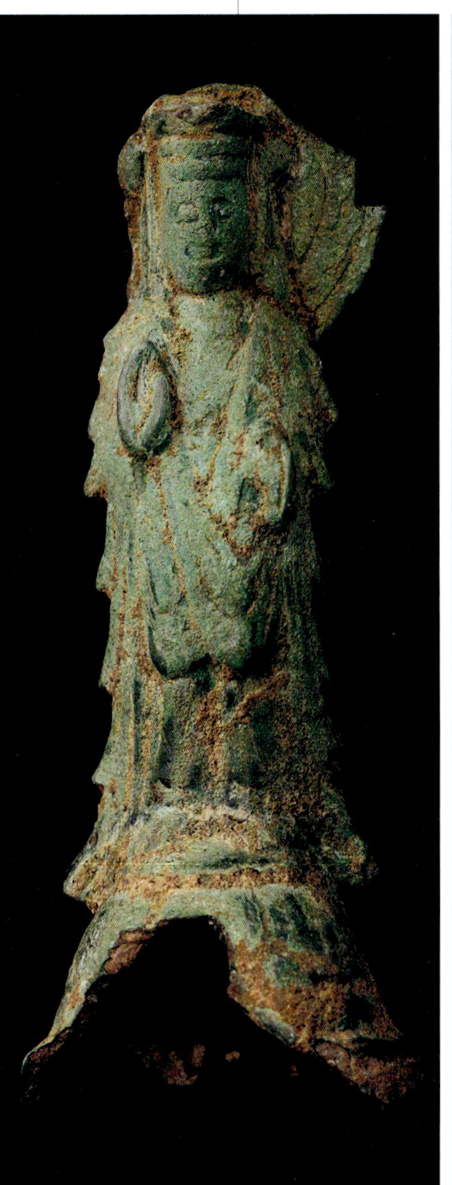

38A

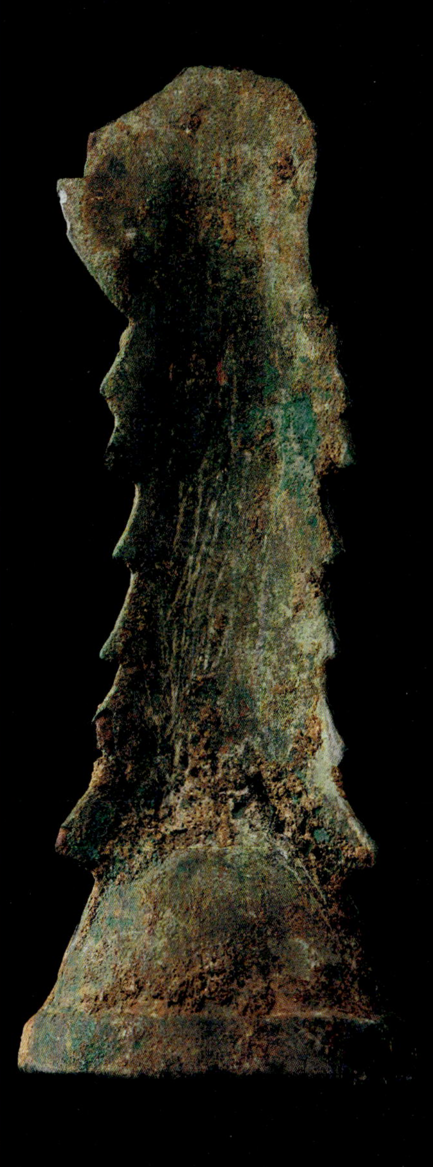

38B

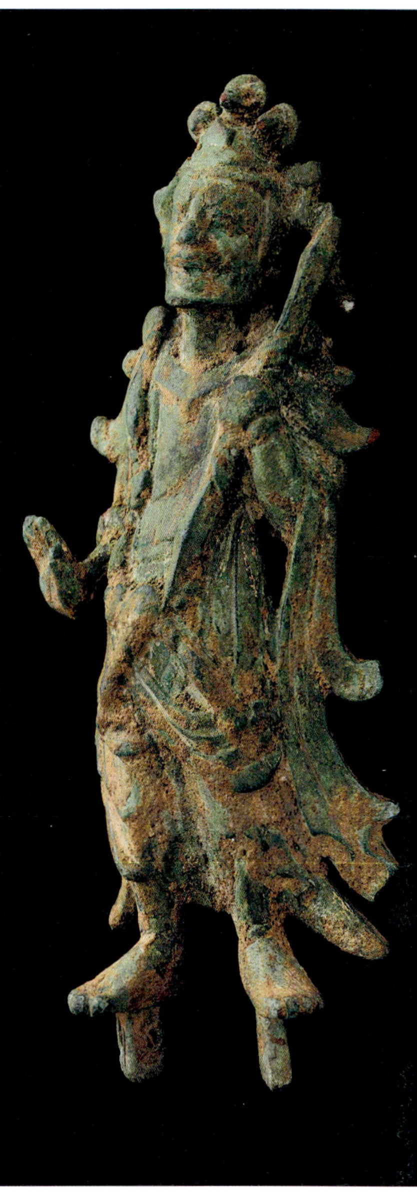

39

38, 38A, and 38B Bodhisattva
see also fig. 16, page 83 for after conservation
China, 6th century
Bronze with traces of gilding; 9.5 × 3 × 3 cm
National Museum of Cambodia, Ga6942

Before cleaning and conservation (left).
Back of figure (center).

39 Vajra-bearing Guardian
(before conservation); see also fig. 17
China, Sui or Tang dynasty, late 6th–7th century
Bronze with traces of gilding; 16.5 × 6 × 3 cm (including tangs)
National Museum of Cambodia, Ga6943

Before cleaning and showing tangs (right).

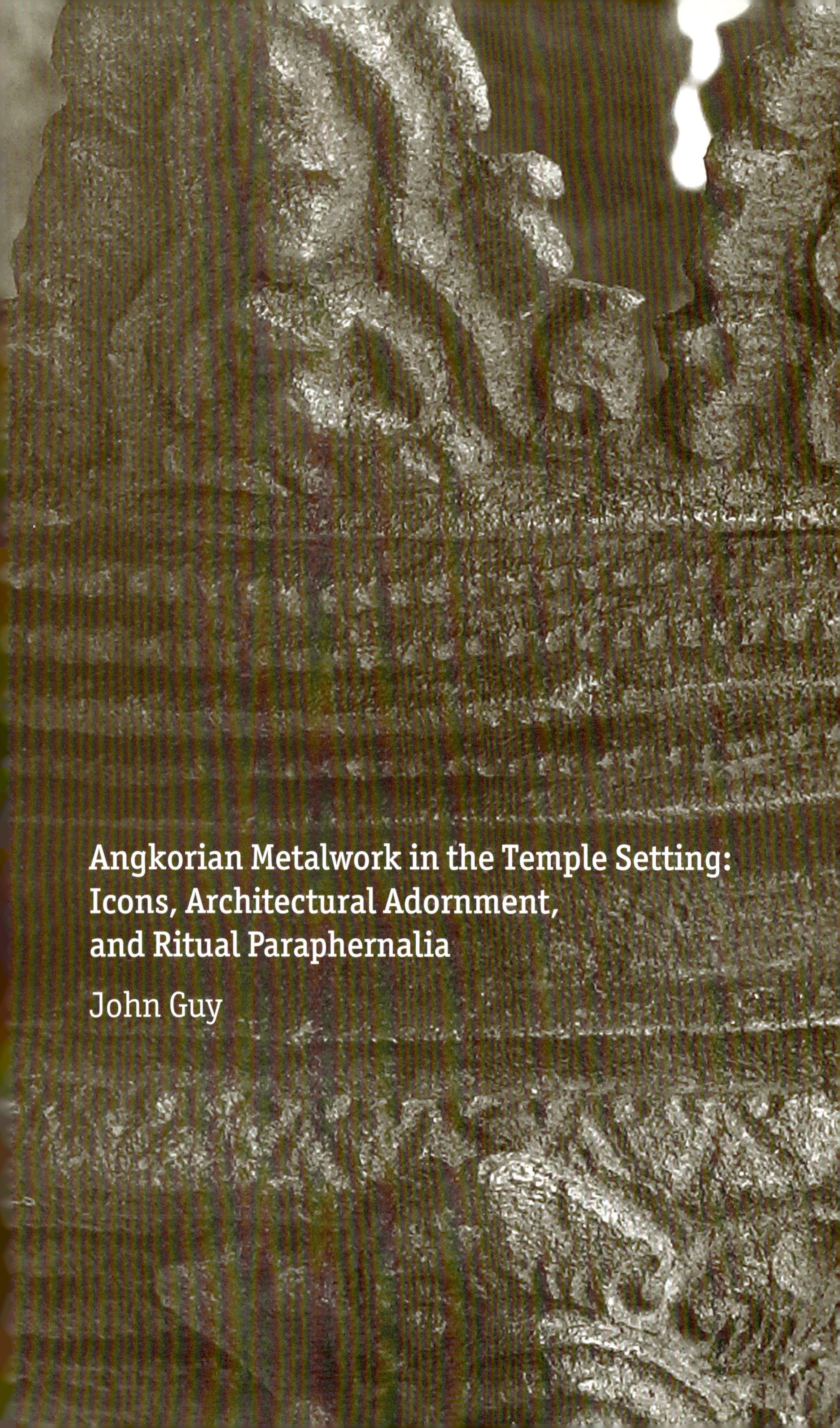

Angkorian Metalwork in the Temple Setting: Icons, Architectural Adornment, and Ritual Paraphernalia

John Guy

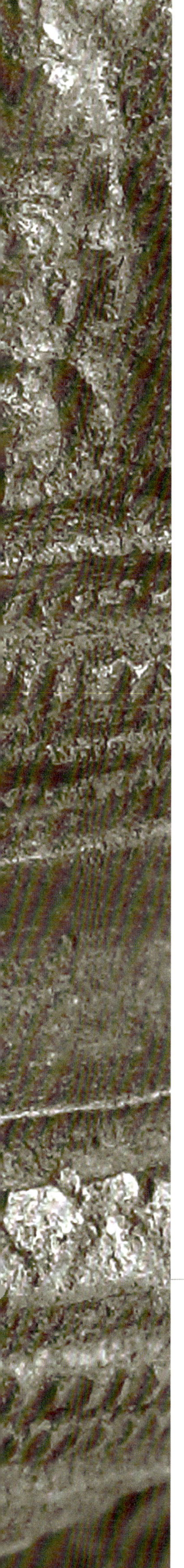

The wall of the city [Angkor Thom]...has five gates. Above each gate are grouped five gigantic heads of Buddha, four of them facing the four cardinal points; the fifth head, brilliant with gold, holds a central position.... At the centre of the Kingdom rises a Golden Tower [Bayon], flanked by more than twenty lesser towers and several hundred stone chambers. On the eastern side is a golden bridge guarded by two lions of gold, one on each side, with eight golden Buddhas spaced along the stone chambers. North of Golden Tower [Bayon], at a distance of about two hundred yards, rises the Tower of Bronze [Baphuon], higher even than the Golden Tower: a truly astonishing spectacle, with more than ten chambers at its base. A quarter of a mile further north is the residence of the King. Rising above his private apartments is another Tower of Gold [Phimeanakas]. These are the monuments which have caused merchants from overseas to speak so often of "Cambodia the rich and noble."[1]

—Zhou Daguan, 1296–97

A member of the Chinese Mongol embassy to Yasodharapura (Angkor) at the close of the thirteenth century, Zhou Daguan left vivid firsthand descriptions of the city, its royalty and daily life, and its riches. He devoted considerable comment to the visual splendor of the temples and palaces of the capital in the final decades of its prosperity. Three centuries later, Portuguese and Spanish visitors to Angkor, missionaries and mercenaries, again provided firsthand accounts. The Spaniard Gabriel de San Antonio wrote of his compatriots' "discovery" of Angkor in 1570 and reported their descriptions of "a marvellous construction.... [T]here are in this town five towers, at the top of each is found a ball of gilded bronze."[2]

Golden metal objects once formed a critical component of the appearance of Angkor. These were not limited to the "golden towers" described by Zhou Daguan but extended to all manner of religious imagery, ritual accoutrements, weapons, and battle standards, and to a variety of architectural antefixes, claddings, and applied reliefs. (fig. 40) Temple buildings were embellished with gilt-bronze cladding and housed precious icons of the gods and deified ancestors.

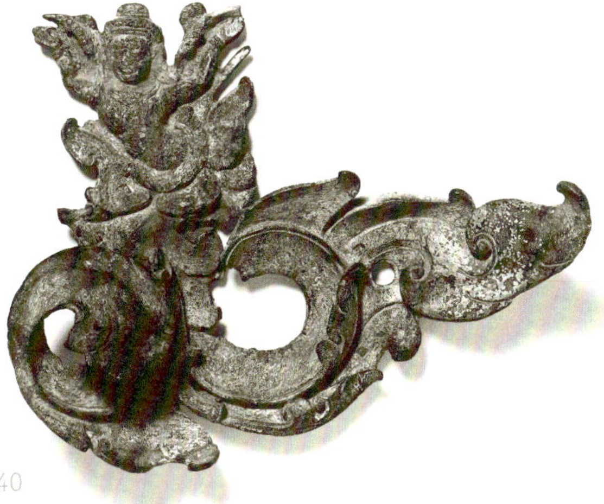

40

40 Architectural ornament depicting a celestial celebrant emerging from a lotus flower and foliage. Cambodia, Angkor period, 11th century. Copper alloy; 28 × 16 cm. Victoria and Albert Museum, London. Gift of the Anthony Gardner Estate, IS87-1993.

The Brahman priests who officiated at state ceremonies used high-value ritual utensils appropriate to the importance of their tasks. Within the palace complex, the king and his inner court enjoyed precious metal vessels for their daily routines (fig. 41), and an array of "ornaments of special design," as Zhou Daguan described them—presumably regalia and military standards—were displayed when the king appeared before his people.

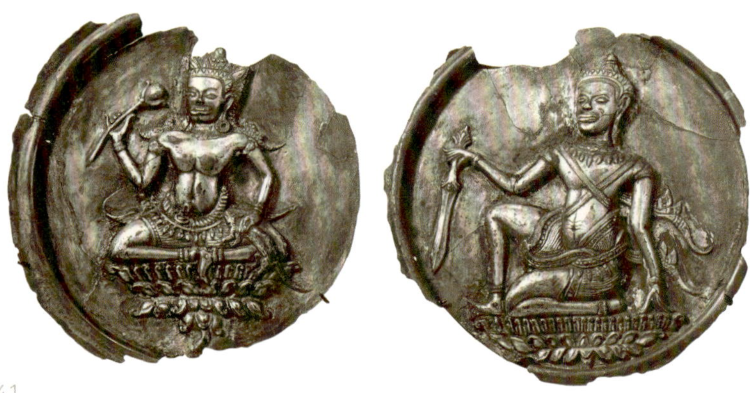

41

Gilt-bronze tridents (*triśūla*), some of which would have stood more than three feet high, were affixed to Shaiva temple towers.[3] The foundation inscription of Ta Keo names the temple as "Mountain with Golden Peaks" and describes it as displaying "five-branched arrows" (*triśūla*) on its towers.[4] Relief depictions of temple towers, such as those at the Bakong, tell us how they looked. The *triśūla* depicted here (fig. 42) was excavated close to the eastern staircase of Phimeanakas, the royal tower within the walled royal palace complex at Angkor Thom. This findspot suggests that it was originally installed as an antefix on that monument. The royal association fits well with the quality of decorative detail, seen in the ornate floral bosses that intercept the shafts of the three prongs.[5]

41 Offering dishes with a repoussé depiction of Kubera, the god of riches, and of a seated nobleman, perhaps a representation of a Khmer king (possibly Suryavarman II or Yasovarman II). Cambodia, Angkor period, early to mid 12th century. Gilt silver; diam. 9 and 9.5 cm. Photograph courtesy of Christies, New York.

Zhou Daguan stated that the Khmer nobility used gold and silver vessels for both their domestic and religious needs, and at death had their ashes thrown into river, interred in a precious metal jar.

42 Trident (triśūla) page 91
Cambodia, Angkor period, 10th century or later
Bronze; 23.5 × 18.6 × 2 cm
National Museum of Cambodia, Ga5635

Shiva's trident weapon, the *triśūla*, serves both as an attribute of the god and as emblematic of the god's presence. As such, it is displayed as an independent icon, affixed to his shrines and carried by devotees. At Angkor, *triśūla*s were a regular feature of temples, as antefixes to the towers and as displayed by Shiva's door-keepers, the *dvarapala*s.

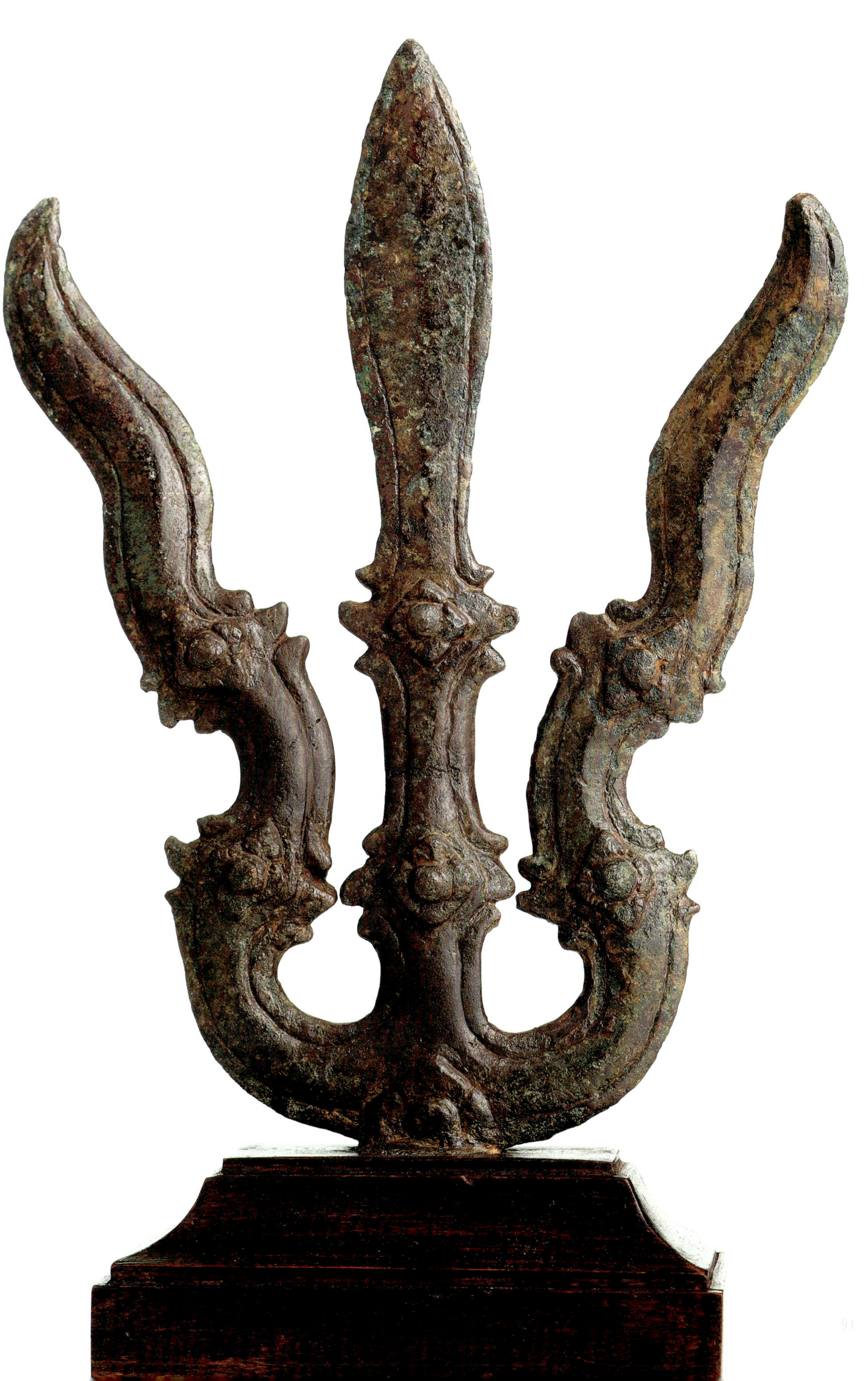

The palaces of the Angkorian courts must have been beautiful structures, gilded and curtained pillared halls with elaborate golden antefixes on the roof eaves and awnings. Henri Parmentier's evocative line drawings—composed of design elements drawn from stone temple architecture and relief depictions of secular buildings, especially as seen at the Bayon—convey a vision of these structures.[6] (fig. 43) The décor may well have included masterful bronzes, such as the kneeling female with raised arms probably supporting a large disk mirror. (fig. 44) Related kneeling figures served as offering receptacles and incense burners.[7] Her finely pleated waist-skirt and jewelry suggest a court retainer.[8] Numerous smaller bronze mirrors have survived from the Angkorian period, presumably objects of everyday use among the elite, as excavated examples would seem to suggest.[9] (fig. 45)

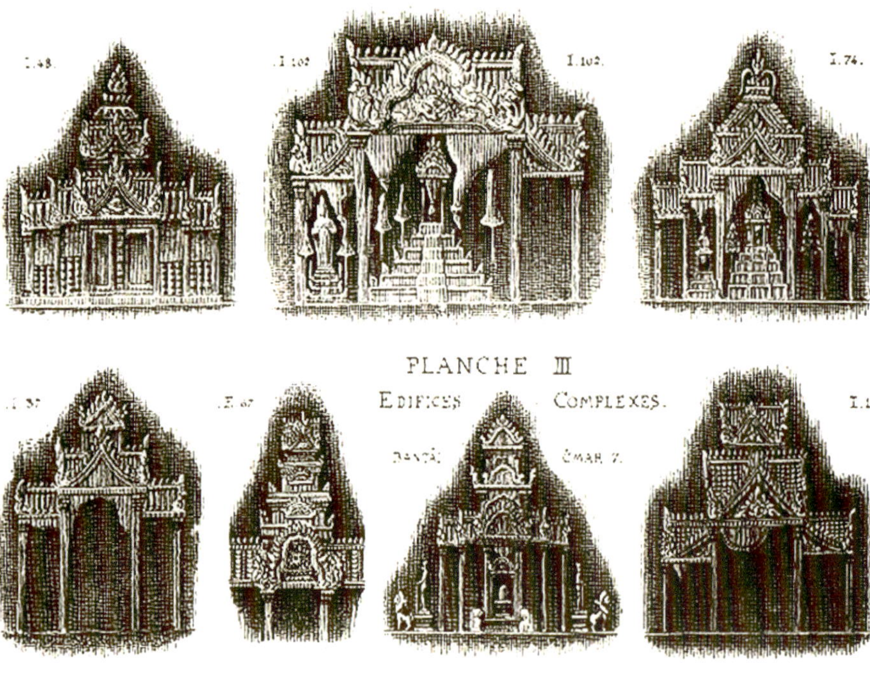

43

43 Composite reconstruction of Angkorian shrines and palace architecture by Henri Parmentier, based on his meticulous study of depictions of Angkorian architecture in reliefs and from his study of extant monuments. A trained architect and founding member of the École française d'Extrême-Orient, Parmentier established the Conservation d'Angkor at Siem Reap and pioneered the restoration of temples at Angkor. He was also a leading figure in the creation of the national museums in Phnom Penh, Hanoi, and Danang. Line drawing after H. Parmentier, "L'Architecture interpretée dans les bas-reliefs du Cambodge," *Bulletin de l'École française d'Extrême-Orient* 14 (1914).

44 Kneeling female figure pages 93–95
Cambodia, Angkor period, first half of the 12th century
Bronze; 34 × 24 × 15 cm
National Museum of Cambodia, Ga5476

The figure probably supported a polished bronze mirror like that in fig. 45.

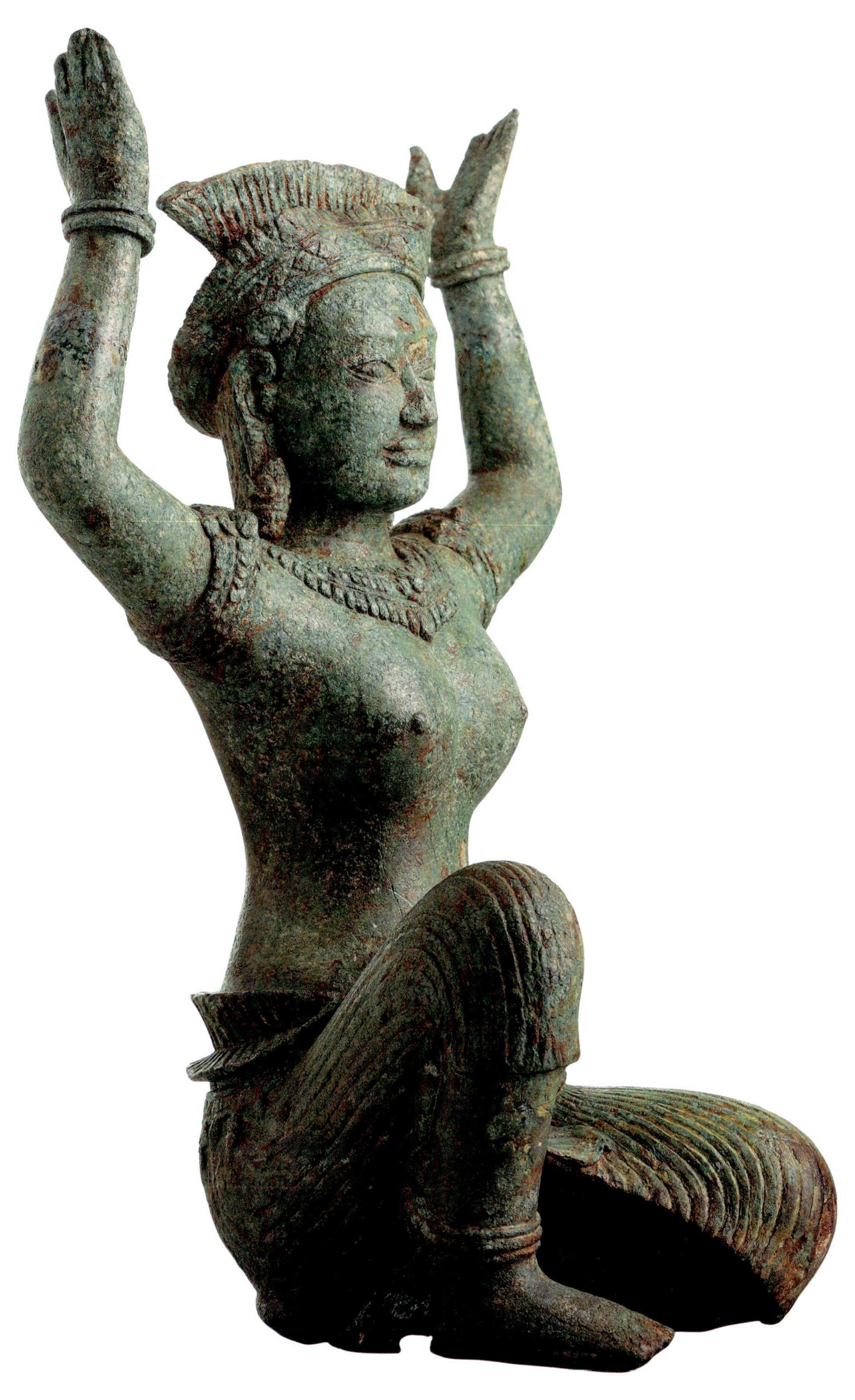

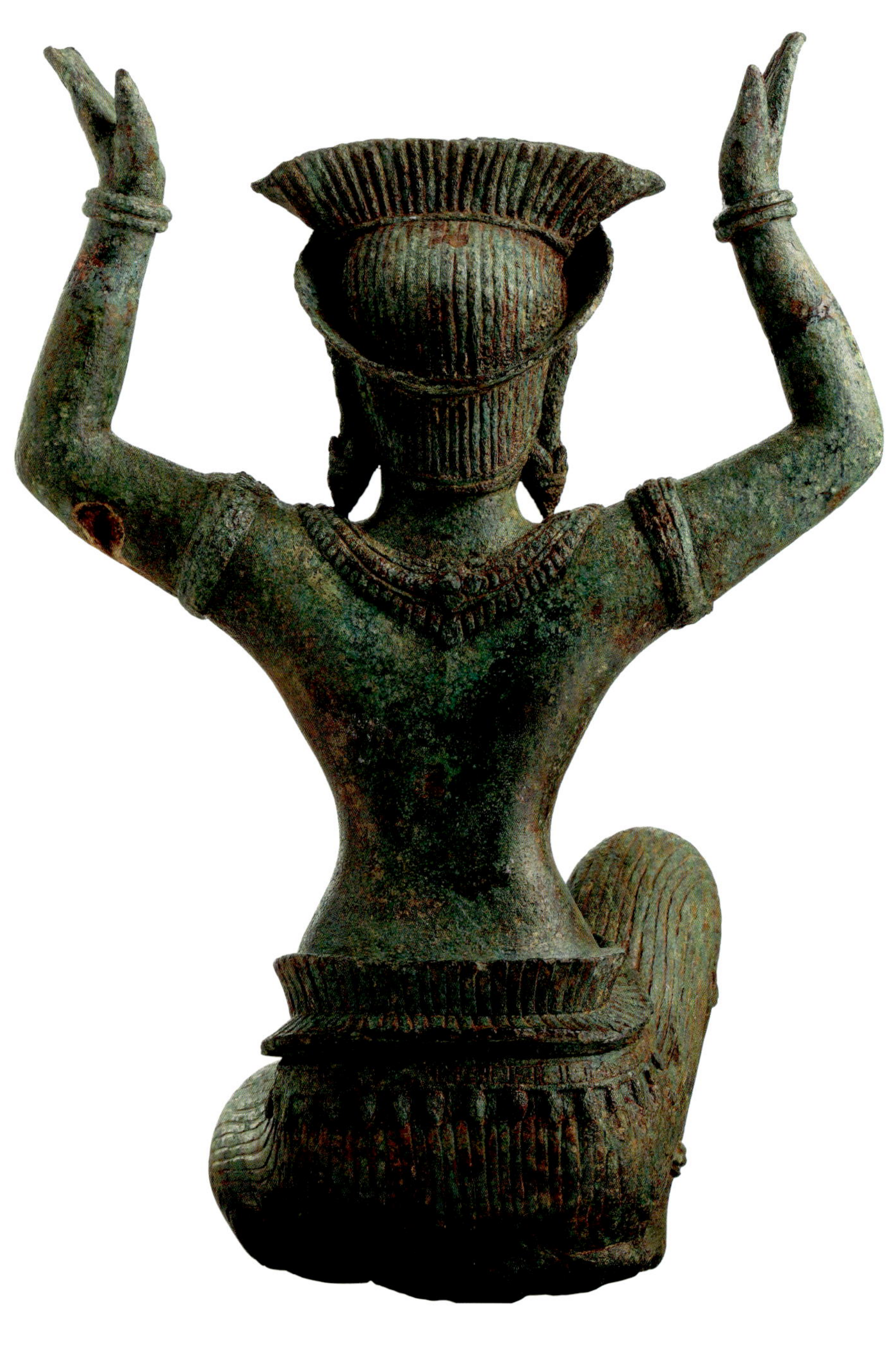

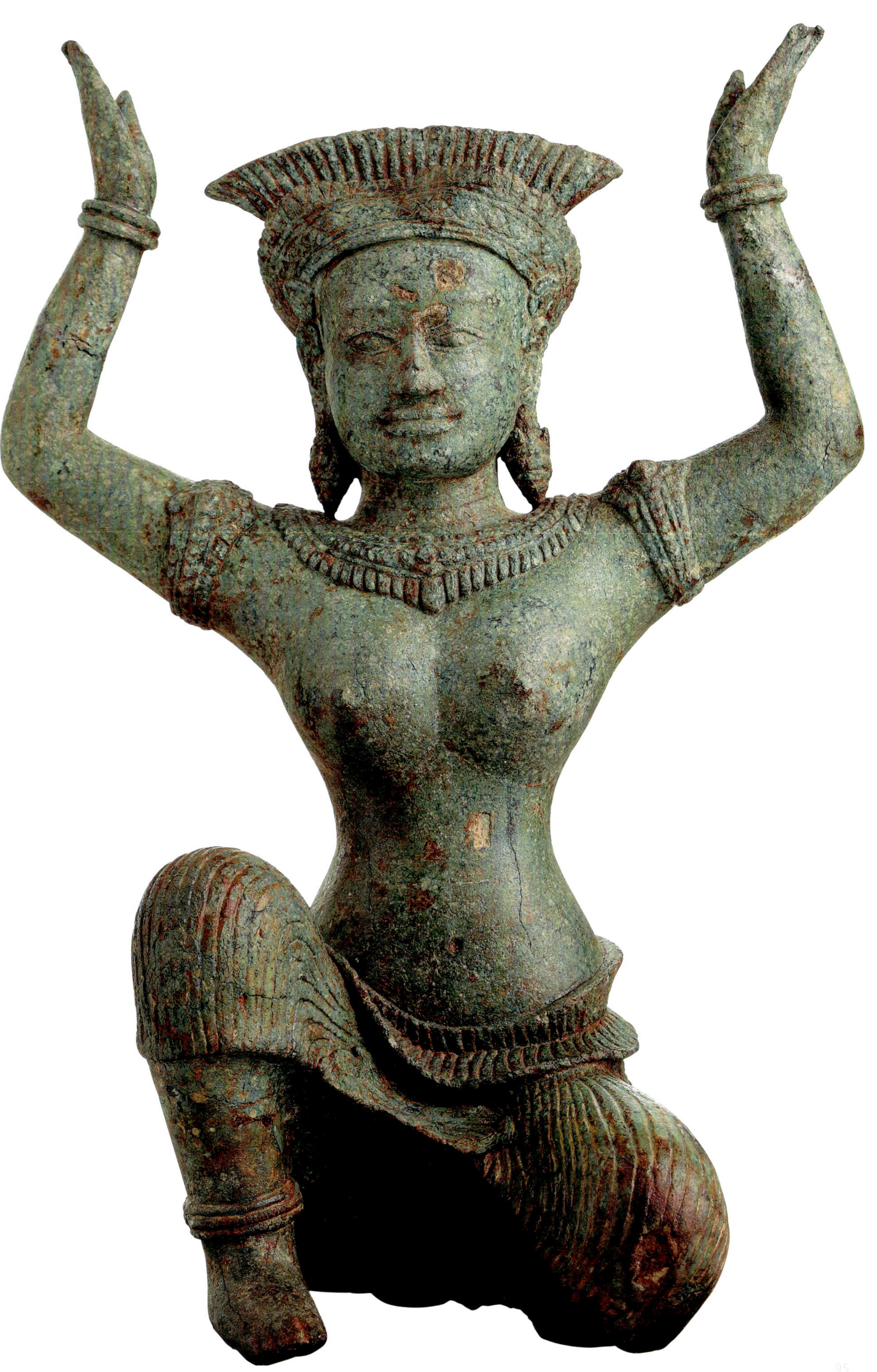

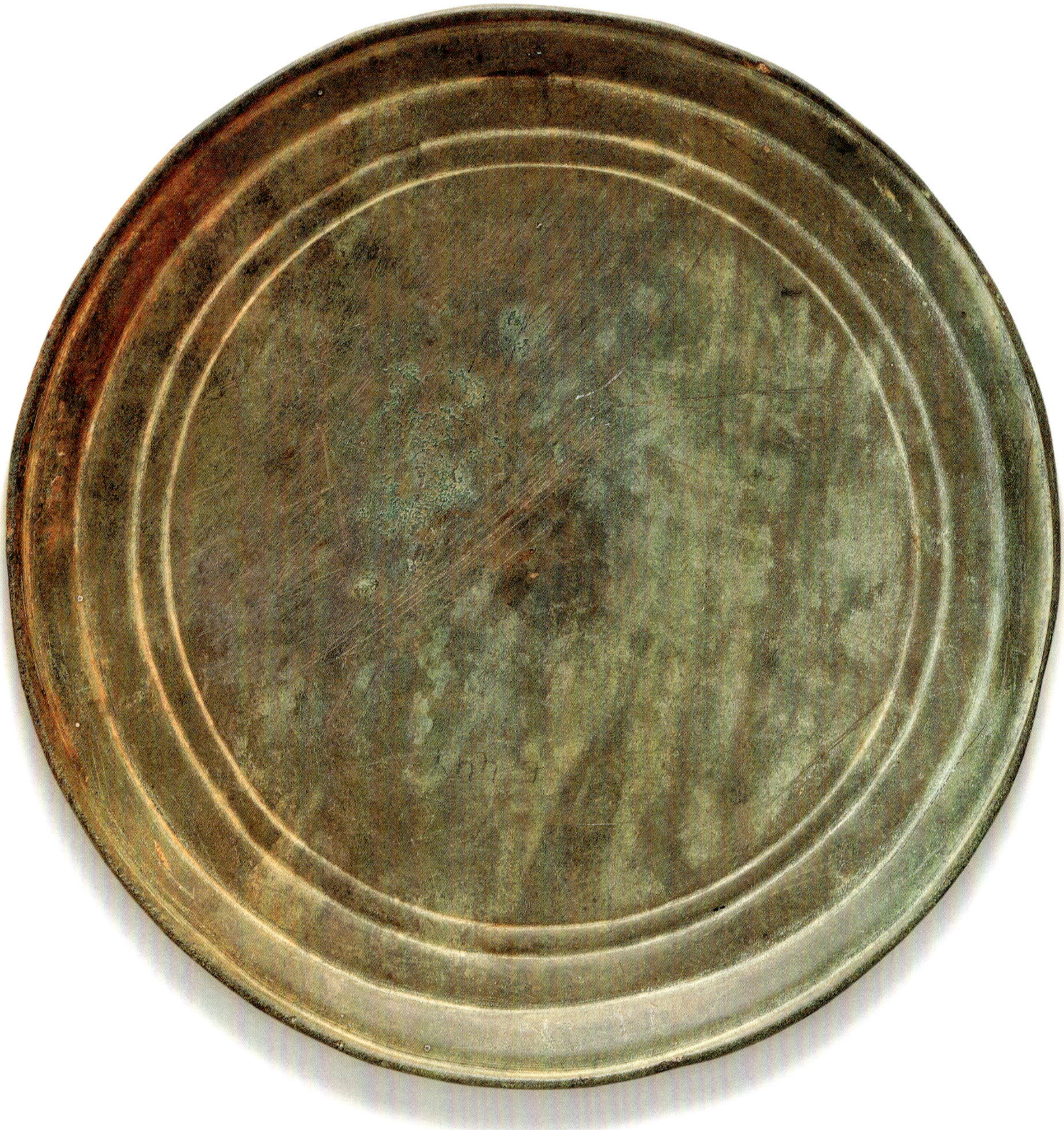

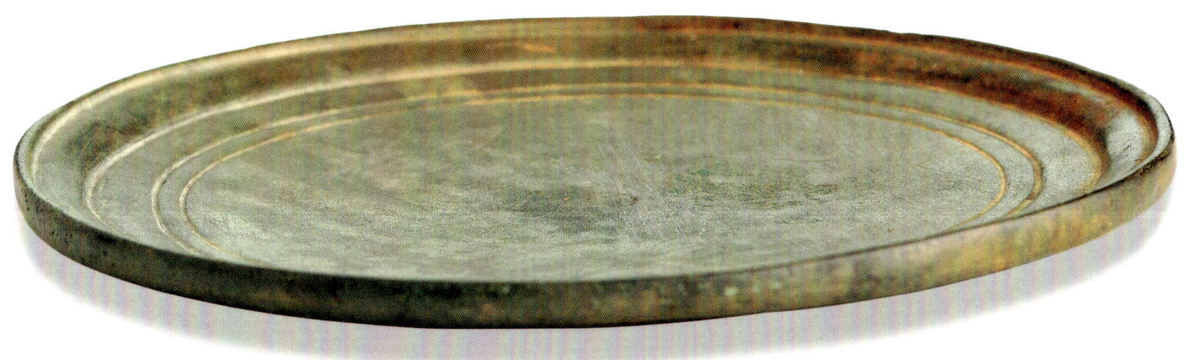

Gods, Guardians, and Vehicles

A profusion of monumental gilded images of deities and animals, mostly guardian creatures such as lions or the vehicles of the gods themselves, adorned the city's temples and palaces. Gilded lions guarded axial staircases and, according to the inscriptional record, secondary sanctuaries housed images of the gods. As many of these chapels have no remaining trace of stone pedestals, we may assume that they probably housed metal icons.

In 1983, a remarkable discovery was made. A life-sized silver-copper alloy sculpture of Shiva's seated calf-bull, Vrsabha (Nandin), was unearthed at the Tuol Kuhea temple site in southern Cambodia in Kandal province, east of Phnom Da, and removed to the Silver Pagoda of the royal palace at Phnom Penh. (fig. 46) With a length of 1.3 meters, the icon is the largest animal sculpture from Angkorian Cambodia discovered to date. It is remarkable for its astute naturalism and the sense that it conveys of embodied divine power,[10] but it is far from a unique find, nor is it the largest Angkorian bronze known. In 1960, fragments of a monumental bronze Shiva were excavated at Kra Lanh, Siem Reap province,[11] and in 1961, the spectacular remains of a standing Maitreya were unearthed at Ban Tanot, Nakhon Ratchasima province, in northeast Thailand.[12] Both approximate double life-size, making them awesome objects of veneration in their original state. In 1989, another monumental bronze, a standing Shiva 1.5 meters in height, was excavated near the south gateway of Prasat Kamphaeng Yai in Sisaket province, northeast Thailand, a temple that was dedicated in 1042.[13]

The largest bronze image from Cambodia ever recorded, and without rival in all of Southeast Asia during this period, is the Vishnu sleeping on the serpent Ananta excavated in 1936 from the island temple of the West Mebon. (fig. 47) In addition to the intact upper section, fragments also were recovered; the complete figure, cast in sections, would have measured more than six meters long. In all probability, the entire figure was gilded, though the gold is no longer visible due to extensive corrosion, and was further enhanced with inlays of contrasting precious metals in the eyebrows, eyes, and mustache. Aesthetically this sculpture is unmatched in the corpus of Angkorian bronzes. The sculptor has created a sublime image of Vishnu in repose, at the moment when he is about to emerge from his cosmic slumber to rescue the universe yet again.[14]

The full radiant beauty and majesty of this figure, installed in its tank of flowing water, would have been inspiring to all who saw it, but its placement on an island in the western *baray* would have ensured access to only a select few, probably the king, his entourage, and an elite corp of Brahman priests.

45 Mirror
Cambodia, China, or Tibet, Angkor period, possibly 11th–12th century
Bronze; 2 × 14 cm
National Museum of Cambodia, Ga5537

According to Zhou Daguan, in late 13th-century Angkor, dozens of mirrors were arranged around the king's audience window, suggesting that such luxury objects were a regular feature of palace life.

Zhou Daguan, describing a shrine in a great lake that had a "bronze reclining Buddha with water constantly flowing from its navel," may have been recording from hearsay the great Vishnu placed under worship some 230 years earlier. The siting of this image in the heart of one of the two greatest reservoirs built in Angkorian history underscores the power of the water symbolism of Hindu creation myths and their compatibility with Khmer cosmologies. We may imagine this icon being worshiped in eleventh-century Yasodharapura in a manner not dissimilar to that still performed today at the Vishnu-Ananta tank-shrine at Budhanilakantha in the Kathmandu valley, Nepal.[15]

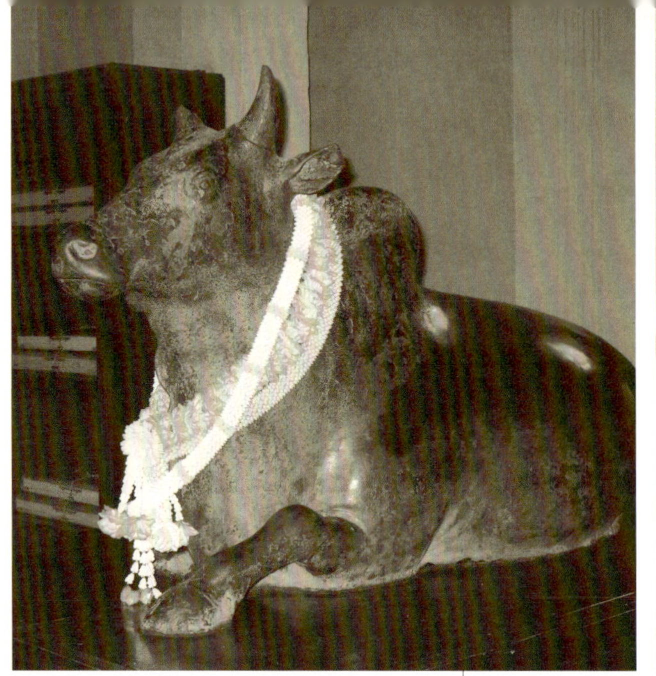

46

Zhou Daguan referred to great numbers of golden and bronze images at major shrines in and around Angkor Thom. His description of the "Northern Lake" corresponds precisely to the late twelfth-century island temple of Neak Pean, a complex water-cosmology mandala. The small-scale and exquisite shrine was built by Jayavarman VII (reigned 1181–circa 1218) as part of the *baray* system serving his royal temple of Preah Khan, to which the shrine was linked. Zhou Daguan described a square tower of gold at the center of the lake and several dozen stone rooms. "If you are looking for gold lions, bronze elephants, bronze oxen, bronze horses," he reported, "here is where you will find them."

The newly discovered Silver Pagoda Nandin bears testimony to the veracity of his account, as do the late Angkorian bronze lion and three-headed elephant, Erawan, the mount of the god of storms Indra, now preserved in Mandalay, upper Burma (Myanmar).[16] These are life-size castings of great sophistication, typically enhanced with mercury gilding. An image of the calf-bull Nandin in the exhibition (fig. 49) belongs to this tradition. The calf-bull is sensitively rendered, poised and alert to the omnipresence of his Lord Shiva.

One of the most detailed accounts of the wealth of metal religious imagery at Angkor is provided in a sixteenth-century Thai source, *The Royal Chronicles of Ayutthaya*.[17] This document includes a highly partial but nonetheless informative account of the raids and plundering of Angkor in 1431. According to the chronicle, the armies of the Thai king Boromaracha II systematically looted the city of its religious images:

At that time the King then had … all the images of sacred oxen and all the images of lions and other creatures brought along. When they reached Ayutthaya, the King therefore had all of the animal images taken and presented as offerings, some at the Phra Si Ratana Maha That Monastery and some at the Phra Si Sanphet Monastery.[18]

This account confirms that significant numbers of large-scale bronzes were still in situ at Angkor in the fifteenth century.[19] Compelling circumstantial evidence suggests that the seven late Angkorian bronze icons preserved at the Arakan Monastery, Mandalay—consisting of three male guardians

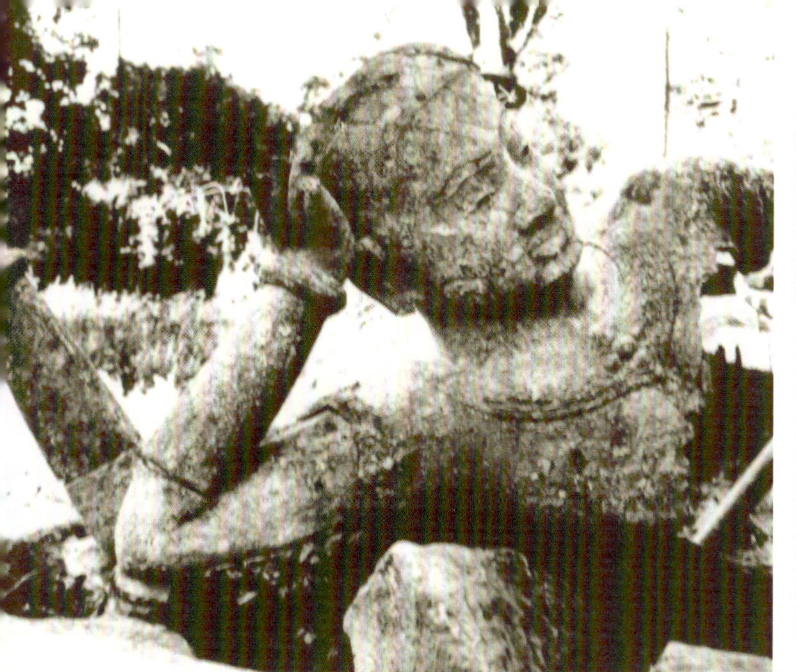

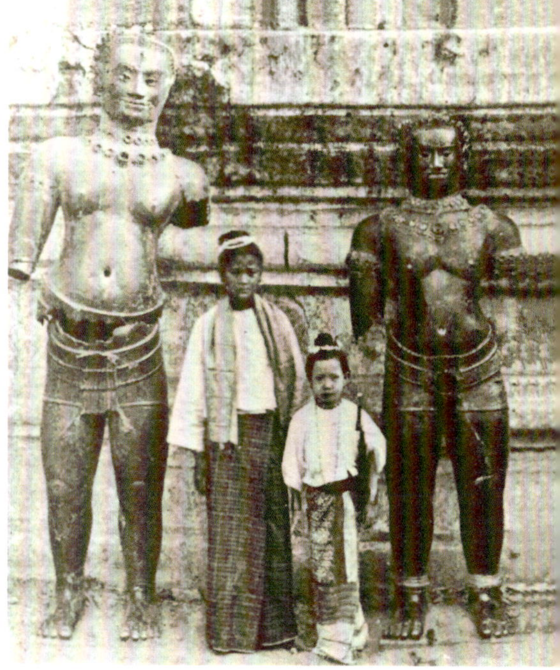

47 48

(*dvarapala*), three lions, and the representation of Erawan—are the remnants of the original group of images looted from Angkor by the Thais in 1431. The looted icons remained in Ayutthaya until the Burmese army sacked the city in 1569 and took them to Pegu in lower Burma. Around 1594 they were plundered in turn by the ruler of Arakan and taken to Mrohaung, then finally installed in Amarapura (Mandalay) at the end of the seventeenth century.

46 Life-size silver-copper alloy sculpture of Nandin, discovered in 1983 at Tuol Kuhea in Kandal province and now under worship in the manuscript library shrine of the Silver Pagoda, Royal Palace, Phnom Penh.

47 Vishnu sleeping on the serpent Ananta. This sculpture is the largest bronze icon ever recovered from Angkorian Cambodia. It was discovered in 1936 by the French archaeologist Maurice Glaize in the ruins of the West Mebon, a temple constructed on a manmade island in the western *baray* by Udayadityavrnan II in the mid-11th century. National Museum of Cambodia.

48 Two monumental bronze guardians of late Angkorian production, the property of the Arakan Pagoda Monastery, Mandalay, photographed circa 1900. These Khmer bronzes were part of a cache of bronze temple sculptures looted from Angkor by the Thai king in 1431 and in turn appropriated by the Burmese during the sacking of Ayutthaya in 1569. After V. C. Scott O'Connor, *The Silken East: A Record of Life and Travel in Burma* (London: Hutchinson, 1904).

49 Shiva's bull, Nandin pages 100–101
Cambodia, Angkor period, 12th–13th century
Bronze with mercury gilding; 36 × 64 × 32 cm
National Museum of Cambodia, Ga5739

Large-scale icons of Nandin were installed for worship in an anteroom adjacent to a temple's central sanctuary housing the Shivalinga, or in a freestanding pavilion (*mandapa*) removed from the temple proper but orientated on the same axis, facing Shiva's sanctuary.

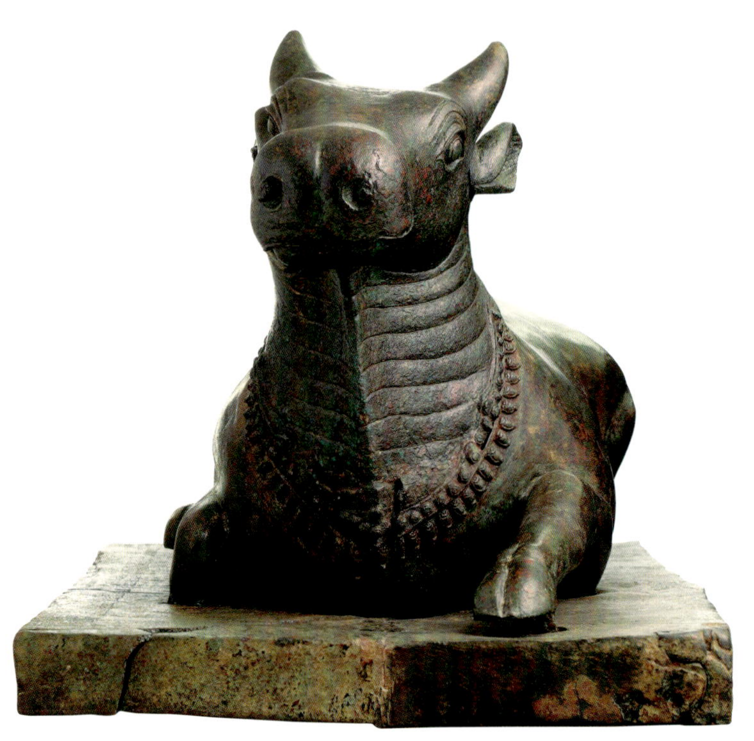

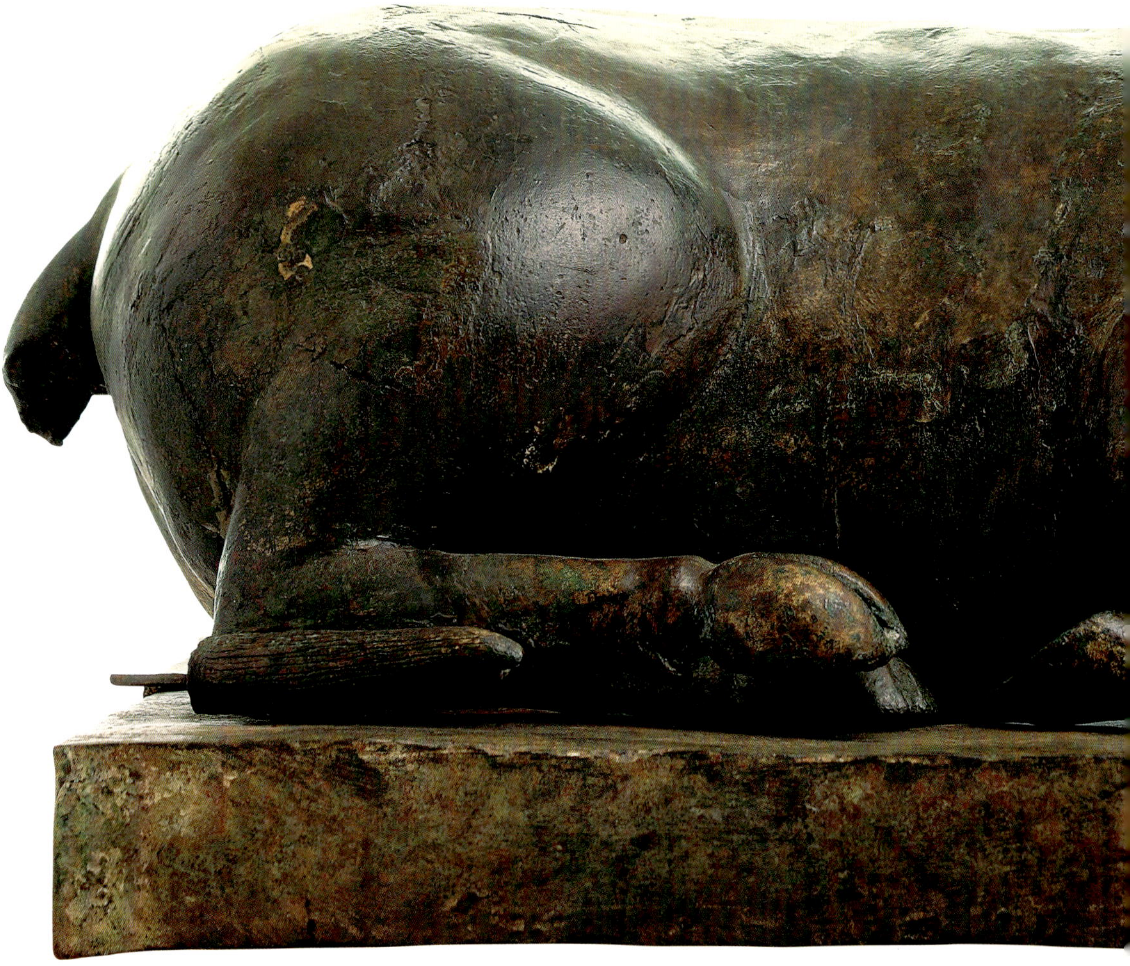

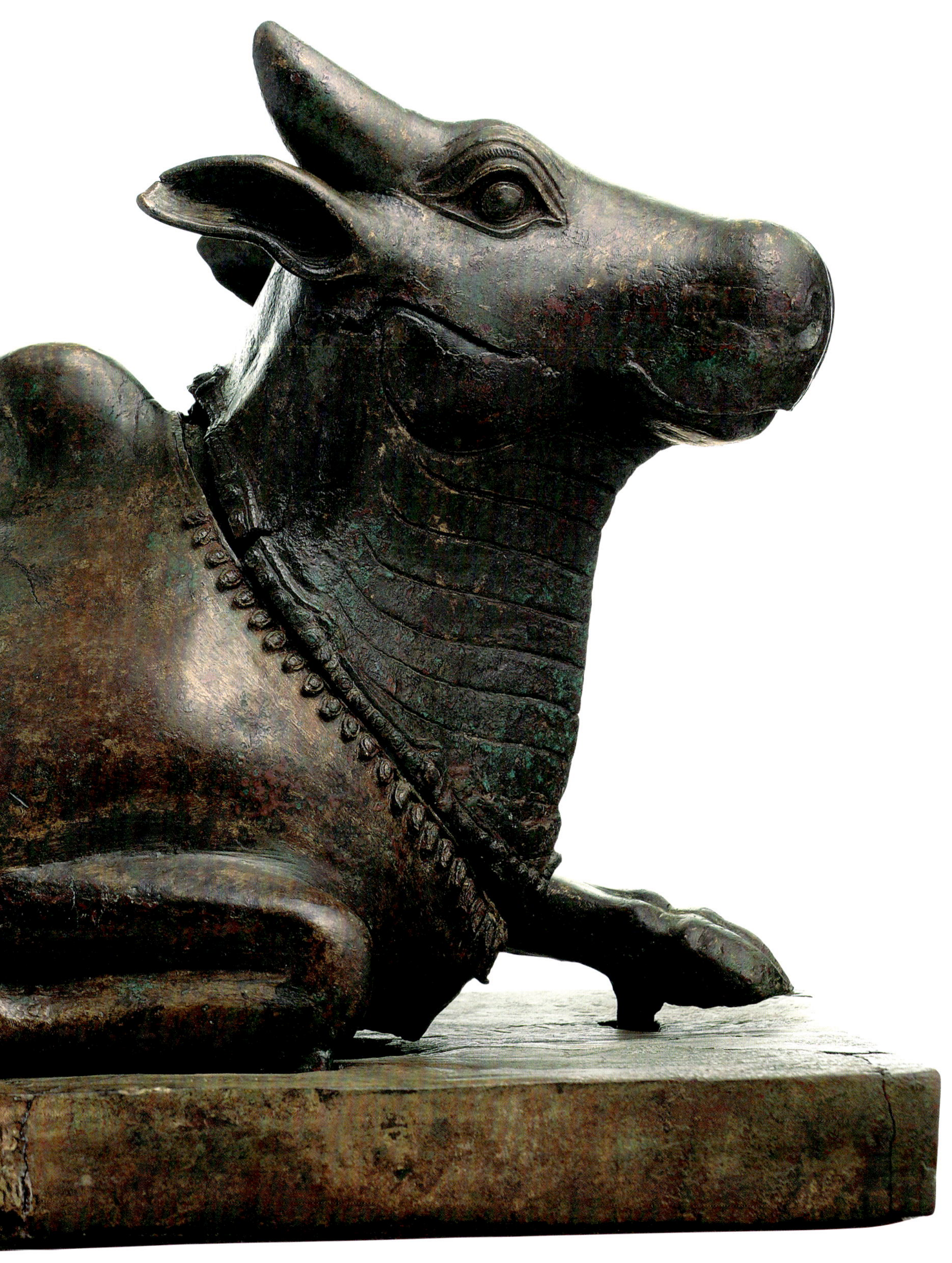

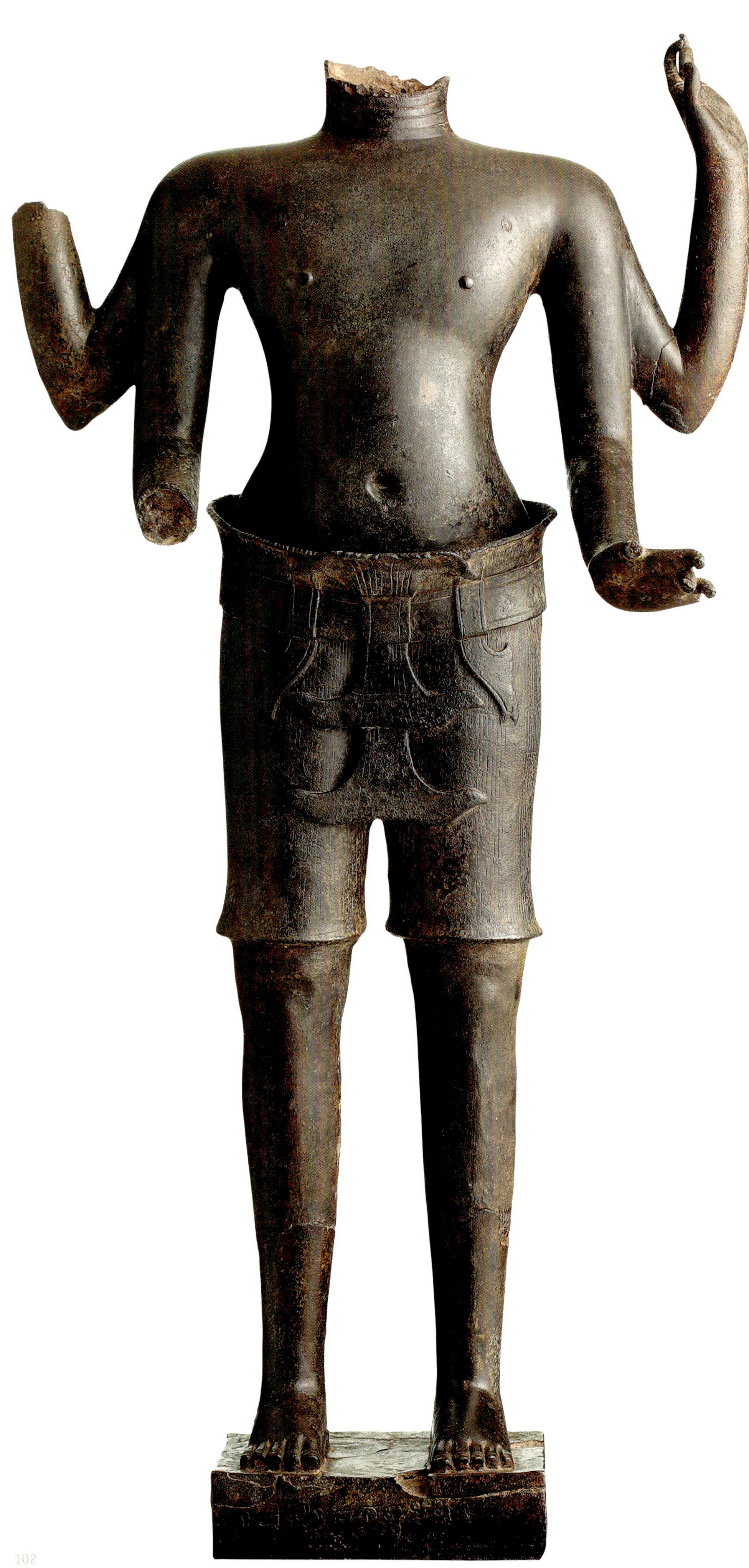

Earlier, in 1177, the Cham army had invaded and occupied Angkor, probably pilfering the treasuries at that time. If the "Mandalay bronzes" were cast after the Cham looting, they may date between the restoration of Khmer authority around 1182–83 by Jayavarman VII and the second half of the thirteenth century.[20] That they are among the great achievements of the late Angkorian bronze-casting tradition to have come down to us is made all the more extraordinary by their remarkable journey from Angkor to Mandalay.[21] The monumental guardians (fig. 48), standing at nearly two meters, display extensive use of contrasting metal inlays to heighten their realism. The Mandalay group are the only monumental Angkorian bronzes to have survived in a non-archaeological context.

Icons

Angkorian Cambodia distinguished itself as a major center for monumental lost-wax casting. As this exhibition demonstrates, however, the bronze sculptures were not all monumental. Many, including those of the principal deities, also were cast as smaller-scale icons suitable for use in festival processions as well as in shrines. Three highly important bronzes of this scale are exhibited: the eight-armed Maitreya (see fig. 5), datable to around 900 in the reign of Yashovarman I (899–circa 915); an unidentified four-armed standing male dated by inscription to 970 (fig. 50); and a two-armed male figure dating from the close of the eleventh century. (fig. 51)

The unidentified deity with the inscription (fig. 50) was recovered from Battambang province, an indication of the extent to which metropolitan castings of major cult icons were distributed to regional centers, presumably serving as costly donations to the province's temples by local governors, senior officials, and generals. The issue of production centers for Khmer bronzes remains unresolved, as no traces of workshop activity have been

50 Male divinity, probably Avalokiteshvara or Shiva page 102; see also fig. 18
Cambodia, Angkor period, 892 *śaka* (970 CE)
Bronze with traces of gliding; 72.5 × 36 × 23 cm
National Museum of Cambodia, Ga5166

The image bears an inscription on the base stating that it was cast in *śaka* 892, equivalent to 970 CE, early in the reign of Jayavarman V. This majestic figure probably represents Shiva, perhaps originally a multi-headed Sadāshiva. The broad-chested figure radiates physical prowess and the four arms confirm his divine status. The distinctive triple-fan pleating of the waistcloth and scarf are associated with stone sculptures from the mid-10th century Pre Rup style.

51 Male divinity, probably Shiva pages 104–105; see also figs. 20 and 20A
Cambodia, Angkor period, late 11th century
Gilt bronze; 57 × 16 × 17 cm
National Museum of Cambodia, Ga2993

The style, distinguished by superb modeling, uniform jewelry, and use of inlaid materials, belongs to the Baphuon period, late 11th century. The identity of this figure is enigmatic, as the attributes once held in each hand are now lost.

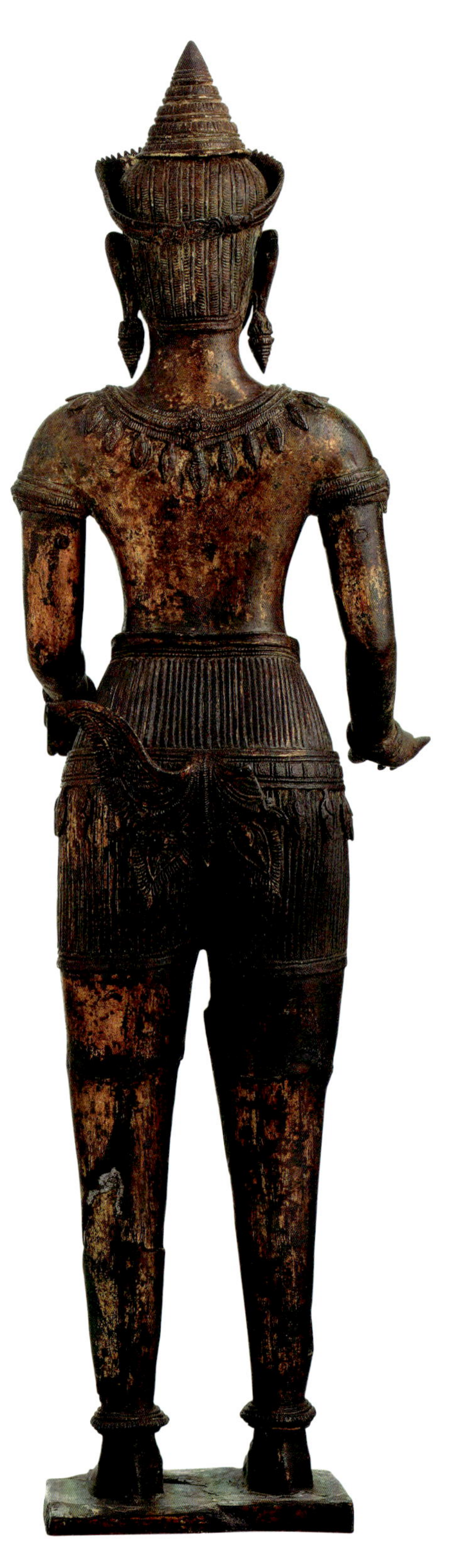

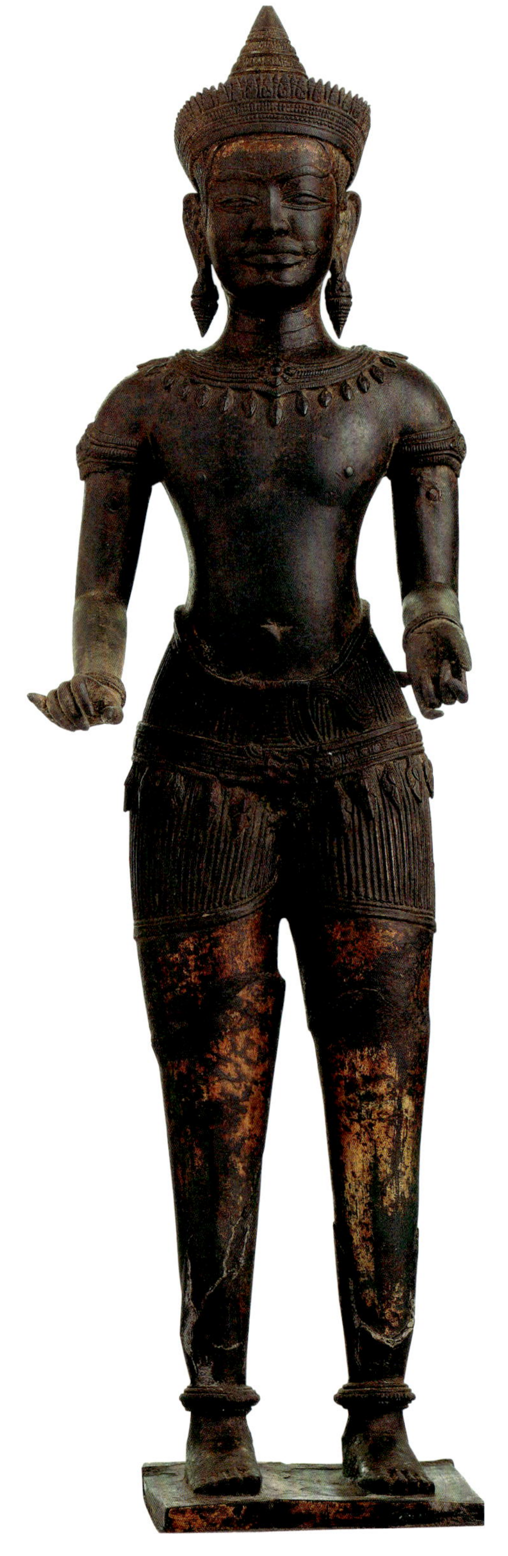

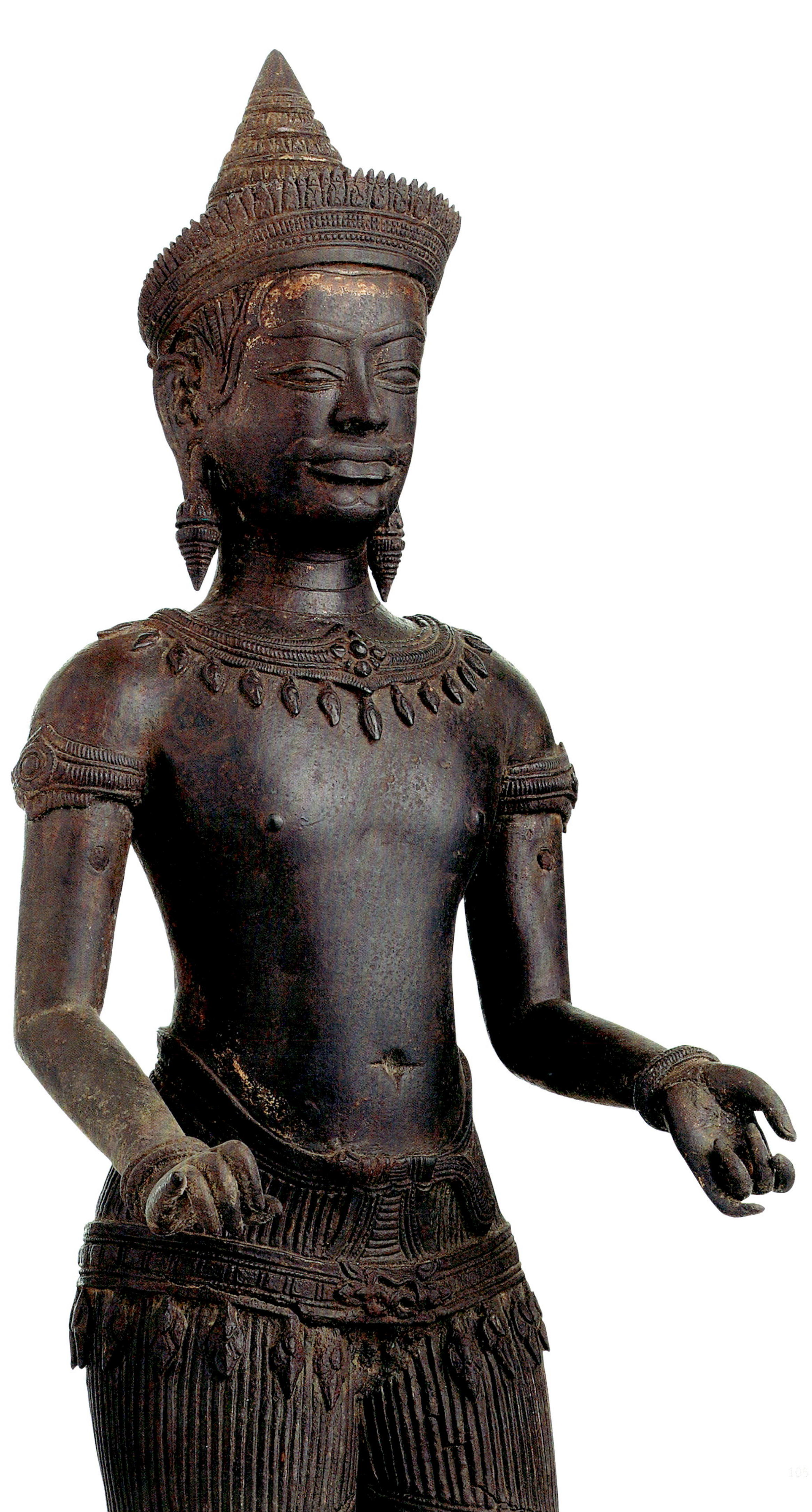

identified. While secondary centers of production probably existed—including Koh Ker at its height of power in the second quarter of the tenth century and important provincial centers such as Phimai in the eleventh and twelfth centuries—the bulk of the output probably was centered at Angkor. The remarkably high skill levels and technical processes required to model and cast such superb copper-alloy imagery precludes the possibility that most images were made where they were found. Portability of religious imagery is a characteristic of mainland Southeast Asia, where such objects were routinely sent from the center to the periphery to demonstrate patronage and assert control, or imported by the local elite to emulate metropolitan

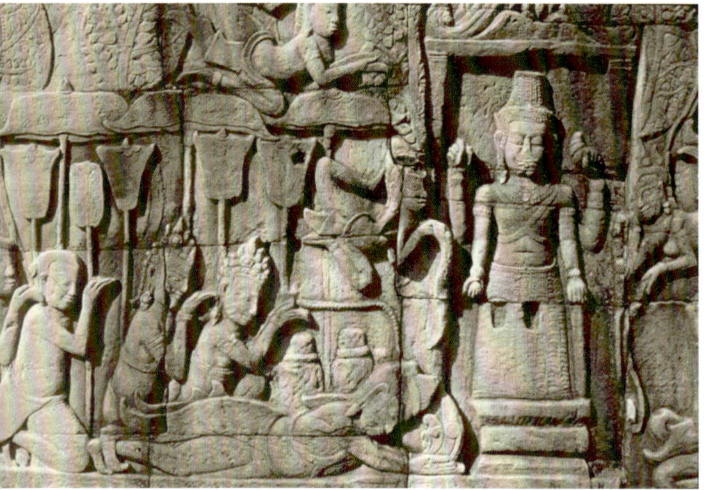

52

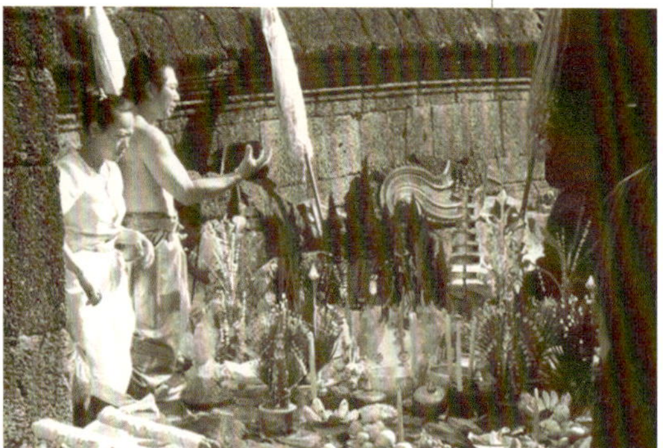

53

donor patterns. This also would appear to be the case with the male figure recovered from Phnom Bayang, Takeo province. (fig. 51) Such a remarkably fine casting, which can be related to a number of the finest surviving gilt bronzes of the period, including the monumental reclining Vishnu, must have been cast in or around Angkor.[22]

Gods in Worship

The three standing deities belong to a category of icon that was intended for use in procession. These are referred to in the Sanskrit ritual literature as *utsavamurti* (images to drive away sorrow)—portable icons temporarily empowered by the enactment of ritual to be deployed in temple festivals.[23] That this Indian concept was familiar in a Khmer temple context is demonstrated by the appearance of the term *utsava* in a number of Angkorian inscriptions.[24] It is worthwhile at this point to reflect briefly on the nature of Khmer temple ritual and what we can begin to reconstruct of it. It is evident that indigenous cults—the most prominent of which was an animistic and ancestor cult worship still practiced today as Neak Ta—were integrated into the adopted, and undoubtedly adapted, Hindu cults.[25] (figs. 52, 53) Dedications honoring one's parents and other lineage ancestors are a regular feature of royal temple foundation inscriptions.

This cult was taken to new levels of complexity in its Vajrayana Tantric guise during the reign of Jayavarman VII. His triad of state temples—Preah Khan (1191), Ta Prohm (1186), and the Bayon (circa 1200 and later), dedicated to his father, mother, and (probably) himself respectively—can be interpreted as mirroring the ruler's cult triad of the *nāga*-protected meditative Buddha (with whom the king may have identified himself) flanked by Lokeshvara (Avalokiteshvara), the embodiment of compassion (his father) and Prajñāpāramitā, the wisdom goddess (his mother). This triad is replicated in numerous images during the latter years of Jayavarman's long reign, in the first quarter of the thirteenth century. The triad recovered from Prei Monti, Roluos (fig. 25) belongs to this period. The sturdy figure of Lokeshvara (see fig. 26), unearthed from a site opposite the royal palace complex at Angkor Thom, is close in style and date to the triad. It may be presumed to have formed part of a similarly configured triad; the central icon of the *nāga*-surmounted celestial Buddha must have exceeded one meter in height, representing an important ensemble. These three icons chronicle the declining quality from the mid- to late twelfth century, as Jayavarman VII demanded greater and greater output from his workshops.

A finial adorned with a meditative Buddha protected by a seven-hooded *nāga* (fig. 54) was also probably part of temple life. It was designed to function as a fixture likely mounted onto a wooden shaft, perhaps on a standard or as a fitting on a preaching platform or palanquin for an important icon. It is an exceptionally high-quality casting for the later twelfth century and a reminder that the workshops, probably monastic and under royal patronage, remained capable of modeling and casting great metal imagery.

Shrine-like icons, such as the triad and the *Hevajra* mandala (see fig. 27) also dating from this reign, were intended as the focus of offerings and to facilitate the enactment of ritual. Much is known about Indian ritual from observations of contemporary Hindu practices and of Buddhist enactment in Nepal, for example. We are less sure how these Angkorian deities were honored. Certainly an array of impressive objects associated with temple activity has survived, the ritual paraphernalia of temple life. Is it valid to extrapolate from the use of such tools of worship in the Indian subcontinent to interpret Angkorian temple practices? If we can judge from a number of

52 A Khmer monarch and his two queens with entourage venerating an icon of Vishnu installed in a sanctuary chapel in the inner gallery of the Bayon, Angkor Thom. This relief dates from the period when the temple was appropriated to Hindu use in the second half of the 13th century. The prostrate figure may be reasonably identified as Jayavarman VIII, the monarch responsible for the conversion.

53 A Khmer professional priest or medium performing a thanksgiving ceremony on behalf of a Cambodian family that sponsored this extravagant offering in the grounds of Banteay Srei temple, 1999. Note the offerings of food, the presence of (auspicious) umbrellas, and the priest's dress of gold-thread cloth and gold belt. Parallels can be drawn with the worship scene in the 13th-century relief in fig. 52.

54 **Finial with crowned nāga-protected Buddha** pages 108–109
Cambodia, Angkor period, late 12th–early 13th century
Bronze; 48.5 × 21 × 5 cm
National Museum of Cambodia, Ga5593

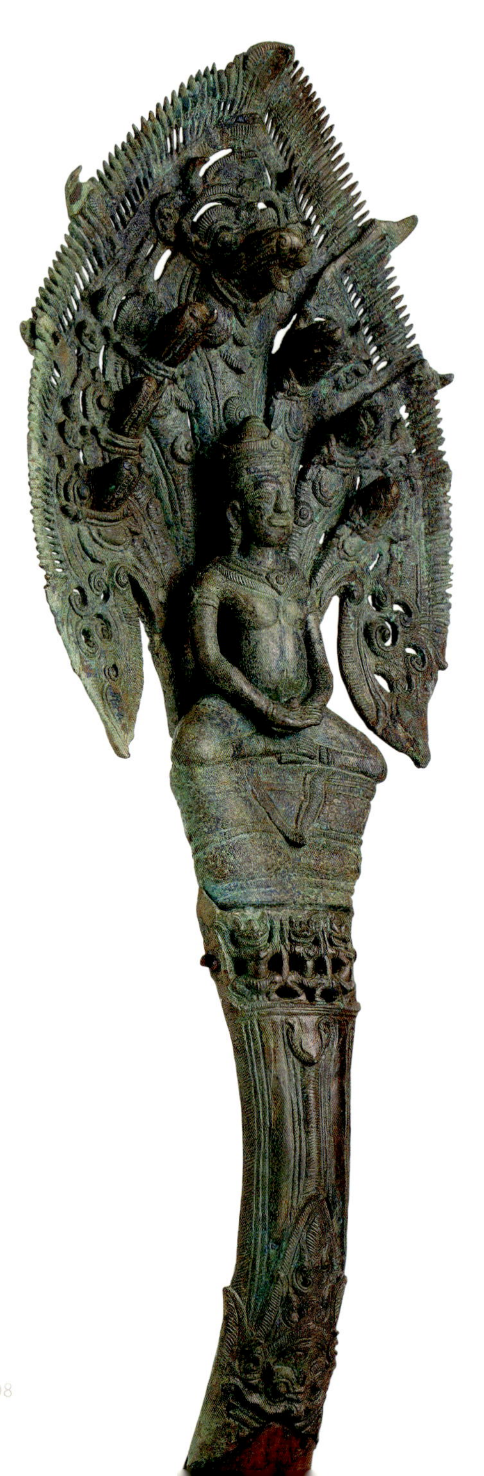

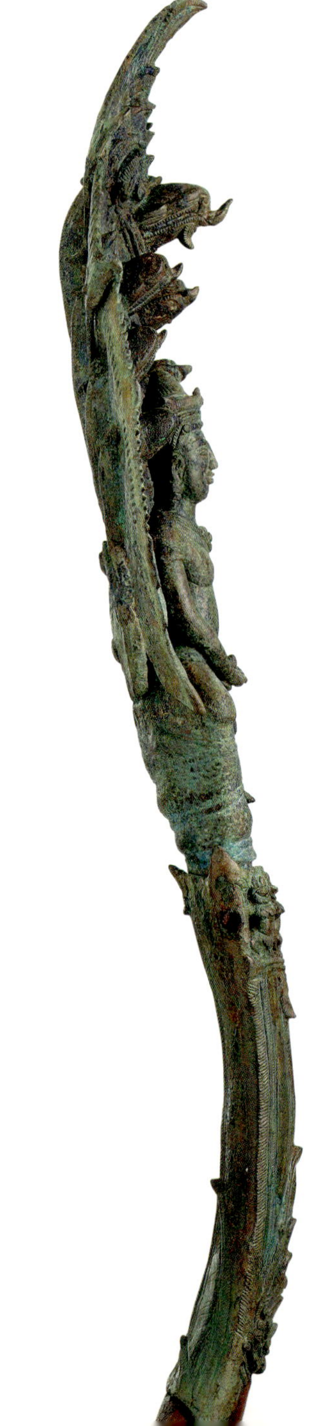

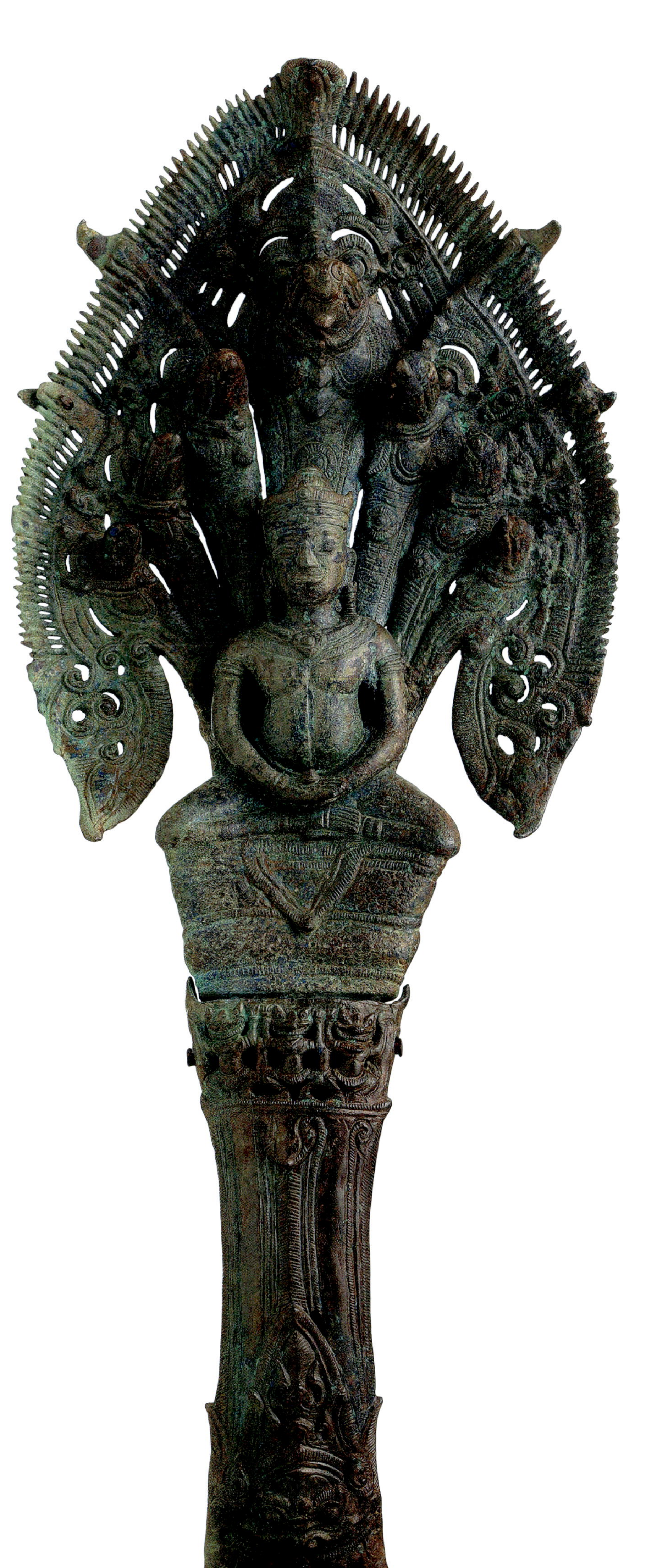

extant Angkorian inscriptions that make clear the prescribed nature of ritual at that time, then the answer is a qualified yes. The observance of Indian ritual was recommended but not, it seems, exclusively.

In an Indian context, temple rituals must be performed according to a strict timetable, at appointed times of the day and at prescribed intervals—daily, weekly, fortnightly, monthly, annually and at periodic cycles of years, most typically every twelve years. In an Indian Hindu setting, these routines of worship are laid out in ritually prescriptive manuals, the *ágamas*; in the Shaiva *ágamas*, for example, the *kriyapada* section deals with image making and the ritual procedures for their worship.[26] The standard South Indian Shaiva *ágama* is the Siddhanta school *Somaśambhu-paddhati*, known in its current form from at least the Chola period (850–1278).[27] We can reasonably assume that, initially, such guidelines were enacted by Indian priests recruited into the Khmer system, but over time we are on less secure ground. Khmer inscriptions provide some guidance here.

An inscription datable to 1306 on the Banteay Srei temple makes clear that the Brahman priests there were guided in the rituals they performed by manuals and that they were following customary practice in this regard:

The personnel of the corporation [priesthood] of Khnar Gran at [the temple] of the goddess are commanded to serve the goddess as [is done] in all [other] deity sites [temples], following the verses of the ordinances of the Sacred Manual on the Procedures for Worship at Sacred Sites.[28]

We do not know the extent that these sacred manuals were closely modeled on Indian antecedents or were heavily "Khmerized." Given that they were based on scriptural sources and enacted within the conventional Indic pantheon of deities, there is good reason to assume that they generally followed Indian models. Nonetheless, rituals also were created anew in Angkorian Cambodia. King Suryavarman I (reigned circa 1002–50) was praised in an inscription of his successor, Udayaditavarman II (reigned 1050–66), for being so learned and skilled in Shaiva ritual that he composed his own manual for honoring his Lord:

And being a born devotee of Siva he was able by virtue of his intelligence to compose a fully appropriate [manual for] an excellent ritual of Siva worship taught in [Saiva] scripture as soon as he had heard it [expounded in that source].[29]

Ritual manuals were transmitted via the medium of the palm-leaf manuscript and enacted by Brahmans trained in their interpretation. Here, we witness Suryavarman, a Khmer king steeped in the Shaiva tradition, apparently improvising his own ritual procedures. Such initiatives lay outside Indian practice, where authority rested with the Shaiva teacher, and were not for reinvention by a devotee, no matter how elevated.[30] Nonetheless, to acquire a high command of sacred wisdom and ritual was a desirable attainment for monarchs in India; the Pallava king Narasimhavarman II (reigned 695–728) was described in his foundation inscription at the royal Kailashanatha temple as "one whose means of knowledge is the *ágamas*."[31]

The Preah Khan inscription adds to our understanding of these performances of ritual and the use of images of deities and other instruments of worship, including devotional music and dance.[32] The inscription records the temple's dedication in 1191 as one of the premier temples of Jayavarman VII and, like Ta Prohm and later the Bayon, a key site for the enactment of rituals for the benefit of the sovereign and state.[33] The inscription dedicates the temple to the memory of Jayavarman's father in honor of the supreme bodhisattva Lokeshvara. The cult image was consecrated together with images of the Buddha and Prajñāpāramitā, the favored Buddhist triad of his reign. We are told that images of 430 other deities were honored with their own shrines or tower sanctuaries and that, in addition to stone images of the gods, a vast number of smaller images were provided—the inscription says 20,400 (perhaps a symbolic number) deities in gold, silver, and bronze.[34]

The inscription further commands the presence of another 122 icons, which (presumably) had been distributed previously to state temples in the provinces. Were these sent as "tribute icons" in the same spirit as the gold and silver trees offered by vassals to sovereign in later periods, or "hostage icons," in the manner of younger princes of rival houses held at the ruling court? I suggest that the 122 icons are best seen as religious tribute, icons manufactured at the center and reassembled there to represent each of the provinces whose loyalty was vital to the security of the state. This assembly of the state's portable icons as a show of political as well as religious unity is unprecedented in the inscriptional record before Jayavarman VII. A similar display also appears to have become a part of the annual religious festivals orchestrated at the Bayon a decade or more later. The presence of such icons served to enhance the efficacy of religious rites performed to protect the state. For this reason, religious imagery also attracted the attention of invading armies, who stole such objects not simply as loot but as a means of appropriating the religio-magical power these objects embodied; witness the Mandalay bronzes, which were repeatedly stolen but never melted down for their metal value.

The clear implication is that the icons were principally metal images, employed as processional icons during temple festivals. Such festivals may be assumed to have been a routine part of temple life in Cambodia since the establishment of Indic temple worship there. The Preah Khan inscription makes clear that the festivals followed the lunar cycle of the Indian calendar: Preah Khan's week-long annual festival was to occur on the full-moon day of the month of Phalguna (March–April) and that of Ta Phrom in the following month of Chaitra (April–May).[35] Chaitra is associated especially with rituals to placate Yama, god of death; in the context of these festivals, the Preah Khan inscription expressly names Yama and Kala, the gods who determine one's fate in the afterlife.

The innumerable small images were probably the product of donations by lesser-rank members of the nobility and the monastic community. This would account for the many high-quality small bronze images that have survived from this period, commissioned for presentation to secondary shrines. Others may have been worshiped at home as household divinities, which would explain the apparently random discovery of many such icons away from temple-site locations.

This may be the case with the Ganesha in the exhibition. (fig. 55) The Hindu deity Ganesha was absorbed into the larger Buddhist pantheon, a role he retains today in Cambodia and Thailand. He acquired a status in the early history of Indic religions in mainland Southeast Asia beyond that assigned to him in India and was celebrated in both bronze and stone. Some rare but important monumental stone cult images were created for his invocation in seventh-century Cambodia and Champa.[36] These early representations appear to display an awareness of Ganesha's origins in early India as a *yaksha* deity associated with fertility of the land, and it may well be this aspect—rather than his path-finding, obstacle-remover role that is now worshiped—that secured him such a prominent role in first-millennium Cambodia. Early representations depict him holding a plant form, the radish, which links him to agriculture. In this sculpture he holds in his lower left hand what appears to be an axe or, more properly, a hoe, again having agricultural associations, as does the broken tusk held in his upper right hand, which served as his plough. Ganesha is shown seated in a yogic meditative posture rather than the more typical standing or seated in "royal ease" pose, and the combination of agricultural attributes and this yogic inclination suggests we are witnessing his transformation in Khmer Hinduism from a fertility deity to an auspicious remover of obstacles.

A small stone Shivalinga set upon a bronze lustration pedestal demonstrates the portability of the tools of worship. (fig. 56) Such icons were readily carried by Brahmans, who could enact the daily rituals honoring Shiva at almost any location, requiring only the performance of a purification rite before the invocation to summon the god's presence. Forest communities of ascetics (*rishi*) routinely carved multiple *linga*s into the living rock, preferably in or near riverbeds, so that the seasonal rains would lustrate the images and bring fecundity to the soil. Rock-cut examples of this enlivening of Shiva's land still can be seen at Ang Khna, a *rishi* abode and quarry site near Koh Ker; in the river at Kbal Spean; and at Anlong Pong Phkay on Phnom Kulen. A bronze *linga* and pedestal close in style to the example exhibited was recovered from the riverbed at the foot of a boulder-cut shrine of *linga*s situated mid-stream in the Mekong River at Wat Phu in Laos. This early walled city was built in the shadow of the most famous naturally occurring *linga* in all Khmer territories, the mountain named Sri Lingaparvata in King Devanika's fifth-century inscription found at the site.[37]

It is an indication of the power of the hereditary priesthood in Angkorian Cambodia that sculptural depictions of Brahman *rishi*s routinely appear on Khmer temples. (fig. 19) Senior Brahmans who rose to high office and presided over state rituals acquired great influence and wealth. They first appear on the pre-Angkorian lintel from Wat Ang Khna, officiating at a royal anointing ceremony, and their role in this affirmation of kingship was asserted repeatedly in Angkorian inscriptions.[38] Depictions of *rishi*s at Thma Dap on Phnom Kulen and at Preah Ko, Roluos, demonstrate that this subject was popular from the outset of the Angkor period. They routinely appear in bas-reliefs at the base of pillars, on sanctuary exterior walls, and as antefixes on temple towers, seated with their legs supported by a meditation strap. This bronze head of a Brahman ascetic recovered in the vicinity of the Bayon reveals that substantial icons of such holy men also were cast, underscoring their status within the ritual life of the Angkorian religious system.

Ritual Paraphernalia

The production of metal religious imagery was not confined to figurative sculptures of deities but also included a vast array of auxiliary objects for ritual performance. Among the most numerous is the cast-bronze imitation of the conch shell. This naturally occurring form had a dual role in ancient India, both as a war trumpet (as carried by Vishnu and described in the *Mahabharata* epic) and as a pouring container for ritual lustration.

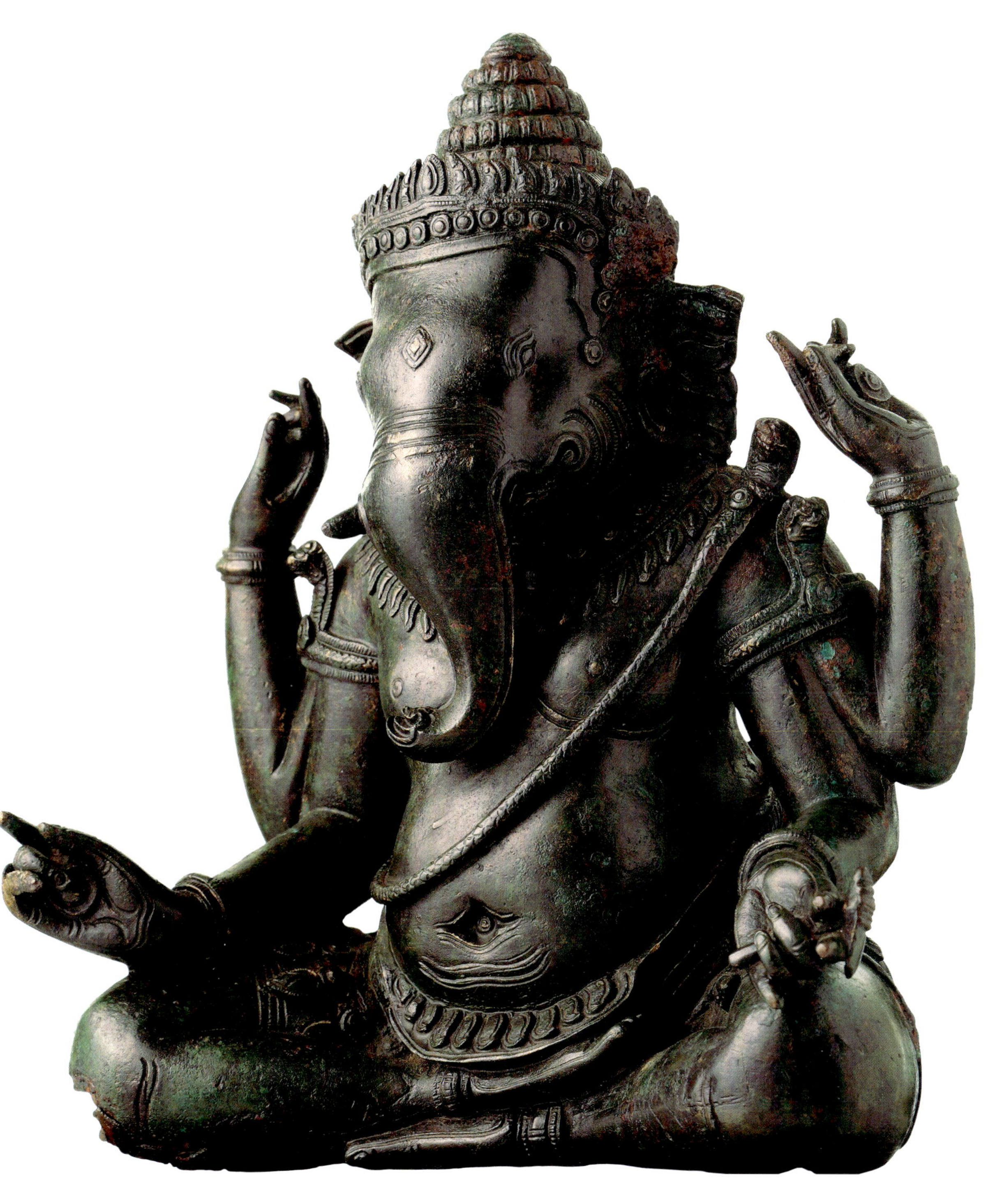

55

55 Ganesha pages 113–115; see also fig. 29
Cambodia, Angkor period, 13th century
Bronze; 26 × 23 × 16 cm
National Museum of Cambodia, Ga5987

Ganesha, the elephant-headed son of Shiva and Parvati, is summoned in prayers as the auspicious beginner of enterprises. His yogic posture of meditation, together with the esoteric gestures of his hands, suggests that he was intended to be worshiped in a religious environment with strong Tantric leanings.

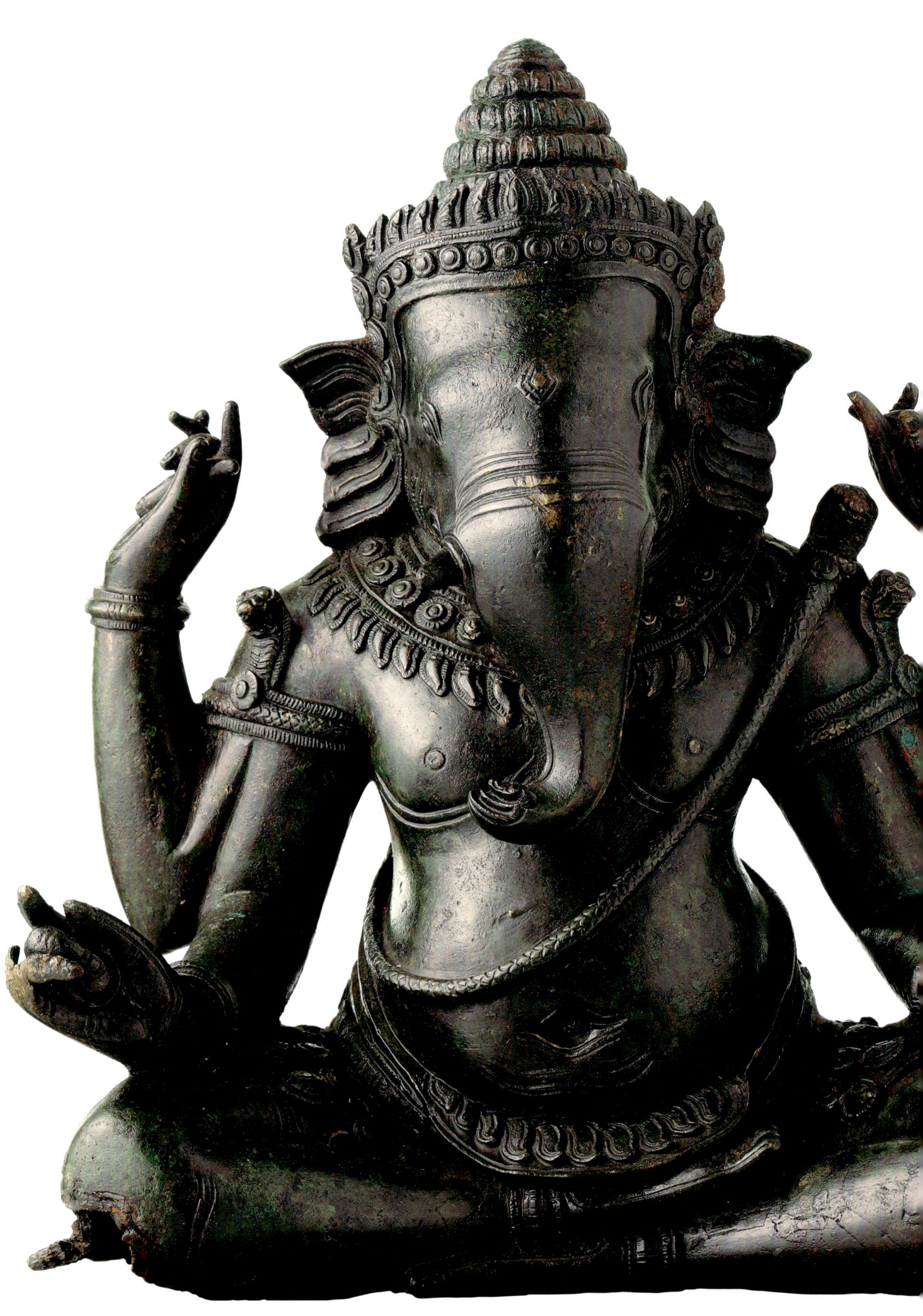

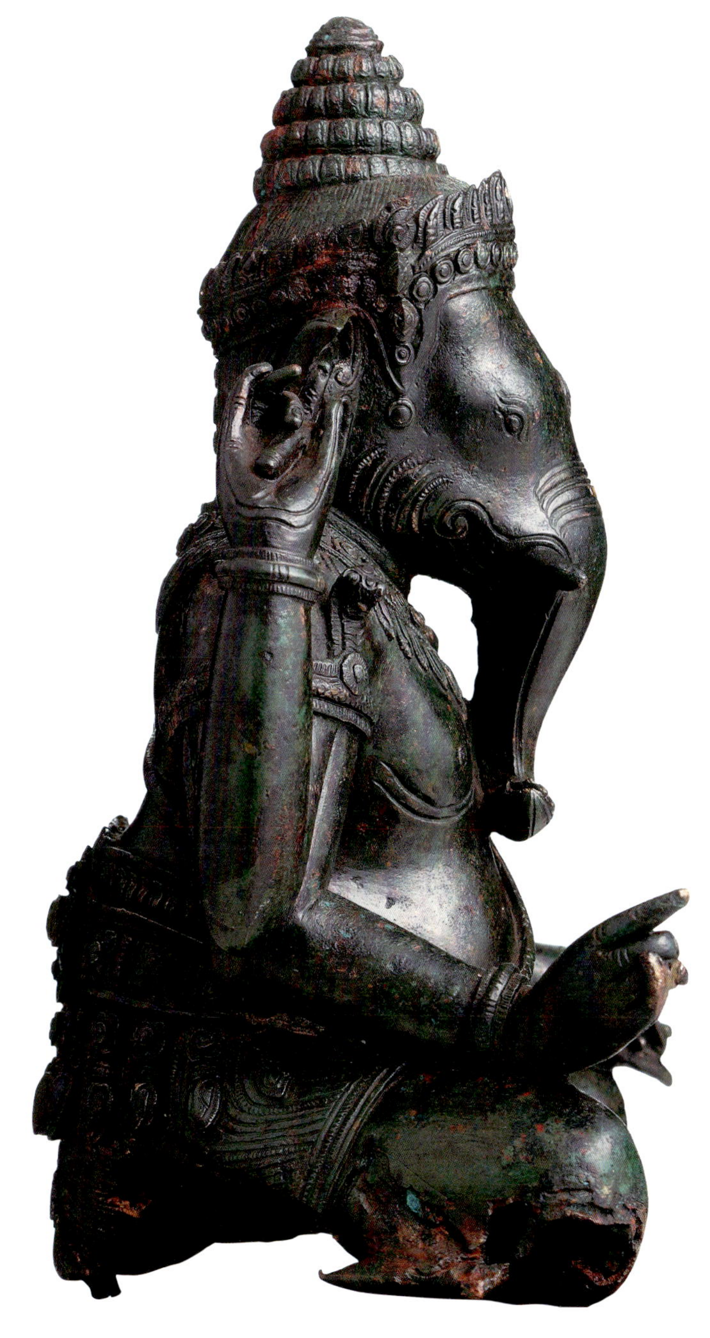

In the latter role, it was widely replicated, no doubt in gold and silver, though none of these have survived from the Angkorian period, and in bronze and ceramic, which have survived.[39] The conch was used as a horn to summon worshipers and evoke the primordial sound of creation. It also served as a holy water vessel to lustrate an icon of a deity in the litany of worship, as described in the *Hevajrasekaprakriya*, a liturgical text known from a surviving Chinese translation.[40] The frontispieces of these conches are decorated with medallions of a variety of deities, but most persistently with an ensemble in which Hevajra and his eight attendant females (*dakinis*) perform their esoteric dance before a presiding celestial Buddha.[41] (fig. 57) According to the *Hevajra Tantra*, an eight-headed Hevajra generates through his Tantric union eight goddess manifestations, who in turn extend compassion in the eight directions of the universe.[42]

The same medallion of Hevajra encircled by his *dakinis* appears as part of a larger and more complex composition on a bronze mold for producing miniature devotional mandala shrines in clay (fig. 28), popularly referred to in Cambodia as *prah patima*, presumably from the Sanskrit *pratima*, an icon of a god (literally the "reflected image" of that god).[43] Here an array of Buddhas, past and future, is serially arranged, presided over by the *nāga*-protected celestial Buddha.

The frequency with which this subject occurs on bronze conches and mandala molds, together with the existence of a number of monumental stone sculptures,[44] suggests that ritual associated with the *Hevajra Tantra* was a major, if not the principal, religious activity in Vajrayana Buddhist worship at Angkor.[45] As this was a feature of the latter half of the long reign of Jayavarman VII, from the construction of the Bayon beginning around 1200 to his death around 1218, many such ritual objects and imagery may be reasonably attributed to this period. A recent re-reading of inscription

56 Linga and pedestal page 117
Cambodia, Angkor period, late 9th–13th century
Granite and bronze; 12 × 13 × 18 cm
National Museum of Cambodia, Ga3449

The possibility exists for Shiva to be worshiped anywhere and in any naturally occurring aniconic form, such as a weathered stone. Miniature *linga* shrines have been recovered from many locations, confirming their role as portable shrines.

57 Ritual conch and stand pages 118–119
Cambodia, Angkor period, late 12th–early 13th century
Bronze; 27 × 11 × 11 cm plus 10 × 13 × 10 cm;
assembled height: 33 cm
National Museum of Cambodia, Ga5484, Ga5485

The decorative border on this bronze conch evokes the precious metal mounts into which shell conches were typically set. The legs of the tripod stand assume the form of rearing *nāgas*, a guardian presence to the ritual tool they support, and a frieze of demigods appears on the antefixes that cradle the conch. The *Hevajra* mandala on the front of the shell makes clear the Tantric orientation of the ritual worship in which this conch was employed.

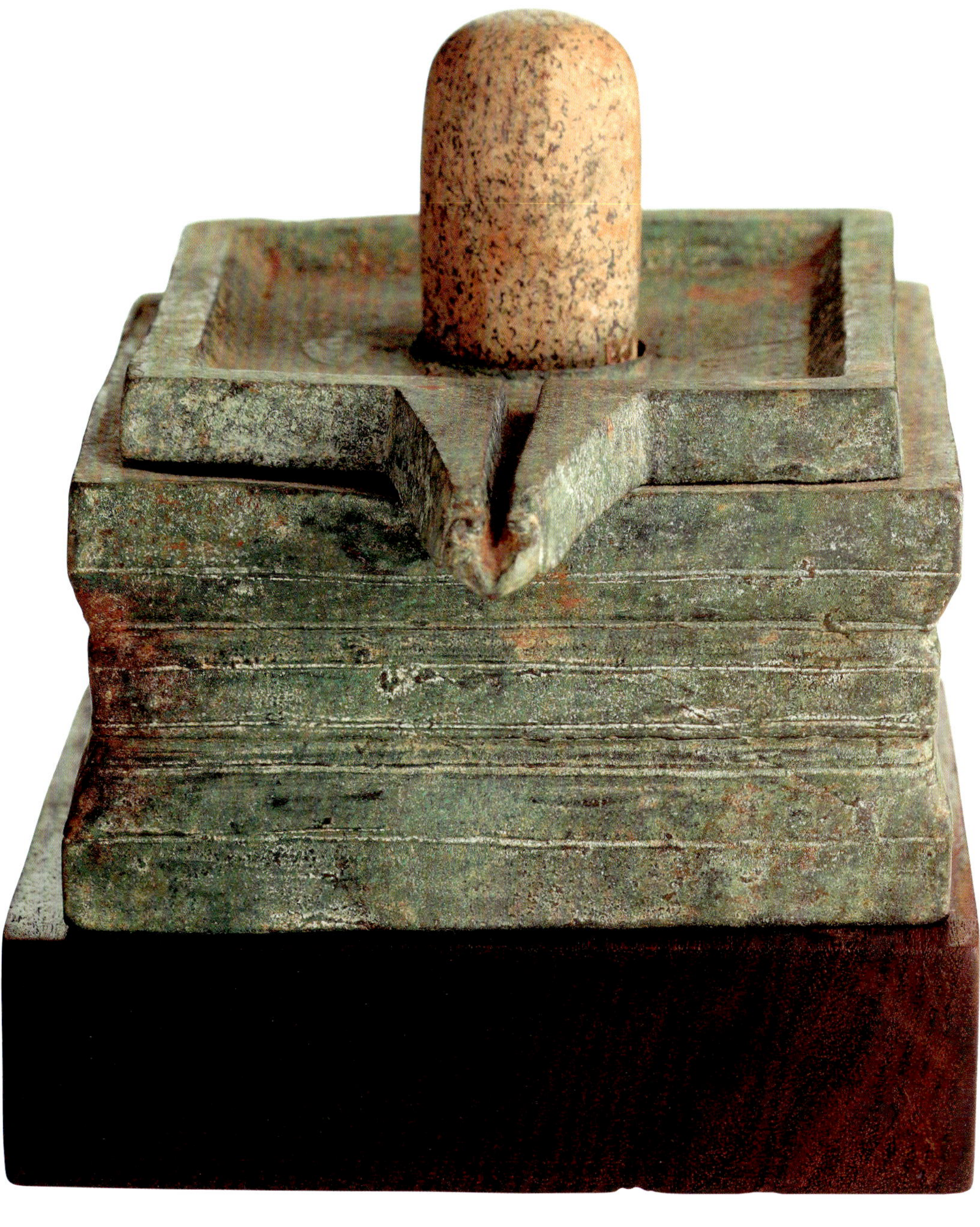

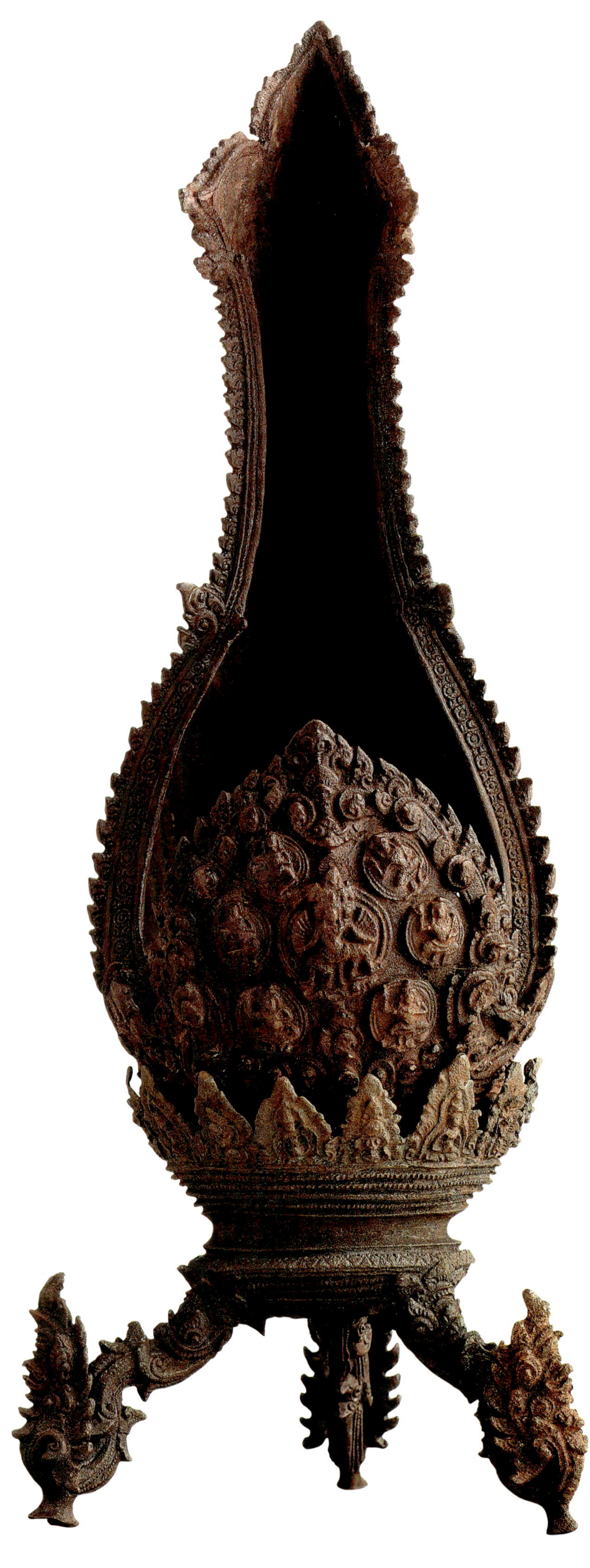

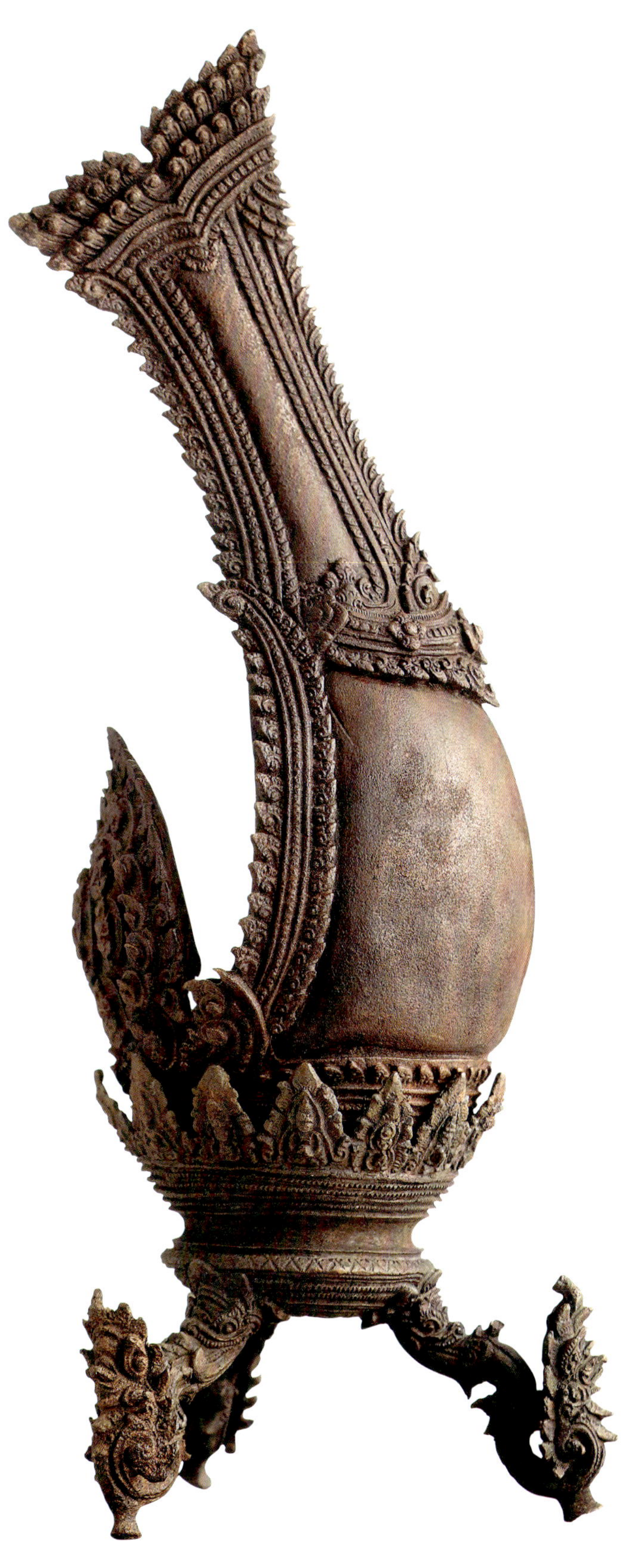

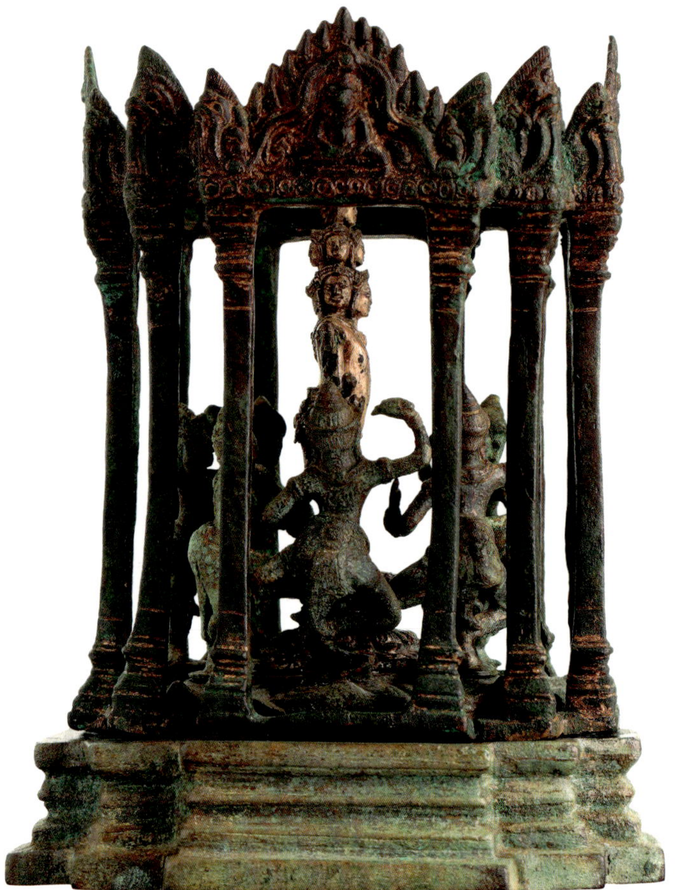

58

K.779, which appears on another bronze Hevajra conch recovered at Preah Khan in 1929 (National Museum of Cambodia, Phnom Penh, Ga3788), links the conch directly to royal activity at that temple in 1196/97.[46]

The miniature shrine of Hevajra (fig. 58; see also fig. 27) replicates in three-dimensional form the architectural elements of the monumental temples of the late Angkorian period. It represents a freestanding pillared hall (its superstructure is missing) on an indented square platform, with the pillars bridged by lintels with pediments displaying reliefs of the Buddha framed by *nāgas*; intervening pillars support projecting *nāga* antefixes. Within its enclosure the blissful dancing Hevajra is surrounded by the fearsome *dakinis*, whose role is to destroy ignorance in the universe. Such a miniature shrine would have allowed the enactment of rituals understood only by *Hevajra Tantra* initiates. The royal palace provenance raises the possibility that Hevajra rituals were performed on occasion for the benefit of royal devotees.

Two objects of great beauty are the lotus flower and stem fragment (fig. 60) and the lotus-flower oil lamp. (fig. 61) The organic form of the lotus stem with leaf and bud projections was part of a large-scale ensemble of some sort. One possibility—that it was part of a large candelabrum—is suggested by an example preserved in the Musée Guimet.[47] But the lotus stem shown in figure 60 is on a much larger scale, and the leaf element does not function as a lamp oil reservoir. Nothing is known about what gilded bronze configurations were created to frame images. Was this magnificent lotus, symbol of purity, intended to rise before an enthroned Buddha image? [48]

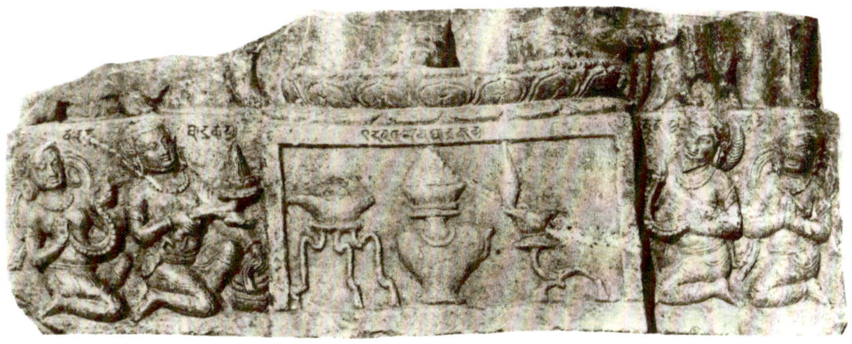

59

A small lotus ensemble provides another solution: it supports a dancing figure described by George Cœdès as an *apsara*, although the vigor of the pose, with the raised leg folded under, suggests that this may be a *dakini*.[49] If this identification is correct, it raises the possibility of a more esoteric setting for the flowering lotus stem, as part of a decorative ensemble accompanying a large-scale image. Esoteric or otherwise, the female dancers that proliferate

58 Miniature shrine with Hevajra in a circle of yoginīs page 120; see also fig. 27

This miniature shrine was designed for the enactment of *Hevajra Tantra* worship by an advanced practitioner. In the Vajrayana system, the bodhisattva Heruka (the Buddhist equivalent of Shiva Nataraja) manifests as Hevajra, and in union with his female consort generates the eight protectors of the universe, the *dakinis*.

59 Relief from the pedestal of a now-lost icon, depicting two donor couples making offerings to a deity above. The two lotus-stem shaped oil lamps depicted provide a close model for the Khmer example in fig. 61, as does the conch shell on a tripod, which can be compared to fig. 57. The center of the ensemble is a flowering vase. Together the ensemble represents fertility (vase of elixir), the driving away of evil (lamps), and instruments for evoking the deity (conch). Bodhgaya, eastern India. Pala dynasty, circa 12th century. (After A. Cunningham, *Mahabodhi*, London, 1896.)

60 Fragment in the form of a lotus plant pages 122–123

Cambodia, Angkor period, 12th century
Bronze with traces of gilding; 49 × 38 × 8 cm
National Museum of Cambodia, Ga5644

Part of a spectacularly large, gilded ornament, which probably served to frame or support an ensemble of Buddhist icons. The imagery of the pure lotus flower—rising from foul waters—alludes to the Buddha and his teachings emerging radiant from the impure, mundane world that is material existence.

61 Incense burner or lamp pages 124–125

Cambodia, Angkor period, 12th century
Bronze; 30.5 × 25 × 13 cm
National Museum of Cambodia, Ga5730

Lotus imagery dominates this beacon of light, an oil lamp with a lotus-bud reservoir and an arching lotus-stem stand. The five-headed snake (*nāga*) emerges from the plant form as a protective presence.

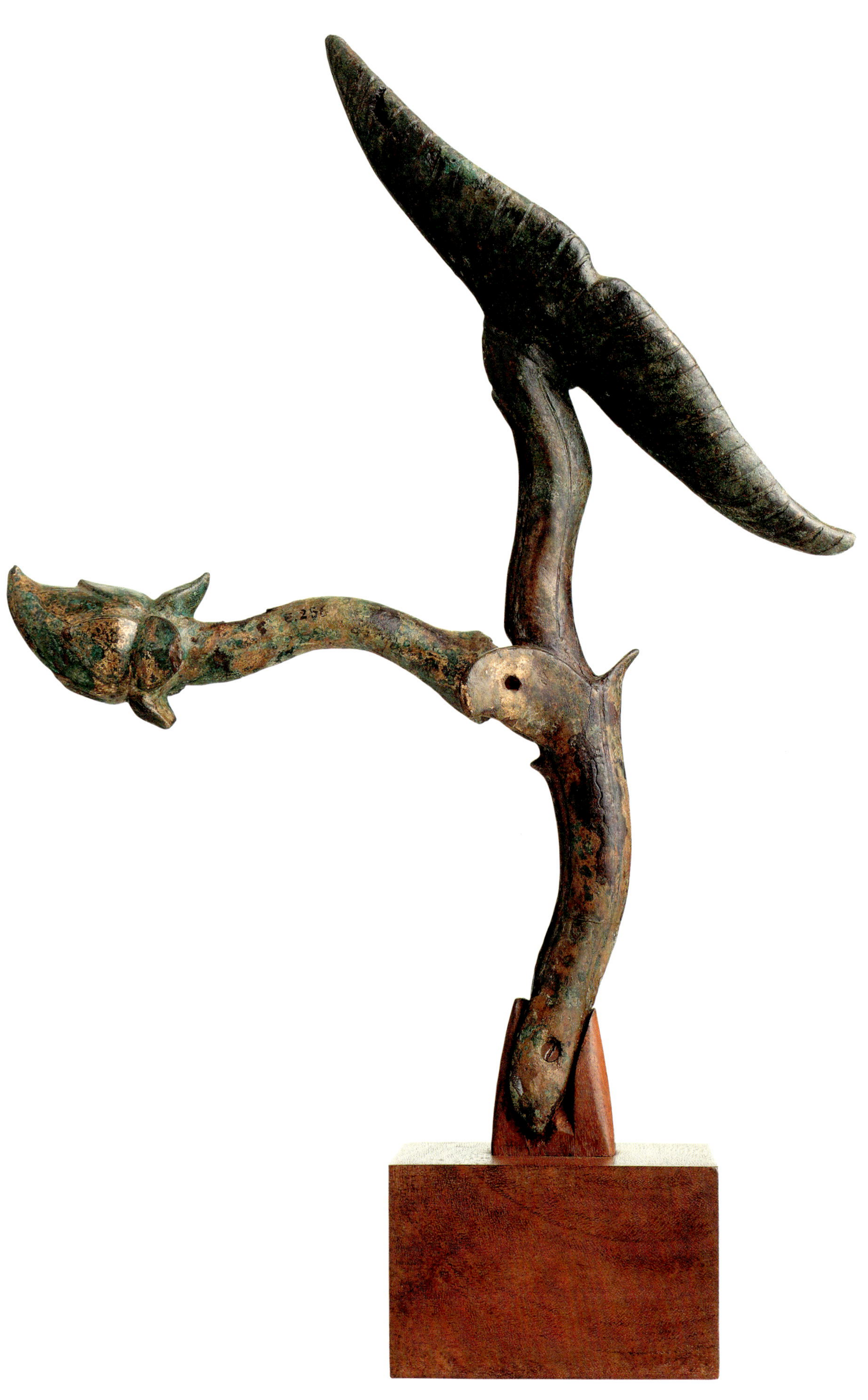

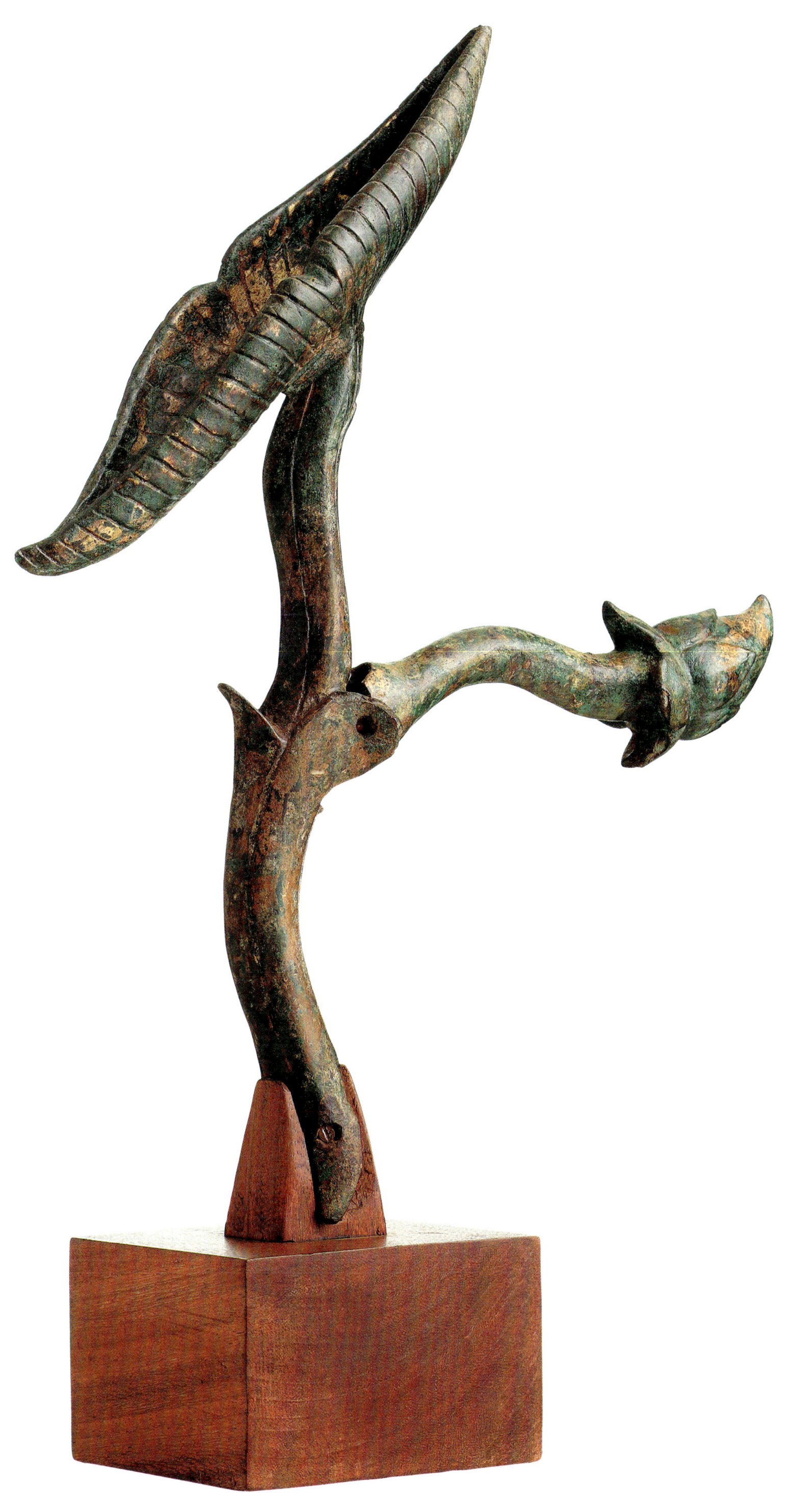

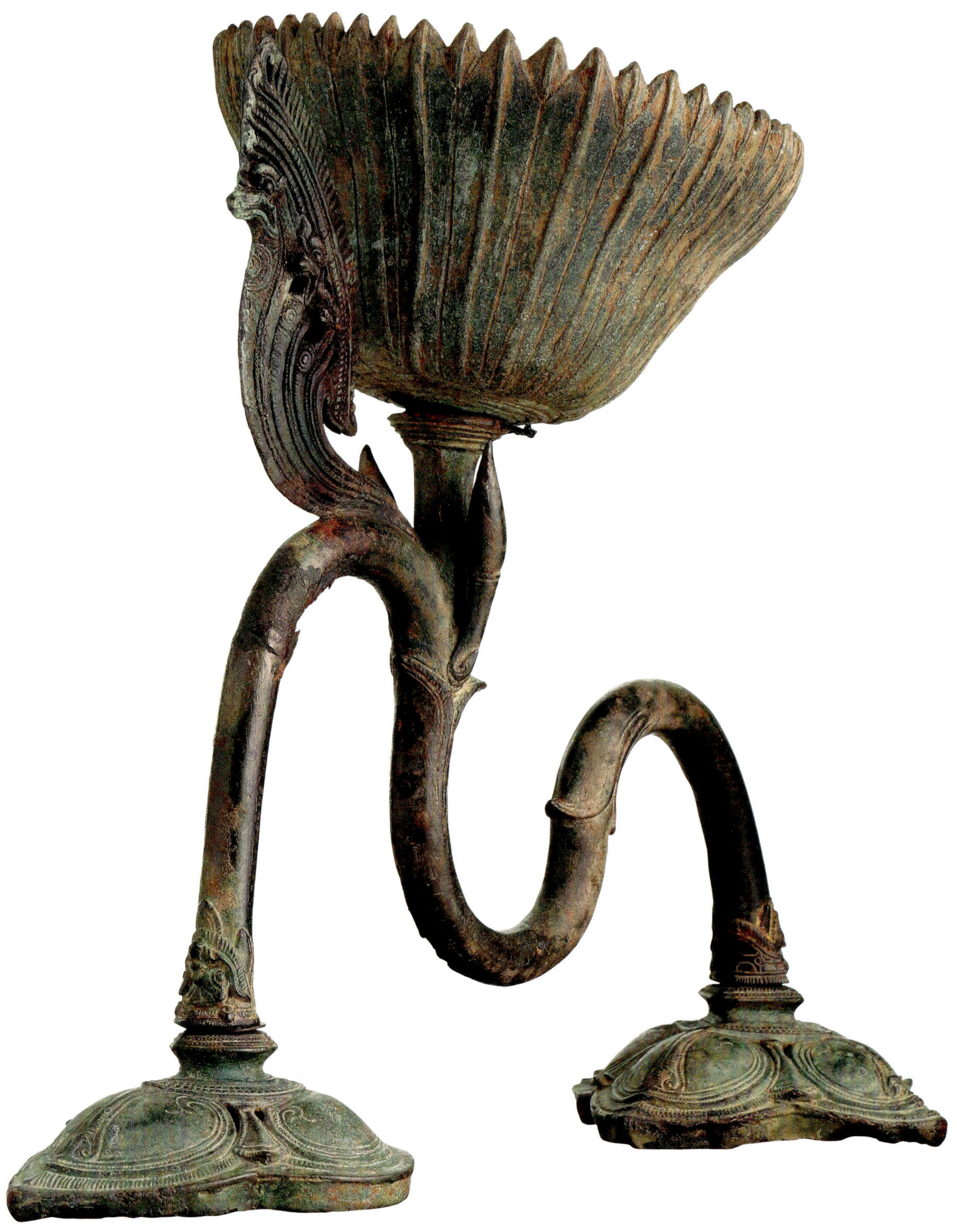

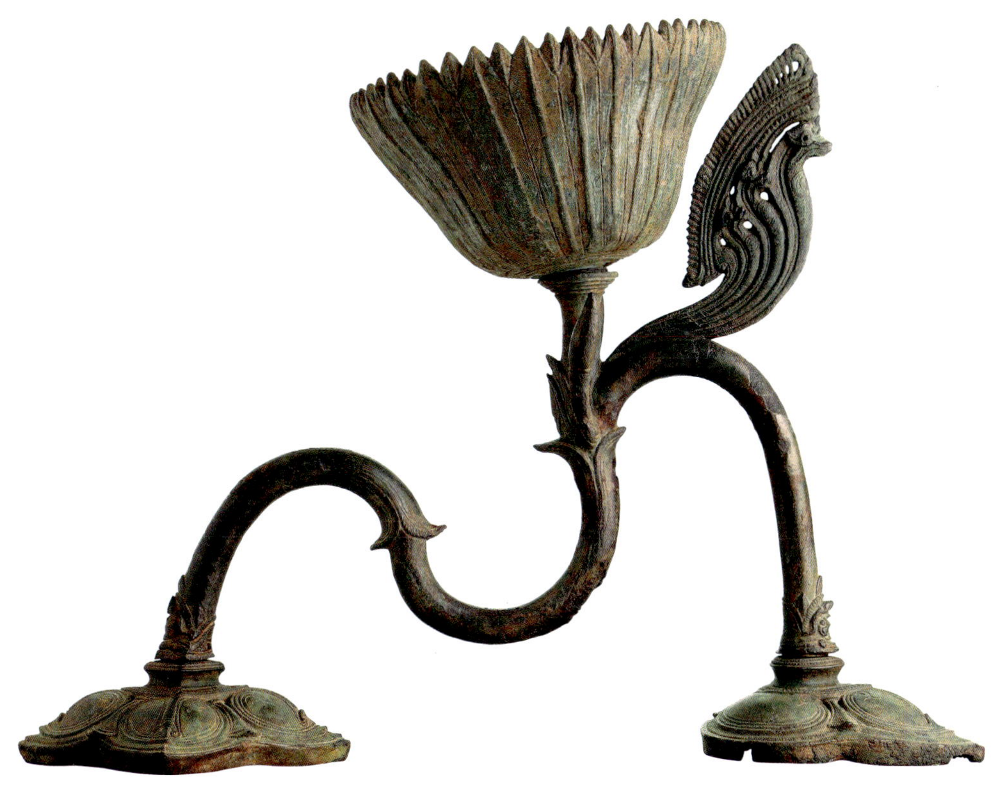

on the pillars of the enclosure terraces of the Bayon and at Preah Khan and Banteay Kdei are closely associated with lotus imagery. All three temples have pillared halls with dancer imagery that has resulted in their identification as dancing halls, potentially spaces where rituals involving dance could have been performed, as so vividly replicated in an esoteric form in the miniature *Hevajra* mandala shrine model.

Esoteric Buddhism was particularly strong in eastern India and early in its development was introduced to western Indonesia; it also appeared in Champa by the tenth century.[50] The presence at Srivijaya, in the second quarter of the eleventh century, of Atisha, the renowned exponent of the *Hevajra Tantra*, may have served as a catalyst in the propagation of that cult. Given the extent of religious dialogue between the royal households of Southeast Asia, these esoteric trends in Buddhist practice probably were introduced from Srivijaya and Champa into Cambodia in the course of the tenth and eleventh centuries. Judging from the art historical evidence, however, esoteric Buddhism came to flourish in Cambodia only somewhat later, at Phimai and for a short period at Angkor under the patronage of Jayavarman VII, to whose reign most known artifacts with Hevajra associations can be assigned.[51] Less problematic is the oil lamp in the form of a serpentine lotus stem, with the open petals of the flower providing the lamp's reservoir. (fig. 61) The form of this elegant object can be seen in a relief from a Buddhist image pedestal at Bodhgaya, Bihar, eastern India, dated to the twelfth century. (fig. 59) Here we can witness the "Khmerization" of an Indian form in the altogether more flamboyant articulation of the lotus-flower petals and in the addition of a five-headed *nāga* as a protector of the holy flame. Such lamps were held by priests and passed before the image under worship to offer light while prayers were recited.

In these rituals, specific utensils were employed. Sacred food must be prepared and served to the gods using temple utensils appropriate to the sanctity of the task. The ritual rice spoon (fig. 62) illustrates the type of utility object traditionally fabricated from wood and coconut shell, here adapted to high-value metal. Such a spoon would be used both to serve the food presented to the gods and to redistribute it to devotees.

Royal processions at Angkor made extensive use of richly caparisoned elephants, as witnessed by numerous relief sculptures. Zhou Daguan noted that whenever the king ventured outside the palace he rode on an elephant whose tusks were sheathed in gold and was flanked by his royal guards, also on elephants.[52] The bronze bell (fig. 63) is like many recovered from the Angkor area which might be expected to have been found in the vicinity of the militia's stables, although no such locations have been securely identified to date.

62 Rice ladle
Cambodia, possibly Angkor period or later
Bronze; 34 × 10.5× 6.5 cm
National Museum of Cambodia, Ga5608

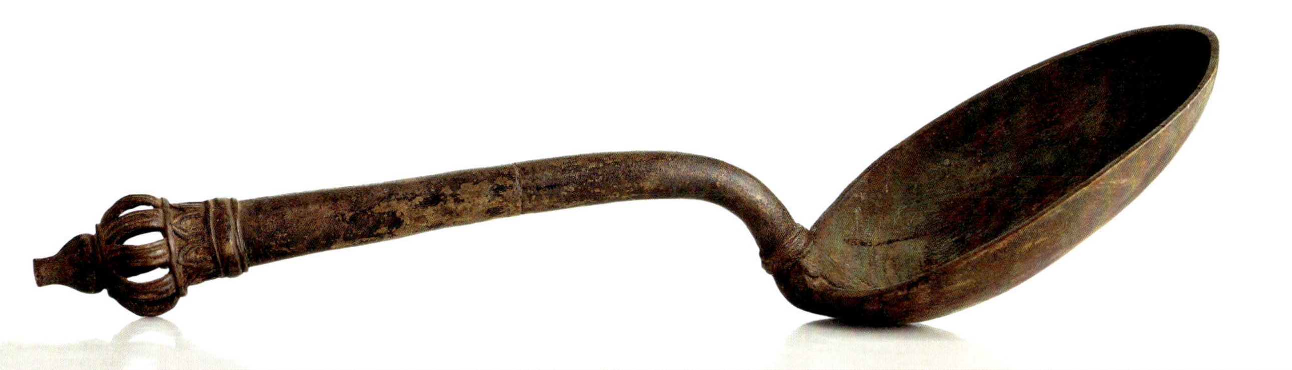

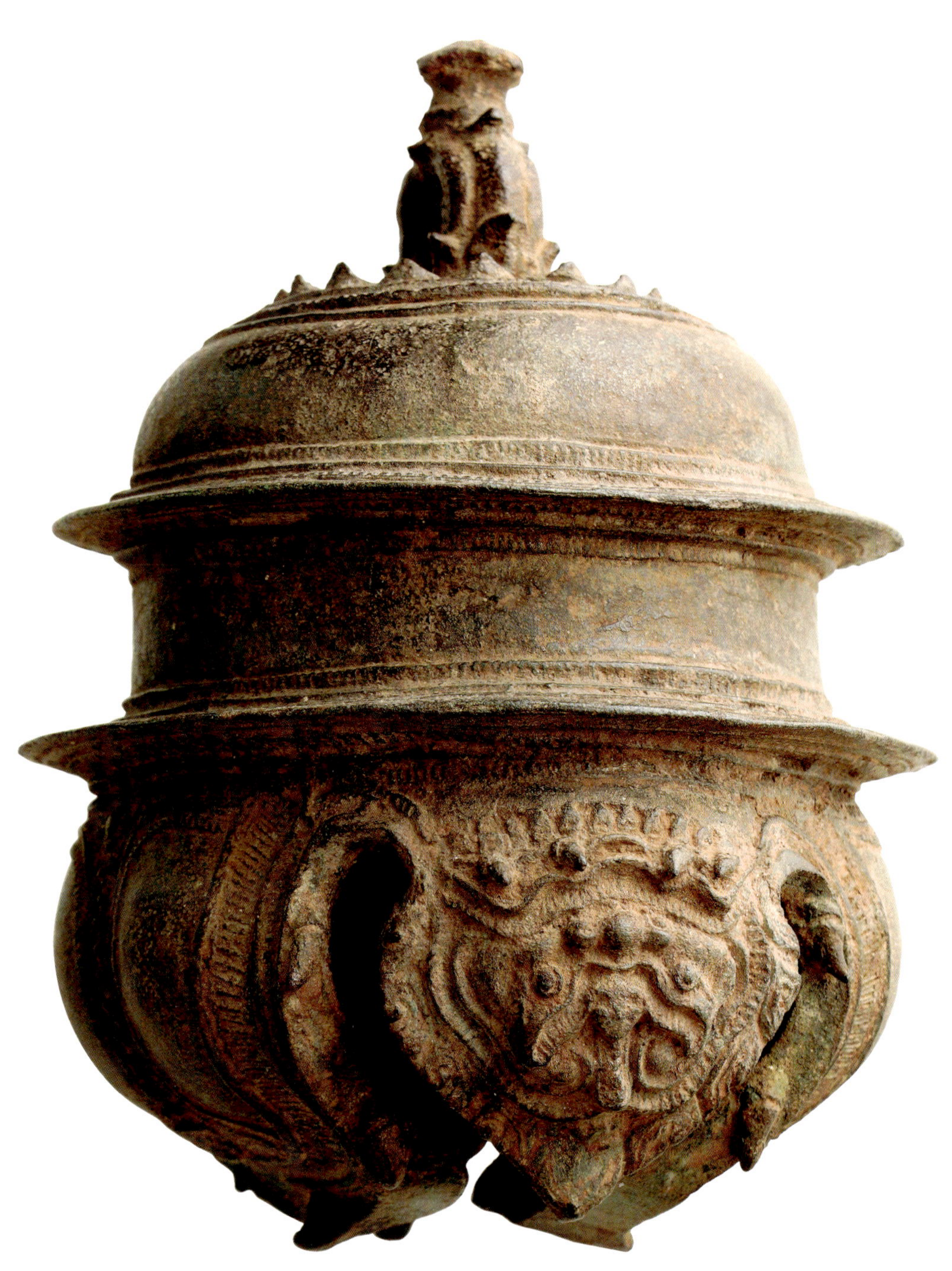

Architectural Ornamentation

Angkorian bronzes employed in the ornamentation of temples enhanced the vision of heavenly splendor that the temples were intended to evoke. The inscriptions at both Preah Khan and Ta Prohm provide detailed inventories of the precious and rare objects (gold, silver, and pearls are mentioned) that constituted the temples' wealth. They record the cumulative weight of gold, silver, and copper vessels (presumably ritual utensils) and also refer, somewhat enigmatically, to significant quantities of brass associated with the enclosure walls.[53] This becomes more comprehensible when, elsewhere in the same inscription set at Preah Khan, we are told that a sanctuary there was lined with golden sheets of bronze.[54]

My examination of the central sanctuary with which this description always has been associated does not support the claim. The fixing holes in the brick interior show traces of wooden pegs and lime plaster, suggesting that their function was to provide a keyed surface upon which to support a stucco render, which was probably polychromed.[55] The pillared hall immediately to the west is another story, however; there the square-section sandstone pillars—with rough chisel marks indicating that these surfaces were not intended to be seen—are routinely pitted with fixing holes that display traces of iron and small particles of copper-rich bronze, sometimes fused to the iron remains. This provides unequivocal evidence that the unfinished surfaces of these pillars were decorated with copper-alloy cladding or ornamentation secured onto the stone with iron pins. This then is probably the golden sanctuary described in the Preah Khan inscription.[56]

On the basis of this evidence, and as witnessed by the array of wondrous Khmer bronzes in this exhibition, we may reasonably evoke an image of the pillared hall of the Preah Khan temple: Its golden surfaces were illuminated by oil lamps of flowering lotus form. Its interior housed gilded bronze images of the presiding deities arrayed beneath gilded silk textiles forming a heavenly canopy above.[57] And it was enlivened periodically by female temple dancers performing in celebration of their Lord, be it for a temple festival or as part of some ritual requirement of Vajrayana Tantrism. The evidence proffered by this exhibition, and by the many fragmentary bronze cast reliefs that have been brought to light and are now being studied, strongly suggests that Angkorian temples were lavishly adorned and appointed, both externally and internally, with gilded bronze. The poetic vision of Angkor as a golden city is not without foundation.

63 Elephant bell

Cambodia, Angkor period, 12th–13th century
Bronze; 21 × 16.5 cm
National Museum of Cambodia, Ga5655

Reliefs of Kala, a god associated with the afterlife, and lotus-petal detailing decorate this elephant bell. Monolithic stone sculptures of harnessed elephants, complete with large bells of this type, typically stand guard at the corners of Angkorian temple platforms, as witnessed today at the East Mebon temple and elsewhere.

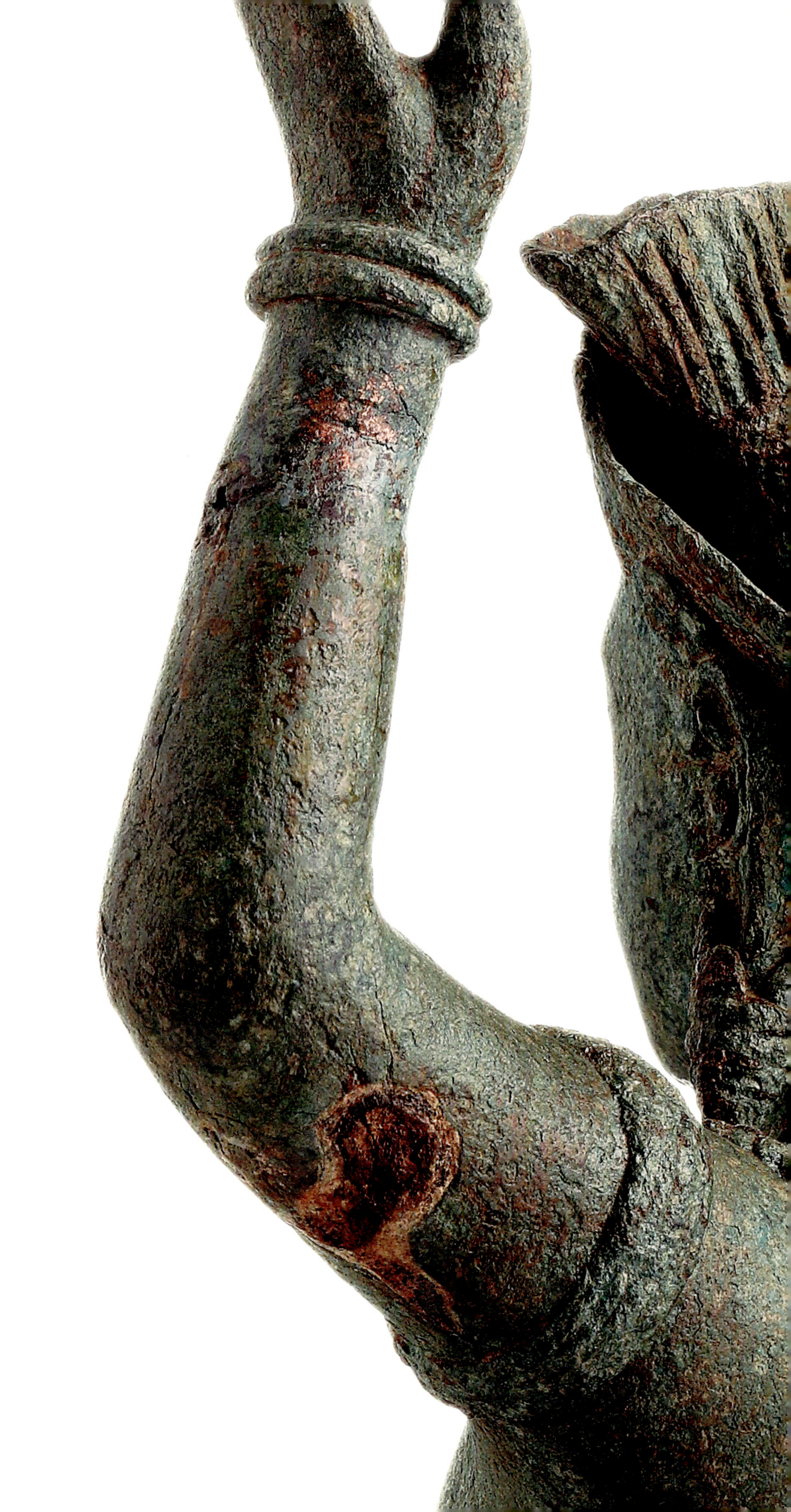

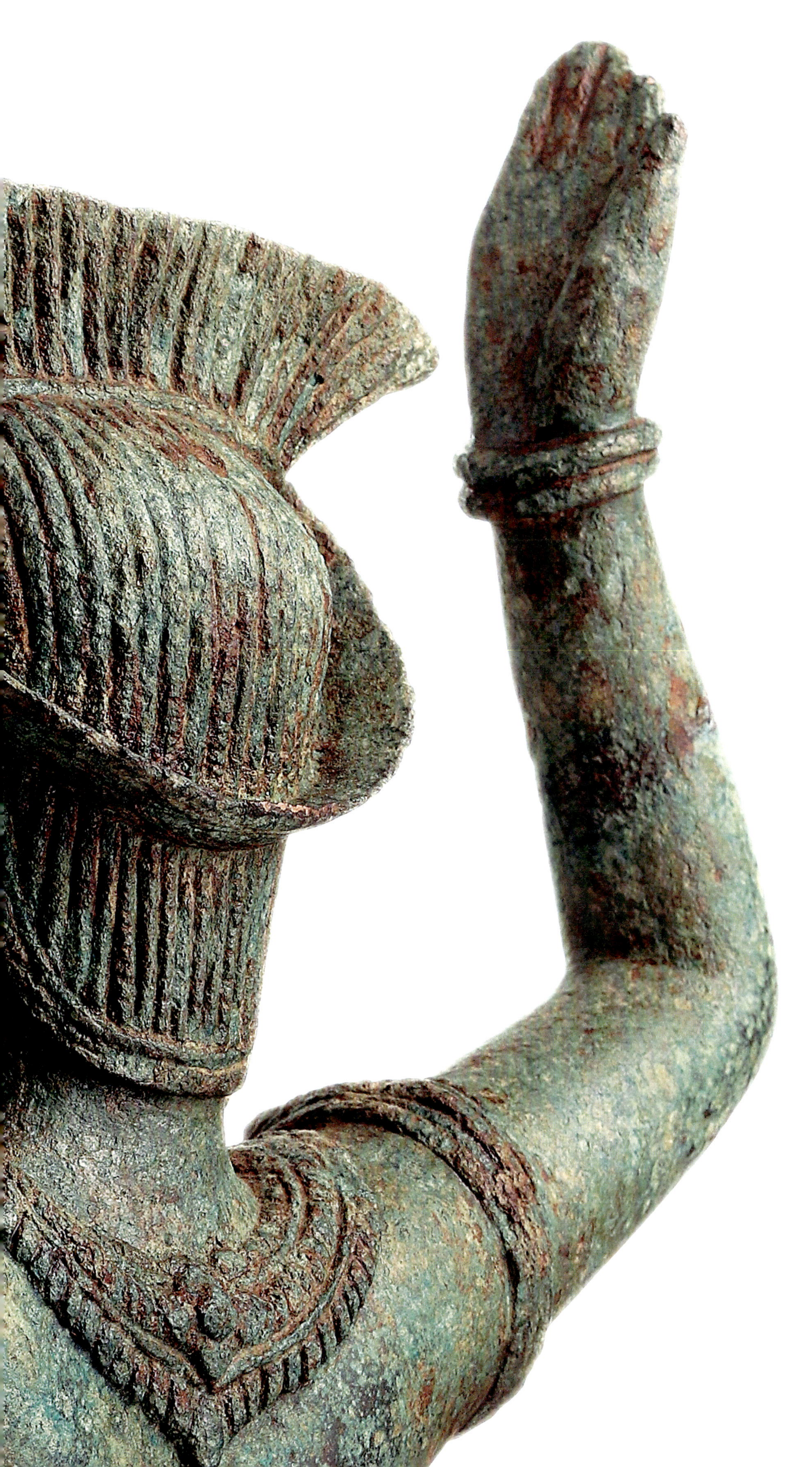

Exhibition Checklist

This list represents the objects in the exhibition *Gods of Angkor: Bronzes from the National Museum of Cambodia*, Arthur M. Sackler Gallery, Washington, D.C., May 15, 2010–January 23, 2011, and the J. Paul Getty Museum, Los Angeles, February 22–August 14, 2011. The images are reproduced on each page according to scale. Captions should be read top to bottom and images, left to right.

Ritual vessel, the "Kandal urn" (figs. 3, 3A)
Probably Cambodia, prehistoric, 4th century BCE–2nd century CE
Bronze; 55.2 × 28.7 × 13 cm
Provenance: Kandal province, Chak Angre commune; acquired 21 June 1948
National Museum of Cambodia, Phnom Penh, Ga2083

Bell (figs. 4, 4A)
Probably Cambodia, prehistoric, 4th century BCE–2nd century CE
Bronze; 57.7 × 30.5 × 24 cm
Provenance: Pursat province, Phnum Kravanh district, Phteah Rung commune, Chrey Kroem village; acquired 19 August 2002
National Museum of Cambodia, Phnom Penh, Ga6854

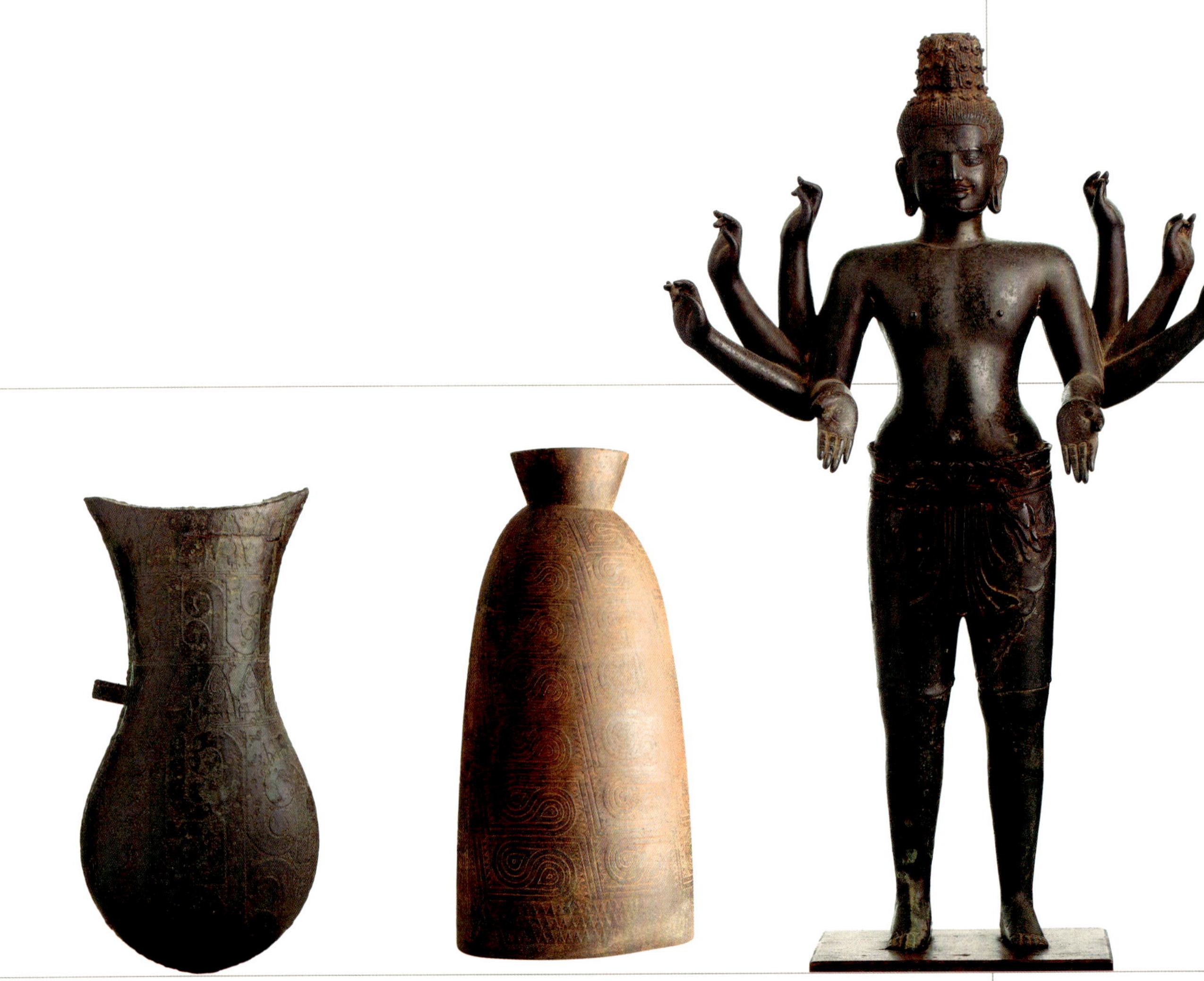

Maitreya (figs. 5, 5A)
Cambodia, Angkor period, early 10th century
Bronze; 75.5 × 50 × 23 cm
Provenance: Kampong Chhnang province, Wat Ampil Tuek; acquired 21 September 1926; transferred from Royal Library, Phnom Penh
National Museum of Cambodia, Phnom Penh, Ga2024

Buddha (fig. 8)
Cambodia, pre-Angkor period, 7th century
Bronze; 27 × 11.8 × 7.7 cm
Provenance: Battambang province, Battambang, Wat Banan; acquired 17 February 1921
National Museum of Cambodia, Phnom Penh, Ga5412

Buddha (fig. 9)
Cambodia, pre-Angkor period, 7th century
Bronze; 49 × 16 × 10 cm
Provenance: Kampong Chhnang province, Kampong Leaeng district, Sangkat Da; acquired 11 March 1967
National Museum of Cambodia, Phnom Penh, Ga5406

Buddha (figs. 10, 33, 33A)
Cambodia, pre-Angkor period, second half of the 7th century
Bronze; 39 × 11.5 × 10.5 cm (figure and base)
Provenance: Kampong Cham province, Cheung Prey district, Sdaeung Chey village; acquired 2006
National Museum of Cambodia, Phnom Penh, Ga6937

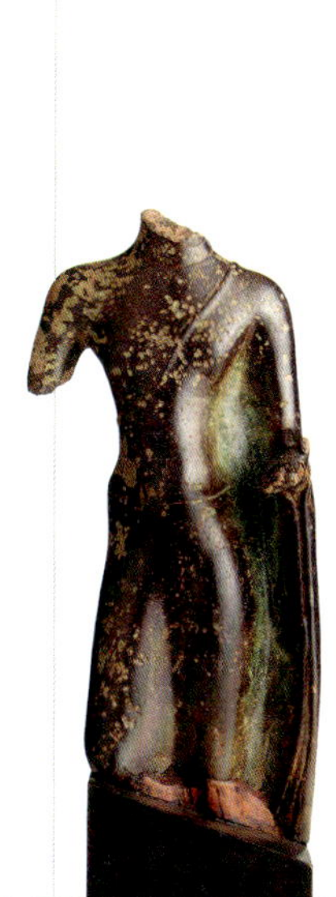

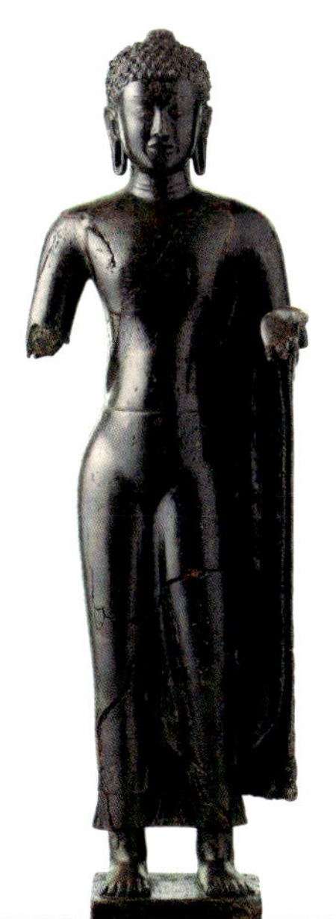

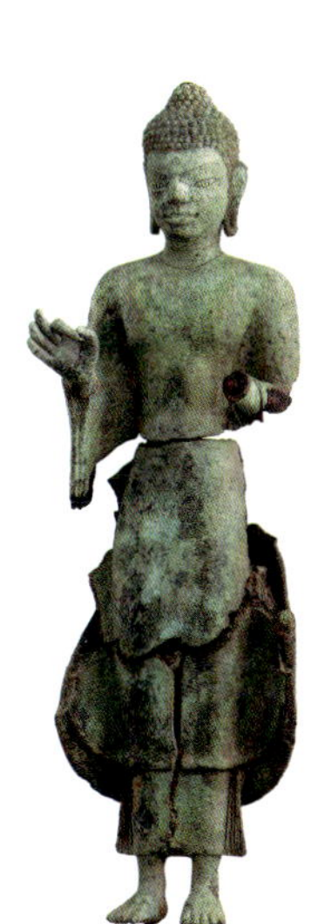

Buddha (figs. 11, 34, 34A)
Cambodia, pre-Angkor period, second half of the 7th century
Bronze; 14 × 5 × 3 cm
Provenance: Kampong Cham province, Cheung Prey district, Sdaeung Chey village; acquired 2006
National Museum of Cambodia, Phnom Penh, Ga6938

Buddha (figs. 12, 35)
Cambodia, pre-Angkor period, second half of the 7th century
Bronze; 25 × 8 × 5 cm (figure and base)
Provenance: Kampong Cham province, Cheung Prey district, Sdaeung Chey village; acquired 2006
National Museum of Cambodia, Phnom Penh, Ga6939

Avalokiteshvara (figs. 13, 37)
Cambodia, pre-Angkor period, second half of the 7th century
Bronze; 13 × 3 × 2 cm
Provenance: Kampong Cham province, Cheung Prey district, Sdaeung Chey village; acquired 2006
National Museum of Cambodia, Phnom Penh, Ga6941

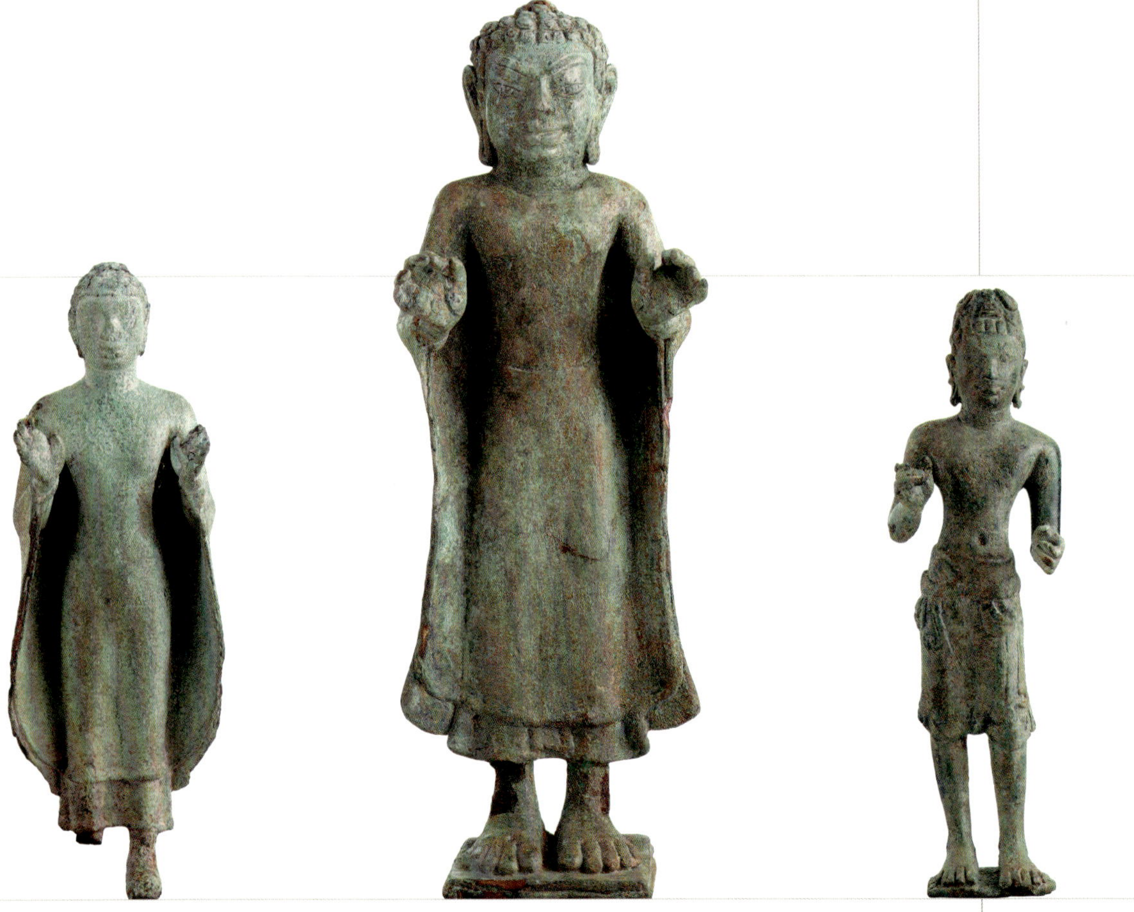

Maitreya (figs. 14, 36)
Cambodia, pre-Angkor period, second half of the 7th century
Brass; 17 × 4.5 × 4 cm
Provenance: Kampong Cham province, Cheung Prey district, Sdaeung Chey village; acquired 2006
National Museum of Cambodia, Phnom Penh, Ga6940

Bodhisattva (figs. 16, 38, 38A, 38B)
China, 6th century
Bronze with traces of gilding; 9.5 × 3 × 3 cm
Provenance: Kampong Cham province, Cheung Prey district, Sdaeung Chey village; acquired 2006
National Museum of Cambodia, Phnom Penh, Ga6942

Vajra-bearing Guardian (figs. 17, 39)
China, Sui or Tang dynasty, late 6th–7th century
Bronze with traces of gilding; 15 × 6 × 3 cm
Provenance: Kampong Cham province, Cheung Prey district, Sdaeung Chey village; acquired 2006
National Museum of Cambodia, Phnom Penh, Ga6943

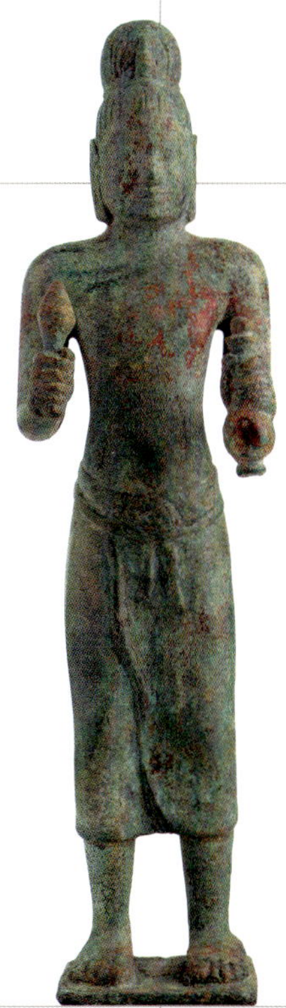

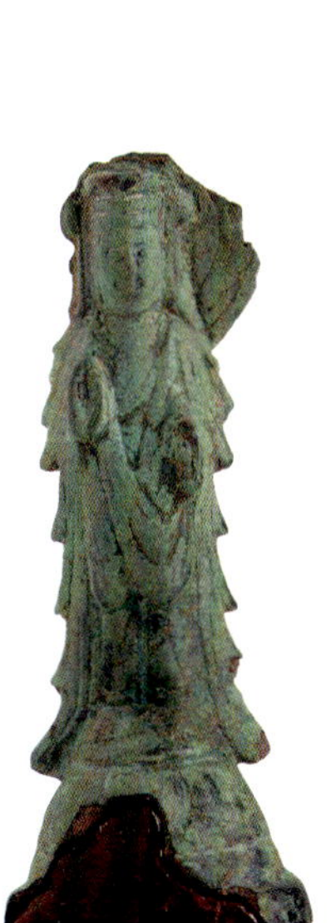

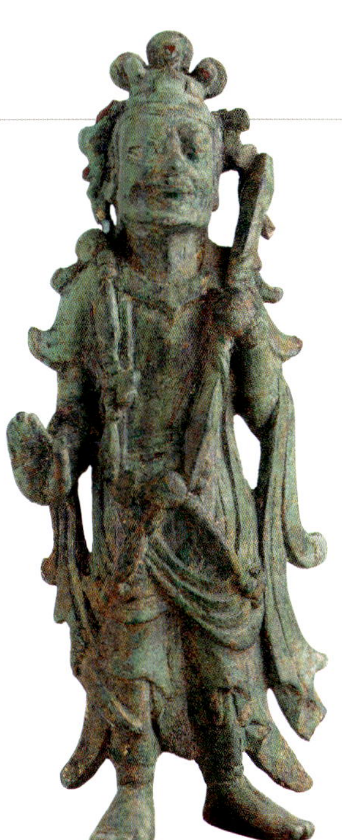

Linga and pedestal (fig. 56)
Cambodia, Angkor period, late 9th–13th century
Granite and bronze; 12 × 13 × 18 cm
Provenance: Prey Veng region; acquired 26 July 1958
National Museum of Cambodia, Phnom Penh, Ga3449

Male divinity, probably Avalokiteshvara or Shiva (figs. 18, 50)
Cambodia, Angkor period, 892 *śaka* (970 CE)
Bronze with traces of gilding; 72.5 × 36 × 23 cm
Provenance: Battambang province, Anlong Koub village, Moung River; acquired 1930s
National Museum of Cambodia, Phnom Penh, Ga5166

Rishi (fig. 19)
Cambodia, Angkor period, 11th century or later
Bronze with traces of leaf gilding; 18.5 × 8 × 6 cm
Provenance: Siem Reap province, Angkor Thom (possibly the Bayon); acquired 1 August 1920; transferred from Conservation d'Angkor, Siem Reap
National Museum of Cambodia, Phnom Penh, Ga5288

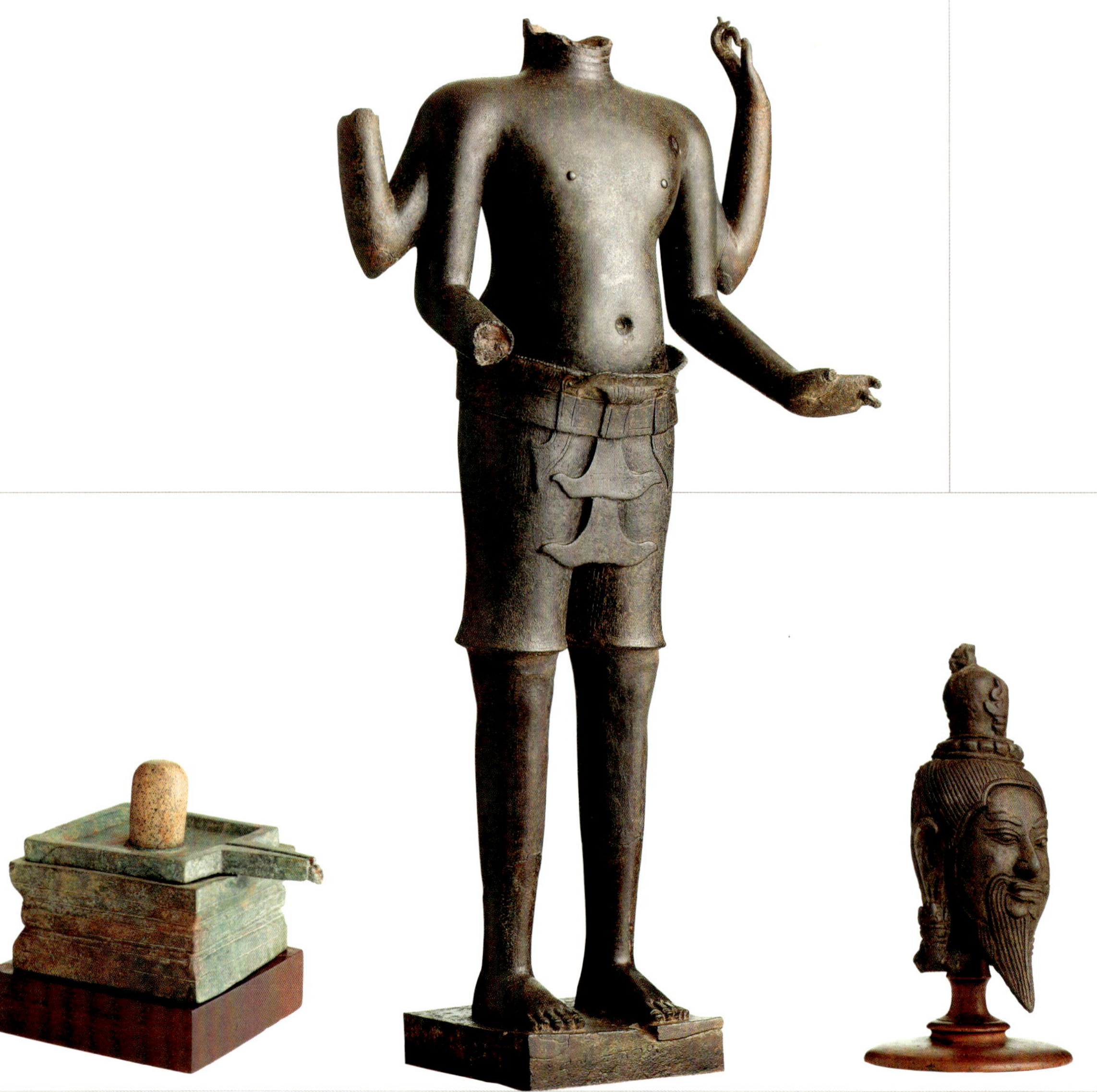

Male divinity, probably Shiva (figs. 20, 20A, 51)
Cambodia, Angkor period, late 11th century
Gilt bronze; 57 × 16 × 17 cm
Provenance: Takeo province, Prasat Phnom Bayang; acquired 18 July 1936
National Museum of Cambodia, Phnom Penh, Ga2993

Vishnu-Vasudeva-Nārāyaṇa (fig. 21)
Cambodia, Angkor period, late 11th–first half of 12th century
Bronze; 40 × 18 × 11 cm
Provenance: Siem Reap province, Angkor, Prasat Kapilapura; acquired 25 November 1925
National Museum of Cambodia, Phnom Penh, Ga5291

Kneeling female figure (fig. 44)
Cambodia, Angkor period, first half of the 12th century
Bronze; 34 × 24 × 15 cm
Provenance: Siem Reap province, Angkor Thom (possibly tank of the Bayon); acquired 3 November 1921
National Museum of Cambodia, Phnom Penh, Ga5476

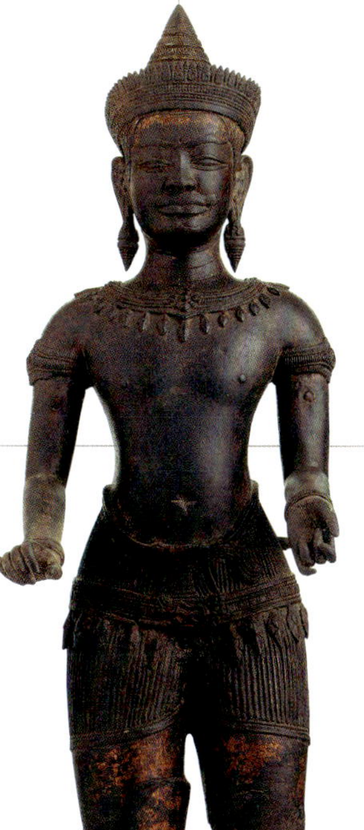

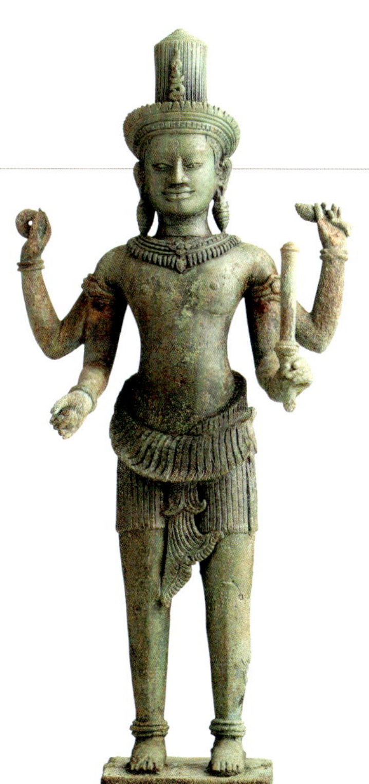

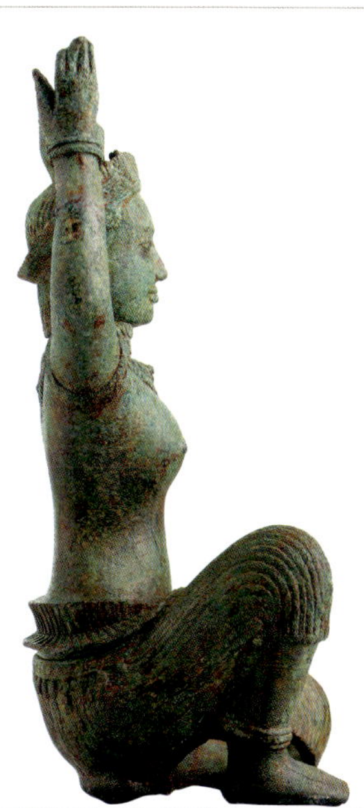

Crowned Buddha (fig. 23)
Cambodia, Angkor period, 12th century
Bronze; 79.5 × 25 × 16.5 cm
Provenance: Siem Reap province, Angkor, Angkor Wat; excavated 1931, Conservation d'Angkor, Siem Reap; acquired 10 January 1955; transferred from Louis Finot Museum, Hanoi
National Museum of Cambodia, Phnom Penh, Ga2081

Crowned nāga-protected Buddha (fig. 24)
Cambodia, Angkor period, second half of 12th century
Bronze; 71 × 31.5 × 18 cm
Provenance: Siem Reap province, Angkor, Sras Srang; acquired 1970; transferred from Conservation d'Angkor, Siem Reap
National Museum of Cambodia, Phnom Penh, Ga5986

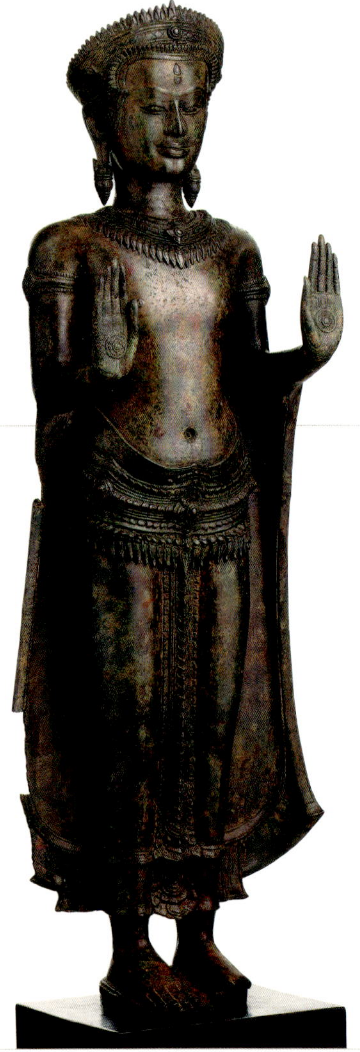

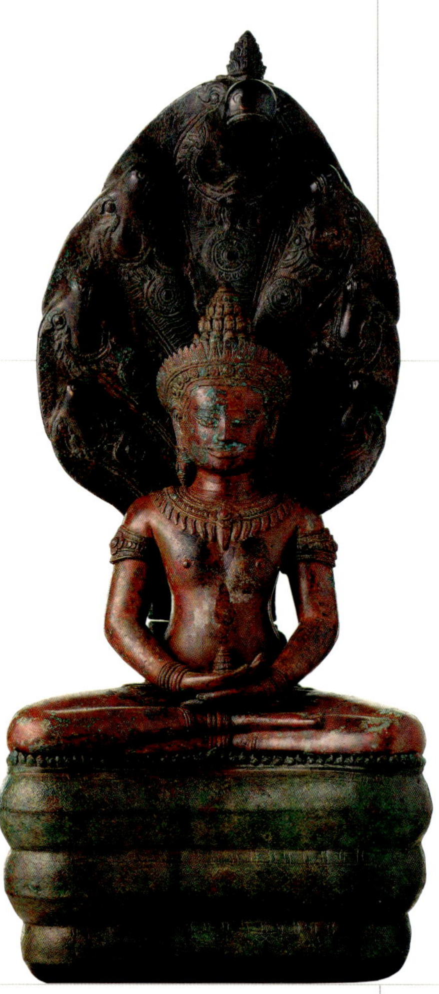

Nāga-protected Buddha with Avalokiteshvara and Prajñāpāramitā (fig. 25)
Cambodia, Angkor period, late 12th–early 13th century
Bronze with mercury gilding; 54.5 × 40 × 15 cm
Provenance: Siem Reap province, Roluos, Prasat Prei Monti;
excavated early 1960s; acquired 1970;
transferred from Conservation d'Angkor, Siem Reap
National Museum of Cambodia, Phnom Penh, Ga5470, Ga2424

Avalokiteshvara (fig. 26)
Cambodia, Angkor period, late 12th–early 13th century
Bronze; 42 × 20 × 13 cm
Provenance: Siem Reap province, Angkor Thom,
Prasat North Khleang; acquired 25 November 1925;
transferred from Conservation d'Angkor, Siem Reap
National Museum of Cambodia, Phnom Penh, Ga5340

Miniature shrine with Hevajra in a circle of yoginīs (figs. 27, 58)
Cambodia, Angkor period, late 12th–early 13th century
Gilded bronze; 20 × 16 × 16 cm
Provenance: Siem Reap province, Angkor Thom, Royal Palace;
acquired 1970; transferred from Conservation d'Angkor, Siem Reap
National Museum of Cambodia, Phnom Penh, Ga2494

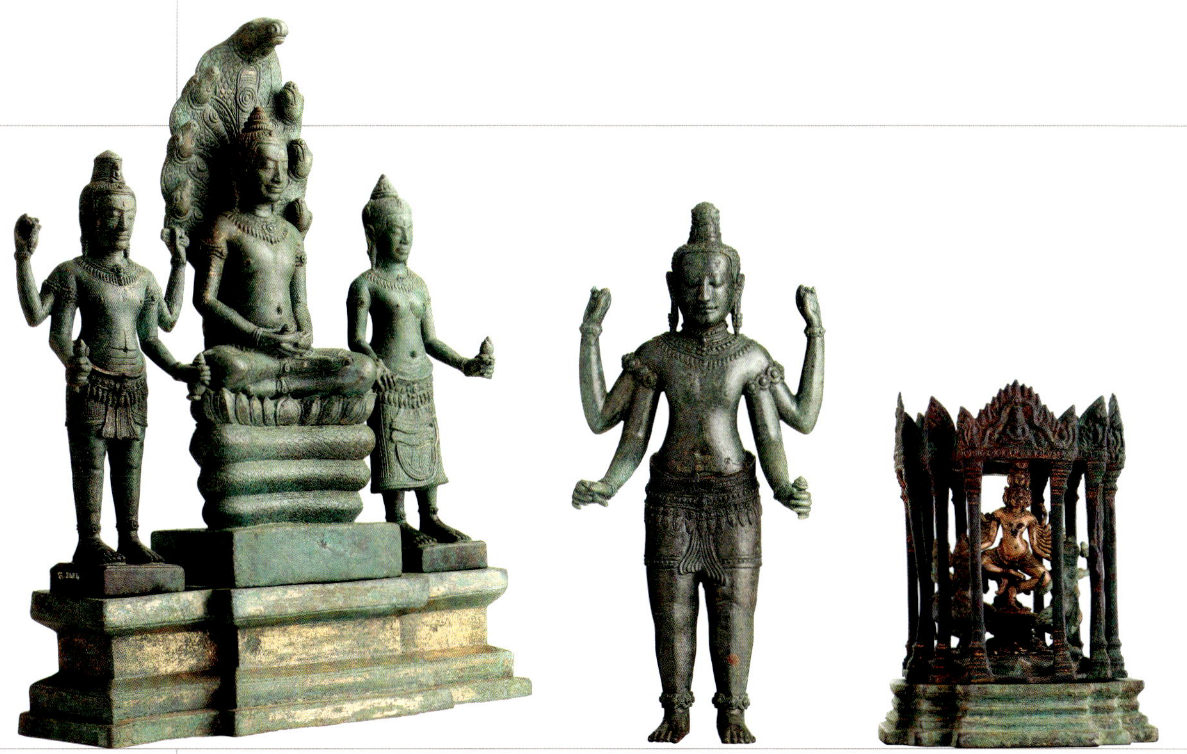

Votive tablet mold with Hevajra shrine and feline handle (fig. 28)
Cambodia, Angkor period, late 12th–early 13th century
Bronze; 22 × 12 × 9 cm
Provenance: Battambang province, Preak Khpob,
Tuol Beng Thmar; acquired 10 October 1922
National Museum of Cambodia, Phnom Penh, Ga5653

Shiva's bull, Nandin (fig. 49)
Cambodia, Angkor period, 12th–13th century
Bronze with mercury gilding; 36 × 64 × 32 cm
Provenance: Siem Reap province, Angkor, west of Angkor Wat;
acquired 1970; transferred from Conservation d'Angkor, Siem Reap
National Museum of Cambodia, Phnom Penh, Ga5739

Ganesha (figs. 29, 55)
Cambodia, Angkor period, 13th century
Bronze; 26 × 23 × 16 cm
Provenance: Siem Reap province, Siem Reap, former airfield;
acquired 1970; transferred from Conservation d'Angkor, Siem Reap
National Museum of Cambodia, Phnom Penh, Ga5987

Five-headed Shiva (Sadāshiva) (fig. 30)
Cambodia, Angkor period, 13th century
Bronze; 34 × 18 × 8.5 cm
Provenance: Siem Reap province, possibly Angkor region;
acquired 1970; transferred from Conservation d'Angkor, Siem Reap
National Museum of Cambodia, Phnom Penh, Ga2682

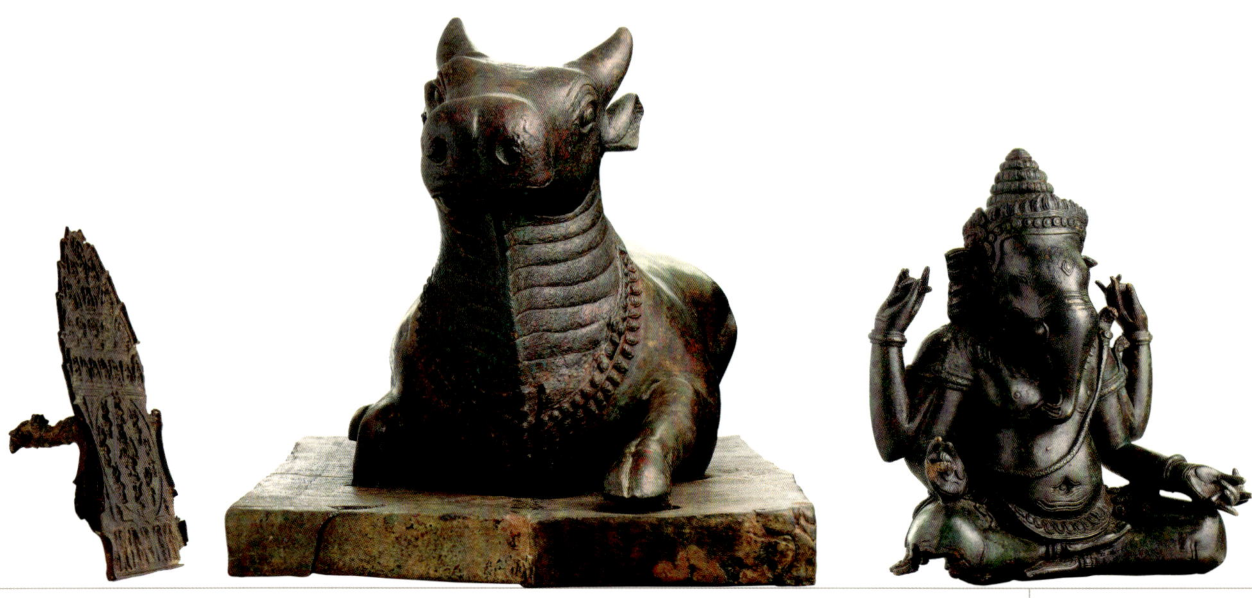

Vishnu-Vasudeva-Nārāyaṇa (fig. 31)
Cambodia, Angkor period, first half of the 14th century or later
Bronze; 67 × 22 × 16 cm
Provenance: Siem Reap province, Angkor Thom, Prasat North Khleang;
acquired 25 November 1925
National Museum of Cambodia, Phnom Penh, Ga5457

Trident (triśūla) (fig. 42)
Cambodia, Angkor period, 10th century or later
Bronze; 23.5 × 18.6 × 2 cm
Provenance: Siem Reap, Angkor Thom, Phimeanakas;
acquired 3 November 1921
National Museum of Cambodia, Phnom Penh, Ga5635

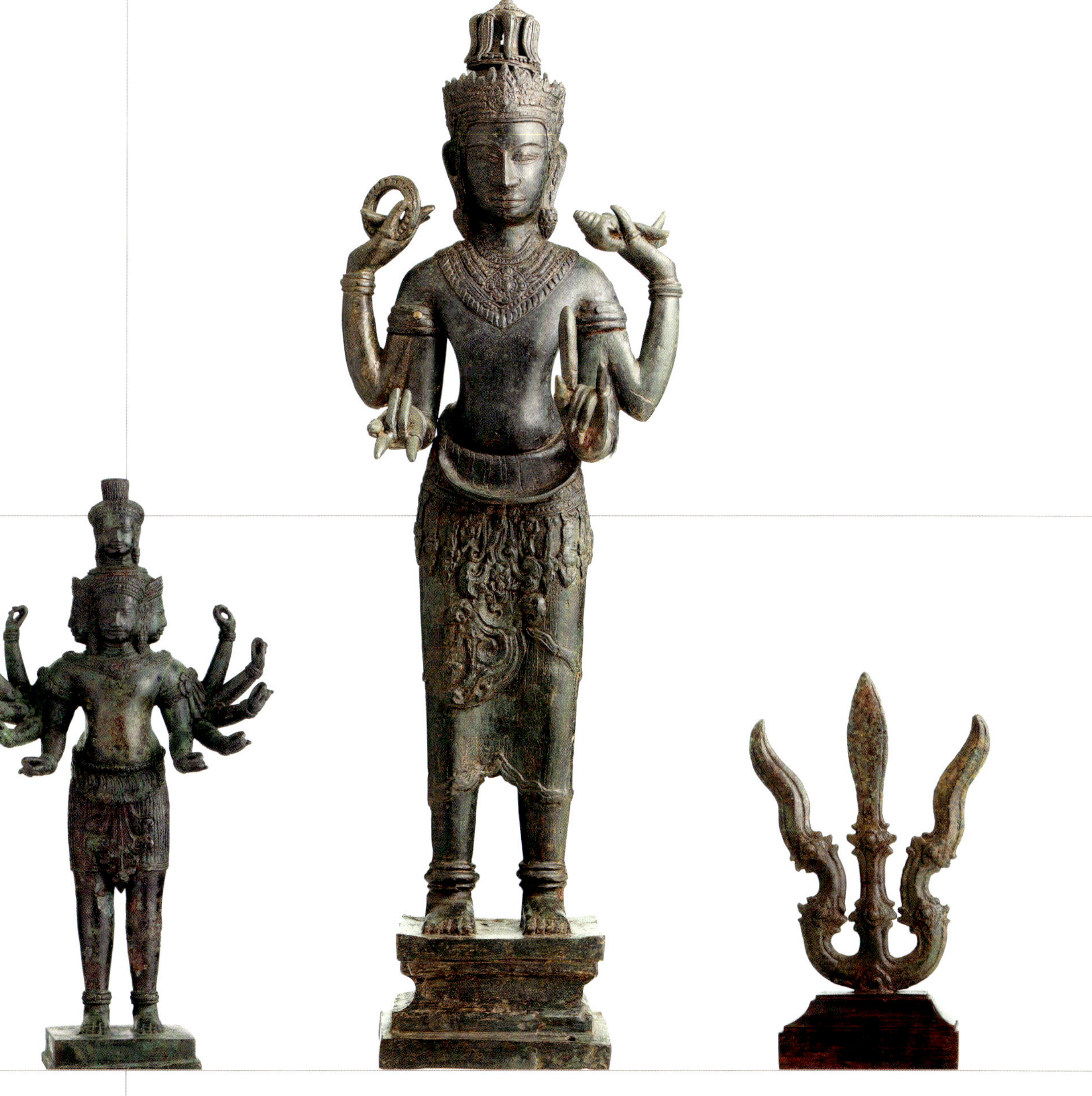

Mirror (fig. 45)
Cambodia, China or Tibet, Angkor period, possibly 11th–12th century
Bronze; 2 × 14 cm
Provenance: Svay Rieng province, Chambak village, Po Sek Kramson; acquired 5 June 1924
National Museum of Cambodia, Phnom Penh, Ga5537

Finial with crowned nāga-protected Buddha (fig. 54)
Cambodia, Angkor period, late 12th–early 13th century
Bronze; 48.5 × 21 × 5 cm
Provenance: Kampong Thom province, Banteay Chha, *baray*; acquired 10 May 1929
National Museum of Cambodia, Phnom Penh, Ga5593

Ritual conch and stand (fig. 57)
Cambodia, Angkor period, late 12th–early 13th century
Bronze; 27 × 11 × 11 cm plus 10 × 13 × 10 cm; assembled height: 33 cm
Provenance: Siem Reap province, Angkor region, shore of the Tonle Sap; acquired 11 June 1921
National Museum of Cambodia, Phnom Penh, Ga5484, Ga5485

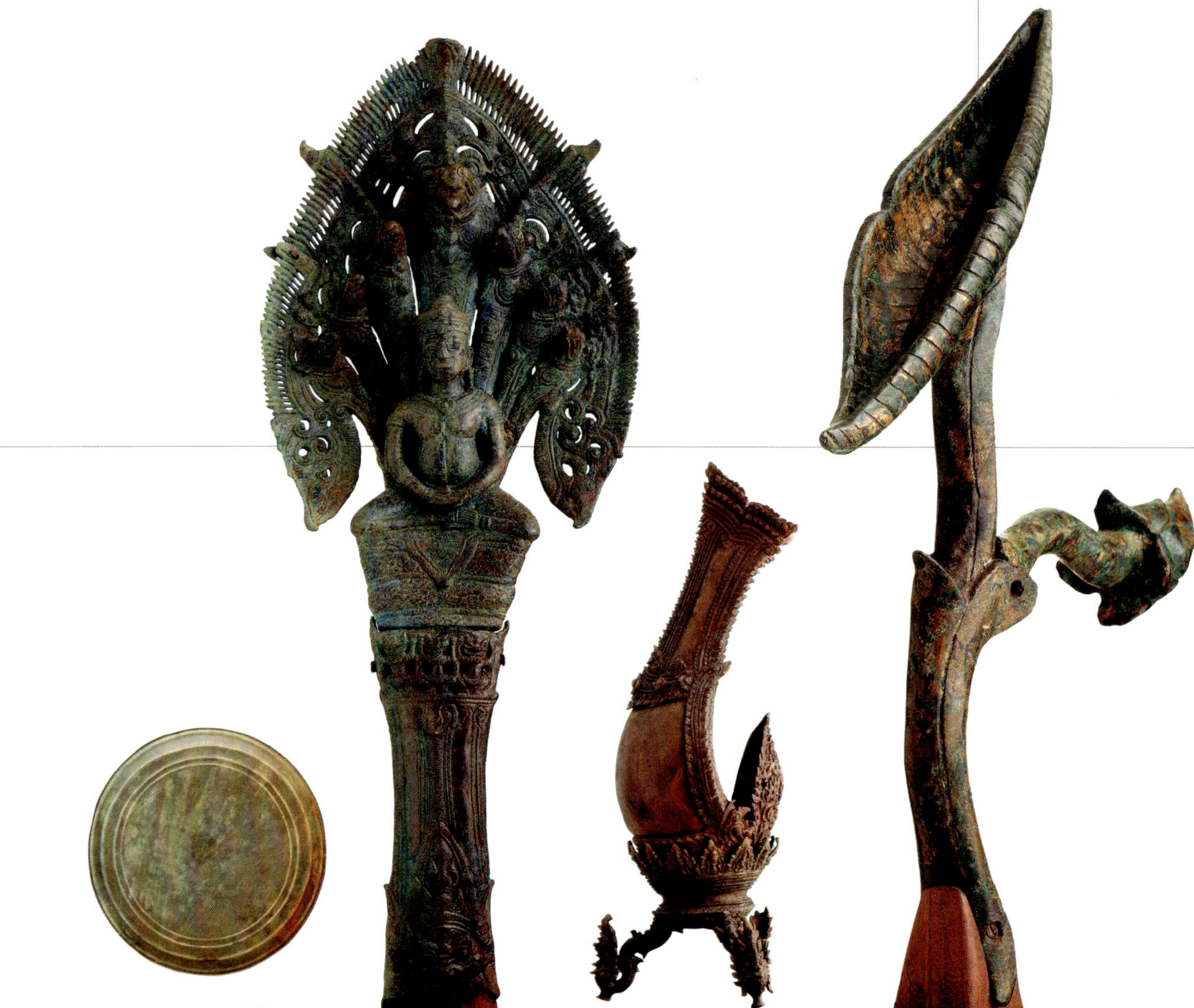

Fragment in the form of a lotus plant (fig. 60)
Cambodia, Angkor period, 12th century
Bronze with traces of gilding; 49 × 38 × 8 cm
Provenance: Siem Reap, Angkor Thom (possibly the Bayon); acquired 3 November 1921
National Museum of Cambodia, Phnom Penh, Ga5644

Incense burner or lamp (fig. 61)
Cambodia, Angkor period, 12th century
Bronze; 30.5 × 25 × 13 cm
Provenance: Banteay Meanchey province, Mongkol Borei district, Dang Run village; acquired 13 October 1925
National Museum of Cambodia, Phnom Penh, Ga5730

Rice ladle (fig. 62)
Cambodia, possibly Angkor period or later
Bronze; 34 × 10.5 × 6.5 cm
Provenance: Kandal province, Oudong; acquired 26 August 1939
National Museum of Cambodia, Phnom Penh, Ga5608

Elephant bell (fig. 63)
Cambodia, Angkor period, 12th–13th century
Bronze; 21 × 16.5 cm
Provenance: Battambang province, Wat Sangker commune; acquired 15 August 1931
National Museum of Cambodia, Phnom Penh, Ga5655

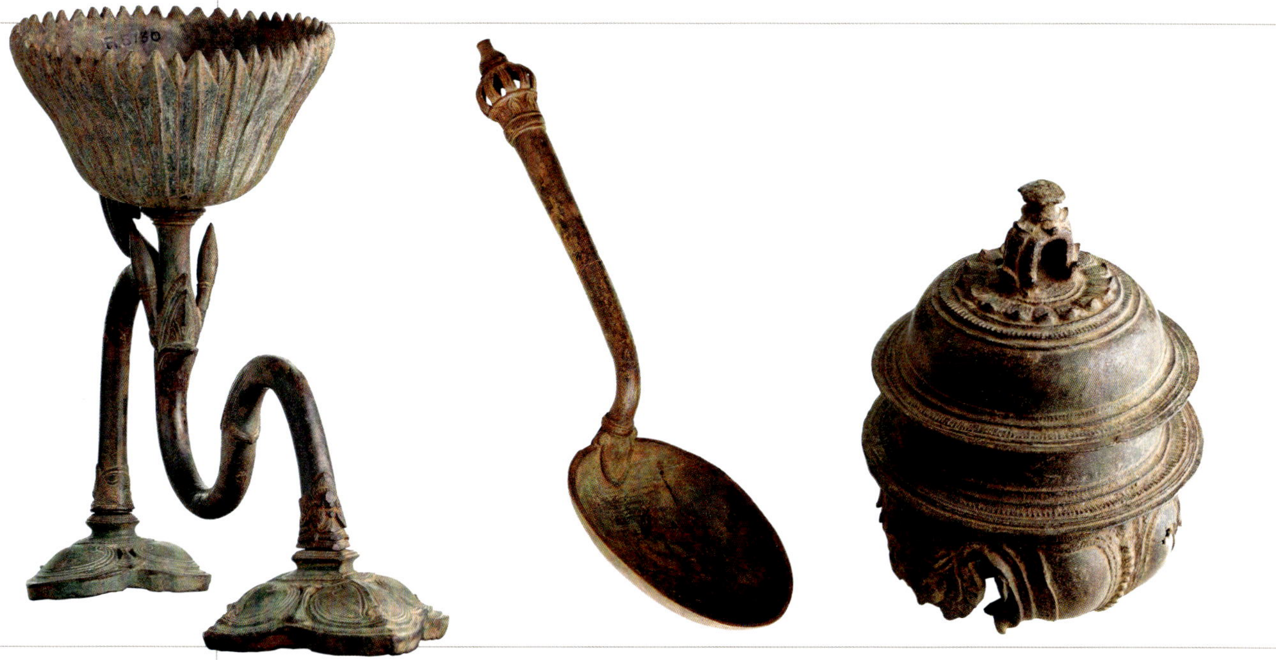

Endnotes

Bronze Drums, Urns, and Bells in the Early Metal Age of Southeast Asia Ian C. Glover

1 Vincent C. Pigott and Roberto Ciarla, "On the origins of metallurgy in prehistoric Southeast Asia: the view from Thailand," in S. La Niece, D. R. Hook and P. T. Craddock, eds., *Metals and Mines: Studies in Prehistoric Archaeometallurgy* (London: British Museum, 2007), pp. 76–88. White and Hamilton point to a Siberian source for the Southeast Asian bronze tradition but still coming through southern China. J. C. White and E. G. Hamilton, "The Transmission of Early Bronze Age Technology to Thailand: New Perspectives," *Journal of World Prehistory* 22, no. 4 (2009), pp. 357–97.

2 Joyce White argues that bronze was present at Ban Chiang in northeast Thailand probably by 2000 BCE and by 1500 BCE at the latest, whereas Charles Higham and T. Higham, after five seasons of excavation at the huge site of Ban Non Wat, also northeast Thailand, place the earliest Bronze Age burials with the time span of 1050–996 cal BCE. Joyce C. White, "Dating Early Bronze at Ban Chiang, Thailand," in J.-P. Pautreau, A.-S. Coupey, V. Zeitoun, and E. Rambault, eds., *From Homo Erectus to the Living Traditions—Papers from the 11th International Conference of the European Association of Southeast Asian Archaeologists* (Chiang Mai, Thailand: 11th International Conference of the European Association of Southeast Asian Archaeologists, 2008), p. 99; Charles F. W. Higham and T. Higham, "A new chronological framework for prehistoric Southeast Asia, based on a Bayesian model from Ban Non Wat," *Antiquity* 83, no. 319 (2009): 134. Of course there is no reason to believe that bronze appeared simultaneously at all sites throughout Southeast Asia, and there the dispute rests at present.

3 Louis Malleret, "Objets de bronze communs au Cambodge, à la Malaisie et à l'Indonésie," *Artibus Asiae* 19 (1956), p. 312. Malleret states that analysis of the Kandal urn shows a composition including 71.8 percent copper, 23.56 percent tin, 2.3 percent lead, and 1.5 percent zinc (p. 323).

4 Pieter Meyers, "A Commentary on the technology of Dông Son vessels," *Arts and Cultures* (2006), pp. 264–67.

5 Anna T. N. Bennett, "Bronze casting in prehistoric Southeast Asia, the technology and its origins," in *From Homo erectus to the Living Traditions*, pp.151–63.

6 Robert E. Murowchick, "The Development of Early Bronze Metallurgy in Viet Nam and Kampuchea: a Re-examination of Recent Work," in R. Maddin, *The Beginning of the Use of Metals and Alloys* (Cambridge, Mass.: Harvard University Press, 1988), pp. 175–81.

7 Franz Heger, *Alte Metalltrommeln aus Südostasien*, 2 vols. (Leipzig: K. von Hierseman, 1902).

8 Victor Goloubew, "L'age du bronze au Tonkin et dans le Nord-Annam," *Bulletin de l'École française d'Extrême-Orient* 29 (1929): 1–46.

9 Bernhard Karlgren, "The date of the early Dong-s'on Culture," *Bulletin of the Museum of Far Eastern Antiquities* 14 (1942): 1–28.

10 Chinese archaeologists consider the Wanjiaba type of drum to be the earliest and identify western Yunnan as the cradle of all bronze drums, but this is disputed by Vietnamese scholars, turning the identification of the earliest drums into a rather sterile nationalistic competition (Xiaorong Han, "Who invented the Bronze Drum? Nationalism, Politics and a Sino–Vietnamese debate of the 1970s and 1980s," *Asian Perspectives* 43, no. 1 [2004]: 7–33).

11 Andreas Reinecke, L. Vin, and S. Seng, "Der Alptraum von Prohear," in

Archäologie in Deutschland 6 (2008): 12–17.

12 Ian C. Glover, "Splendid enigmas from Southeast Asian later prehistory," *Arts and Cultures* (2004): 174–93.

13 This urn is the largest, at 85 cm tall, of all the urns so far known; it is said to have been found in an limestone sea cave close to the present Thai–Cambodian border.

14 Malleret, p. 319.

15 ———, p. 318.

16 Glover, "Splendid enigmas from Southeast Asian later prehistory."

17 The Kandal urn had been in the family of an employee of the Palace Museum for three generations, and it had been used to carry drinking water on his family's travels by bullock cart, although one must doubt whether this was the purpose for which it was originally made.

18 One urn, in a private collection in Bangkok, contains tightly packed red lateritic earth with some small bones visible, raising the possibility that the vessels might have served as cremation urns, but the visible bones seemed to be those of small animals or birds.

19 Malleret, pp. 317–26.

20 Glover, "Splendid enigmas from Southeast Asian later prehistory"; Ian C. Glover, "Bronzes en marge de la culture de Dong Son," in Monique Crick and Helen Loveday, eds., *Art Ancien du Viet Nam—Bronzes et céramiques* (Geneva: Collections Baur, 2008), pp. 31–45.

21 Malleret, fig.1.

22 Andreas Reinecke and Nguyen Thi Thanh Luyen, "Recent Discoveries in Vietnam—Gold masks and other precious items," *Arts of Asia* 39, no. 5 (2009): 58–67.

Bronze Sculptures of Ancient Cambodia Hiram Woodward

1 Inscription of Tep Pranam, K.290: George Cœdès, "La stèle de Thep Pranam," *Journal Asiatique* ser. 10, vol. 8 (1908), pp. 203–25; Cœdès, "Etudes Cambodgiennes XXX – A la recherche de Yaçodharāçrama," *Bulletin de l'École française d'Extrême-Orient* 32 (1932): 84–112.

2 For the date and related sculptures, Emma C. Bunker and Douglas Latchford, *Adoration and Glory: The Golden Age of Khmer Art* (Chicago: Art Media Resources, 2004), pp. 124–25. For bronze images with stylistic connections to fig. 1, ibid., pp. 116–21.

3 The example closest in date is illustrated in Emma C. Bunker and Douglas A. J. Latchford, *Khmer Gold: Gifts for the Gods* (Chicago: Art Media Resources, 2008), p. 59, fig. 4.24a.

4 Bunker and Latchford, *Adoration and Glory*, p. 120.

5 Samuel Beal, *Si-yu-ki: Buddhist Records of the Western World*, 2 vols. (reprint New York: Paragon, 1968), vol. 2, p. 119.

6 Hiram Woodward, "The *Karandavyuha Sutra* and Buddhist Art in 10th-Century Cambodia," in Pratapaditya Pal, ed., *Buddhist Art: Form & Meaning* (Mumbai: Marg Publications, 2007), pp. 70–83, esp. p. 75.

7 Khun Samen, *The New Guide to the National Museum* (Phnom Penh: Department of Museums Ministry of Culture and Fine Arts, 2002), pp. 25–26; Bunker and Latchford, *Adoration and Glory*, pp. 34–37; for *kaccha* style in India, Roshen Alkazi, *Ancient Indian Costume* (New Delhi: National Book Trust, 1996), p. 15.

8 George Groslier, *Les collections khmères du Musée Albert Sarraut à Phnom-Penh*, Ars Asiatica, vol. 16 (Paris: G. van Oest, 1931), p. 48 and pls. XI, 3; Pierre Dupont, *La statuaire préangkorienne*, Artibus Asiae Supplementum XV (Ascona: Artibus Asiae, 1955), p. 206.

9 Nancy Dowling, "New Light on Early Cambodian Buddhism," *Journal*

of the Siam Society 88 (2000): 122–55.

10 For this type elsewhere, Pierre Dupont, *L'Archéologie mône de Dvāravatī*, 2 vols., Publications de l'École française d'Extrême-Orient, vol. 41 (Paris, 1959), plate vol., group P, figs. 456–63; Hiram Woodward, *The Art and Architecture of Thailand* (Leiden and Boston: Brill, 2003), p. 94.

11 The Harihara of Sambor Prei Kuk, National Museum of Cambodia, Phnom Penh, Ga1607; Nadine Dalsheimer, *Les collections du musée national de Phnom Penh: L'art du Cambodge ancien* (Paris: École française d'Extrême-Orient, 2001), p. 87. For the Guimet sculpture, Pierre Baptiste and Thierry Zéphir, *L'Art khmer dans les collections du musée Guimet* (Paris: Editions de la Réunion des musées nationaux, 2008), pp. 34–35. The depiction of the hair loops, meanwhile, suggests a date prior to 706, the date of a Harihara in which the hair loops fall at diagonal angles rather than vertically (although indeed the older style was not entirely supplanted): Madeleine Giteau, *Khmer Sculpture and the Angkor civilization* (New York: Abrams, 1965), pl. 20, p. 62; Rita Régnier, "Note sur l'evolution du chignon (Jaṭā) dans la statuaire préangkorienne," *Arts Asiatiques* 14 (1966): 17–40, fig. 9; Maud Girard-Geslan, ed., *Art of Southeast Asia* (New York: Abrams, 1998), fig. 429.

12 National Museum of Cambodia, Phnom Penh, Ga5330; Helen Ibbitson Jessup and Thierry Zéphir, eds., *Sculpture of Angkor and Ancient Cambodia* (Washington, D.C.: National Gallery of Art, 1997), p. 156. The Maitreya (fig. 14), on the other hand, has a bulbous coiffure. The same pairing of coiffure types can be seen on a Dvāravatī stele, Pierre Baptiste and Thierry Zéphir, *Dvāravatī: aux sources du bouddhisme en Thaïlande* (Paris: Réunion des musées nationaux, 2009), fig. 28, p. 95. For the Buddha-flanking figures on this stele as Avalokiteshvara and Maitreya, Nandana Chutiwongs, *The Iconography of Avalokiteśvara in Mainland South East Asia* (Leiden: Proefschrift, Rijksuniversiteit, 1984), pp. 225–26.

13 The two inscriptions are K.49 and K.163: G. Cœdès, *Inscriptions du Cambodge*, 8 vols. (Hanoi and Paris: École française d'Extrême-Orient, 1938–66), vol. 6, pp. 6–9, 100–101.

14 Lin Li-kouang, "Puṇyodaya (Na-t'i), un propagateur du tantrisme en Chine et au Cambodge à l'époque de Hiuan-tsang," *Journal Asiatique* 227 (1935): 83–100. For an exploration of connections between Dvāravatī and China, Nicolas Revire, "À propos d'un 'tête' de *khakkhara* au Musée national de Bangkok," *Aséanie* 24 (December 2009), pp. 111–34.

15 E.g., René Yvon Lefebvre d'Argencé et al., *Chinese, Korean, and Japanese sculpture: The Avery Brundage Collection, Asian Art Museum of San Francisco* (Tokyo and New York: Kodansha, 1974), no. 92, pp. 192–93. This example is later than fig. 17. For opinions concerning the two Chinese sculptures, I am grateful to Emma Bunker, Thomas Lawton, Marylin Rhie, Keith Wilson, and Dorothy Wong.

16 Christine Ho, *The Casting of Religion: A Special Exhibition of Mr. Peng Kai-don's Donation* (Taipei: National Palace Museum: [2004]), no. 106, p. 31, dated to the Northern Qi (550–57).

17 Inscription K.53: Jacques, "Le pays khmer," pp. 77–78; Lawrence Palmer Briggs, *The Ancient Khmer Empire* (Philadelphia: American Philosophical Society, 1951), p. 55.

18 This reflects the views of Sheldon Pollock, "From whatever vantage point we look, if we are prepared to look historically, civilizations reveal themselves to be processes and not things," in *The Language of the Gods in the World of Men: Sanskrit, Culture, and Power in Premodern India* (Berkeley: University of California Press, 2009), p. 538.

19 For an account of Prasat Ak Yom, Bruno Bruguier, "Le Prasat Ak Yum:

État des connaissances," *Recherches nouvelles sur le Cambodge: Études thematiques* (Paris: École française d'Extrême-Orient, 1994), vol. I, pp. 273–96. In regard to the date, where a number of views have been expressed, I am in basic agreement with Helen Jessup (in Jessup and Zéphir, *Sculpture of Angkor*, p. 103) except that I understand the two inscriptions (K.749 and K.753) as being executed prior to the construction of the monument (Brugier, "Prasat Ak Yum," p. 282). For K.753, Cœdès, *Inscriptions du Cambodge*, vol. 5, pp. 58–59; K.749, ibid., pp. 57–58; redated (to 674) in Claude Jacques, "Le pays khmer avant Angkor," *Journal des Savants* 1986 (Jan.-Sept.), p. 88n (entire article, pp. 60–95). On the inscriptions and their content, Michael Vickery, *Society, Economics, and Politics in Pre-Angkor Cambodia: The 7th–8th Centuries* (Tokyo: The Centre for East Asian Cultural Studies for UNESCO, The Toyo Bunko, 1988).

20 The lintel is illustrated in Stern, "Hariharālaya et Indrapura," pl. LVIB, and Jean Boisselier, "Les linteaux khmers du VIIIe siècle: Nouvelles données sur le style de Kampong Preah," *Artibus Asiae* 30 (1968), pp. 101–44, fig. 19. For a sixth-century example of the Chinese design, Jessica Rawson, *Chinese Ornament: The Lotus and the Dragon* (London: British Museum Publications, 1984), fig. 67, p. 90. For epigraphic support of the dating, inscription K.688 at the Roluos monument Prasat Prei Prasat N. (Cœdès, *Inscriptions du Cambodge*, vol. 4, p. 36). Stylistically, the Roluos monuments date from the first two decades of the eighth century: see the lintels at Trapeang Phong S4, Prasat Olok A, and Prasat Olok C. For illustrations, Philippe Stern, "Hariharālaya et Indrapura," *Bulletin de l'École française d'Extrême-Orient* 38 (1938), pp. 175–97, pls. 54C, 57A, 57B; and Boisselier, "Les linteaux Khmers," figs. 6, 11, 12.

21 Edouard Chavannes, *Le T'ai chan: essai de monographie d'un culte chinois*, Annales du Musée Guimet, Bibliothèque d'études, vol. 21 (Paris: E. Leroux, 1910), pp. 322, 326; Howard J. Wechsler, *Offerings of Jade and Silk* (New Haven and London: Yale University Press, 1985), pp. 170–94; Brian R. Dott, *Identity Reflections: Pilgrimages to Mount Tai in Late Imperial China* (Cambridge, Mass. and London: Harvard University Asia Center, 2004), pp. 51–52; Robert E. Harrist, Jr., *The Landscape of Words: Stone Inscriptions from Early and Medieval China* (Seattle and London: University of Washington Press, 2008), pp. 221–56. The Chinese altar to heaven was round; since Prasat Rong Chen is square, if there was a link, it did not extend to roundness. The phenomenon of central and subsidiary towers can be understood in an Indian context but not the pyramid. For Ak Yom and Indian towers, Michael Meister, "Mountain Temples and Temple-Mountains: Mazrur," *Journal of the Society of Architectural Historians* 65, no. 1 (March 2006), pp. 26–49.

22 Jacques Dumarçay, *Architecture and its Models in South-East Asia* (Bangkok: Orchid Press, 2003), pp. 11, 43, 108, 113.

23 Inscription K.847: *Cœdès, Inscriptions du Cambodge*, vol. 6, p. 167.

24 As noted by Jean Boisselier, *La statuaire khmère et son evolution*, 2 vols. (Paris: École française d'Extrême-Orient, 1955), text vol., p. 280.

25 I am grateful for discussions with Brice Vincent.

26 Jessup and Zéphir, *Sculpture of Angkor*, pp. 257–59.

27 The sculptures are: (1) Bunker and Latchford, *Adoration and Glory*, no. 70, pp. 213–15 (dated equivalent to 1044 CE); (2) ibid., no. 73, pp. 220–21; (3) Pratapaditya Pal, *The Sensuous Immortals* (Los Angeles: Los Angeles County Museum of Art), no. 145, p. 239 (currently Metropolitan Museum of Art, New York, L94.48); (4) Wolfgang Felten and Martin Lerner, *Thai and Cambodian Sculpture* (London: Philip Wilson Publishers, 1988), no. 33, pp. 224–27; (5) Michael Brand, ed., *Traditions*

of *Asian Art Traced Through the Collection of the National Gallery of Australia* (Canberra: National Gallery, 1995), p. 47; (6) Martin Lerner and Steven Kossak, "The Arts of South and Southeast Asia," *Metropolitan Museum of Art Bulletin* 51, no. 4 (spring 1994), fig. 83, p. 82 (accession number 1988.355). In two of these, the right hand holds a lotus (nos. 2 and 4). In three of them, there is no attribute in the right hand, but it is positioned in a way that suggests that there was originally a lotus (nos. 1, 2, and 5). In two of them, the left hand performs a gesture like that seen on the Phnom Bayang bronze (nos. 2 and 6). In the case of nos. 3 and 4, the catalogue authors believe that the lotus indicates a connection with Avalokiteshvara. This possibility cannot be eliminated, but my view would be that the primary identification holds: they are only secondarily Lokeshvara (= Avalokiteshvara), that is *–iśvara* (Lord, = Shiva) of the *loka* (world). There has been damage to the coiffure of no. 1, and Bunker and Latchford propose that it originally supported a figure of the Jina Amitabha. I hold that what was there was more likely to have been the magical syllable *oṃ*, in relief, as in fig. 19 in this catalogue. For additional discussions of related eleventh-century bronzes, Woodward, *Art and Architecture of Thailand*, pp. 126–27, and Baptiste and Zéphir, L'Art khmer, no. 59, pp. 204–5.

28 In "Chronique: Phnoṃ Bàyàṅ," *Bulletin de l'École française d'Extrême-Orient* 36 (1936), p. 626, Henri Mauger, its discoverer, wrote that this sculpture would have held "une fleur mobile." For Shiva as lotus bearer, Kamaleswar Bhattacharya, *Les religions brahmaniques dans l'ancien Cambodge* (Paris: École française d'Extrême-Orient, 1961), p. 83.

29 Inscription K.852, as summarized in Bruno Bruguier and Juliette Lacroix, *Guide archéologique du Cambodge*, vol. 1, *Phnom Penh et les provinces méridionales* (Phnom Penh: Reyum, 2009), p. 176.

30 Bhattacharya, *Les religions brahmaniques*, pp. 97–101; Wibke Lobo, "Viṣṇu-Vāsudeva-Nārāyaṇa: a Late Twelfth Century Khmer Bronze," in *Living a Life in Accord with Dhamma: Papers in Honor of Professor Jean Boisselier on his Eightieth Birthday*, ed. Natasha Eilenberg, M. C. Subhadradis Diskul, and Robert L. Brown (Bangkok: Silpakorn University, 1997), pp. 320–29. The inscription is K.165, Thvar Kdei, Cœdès, *Inscriptions du Cambodge*, vol. 6, pp. 132–39.

31 D. Dennis Hudson (edited by Margaret H. Case), *The Body of God: An Emperor's Palace for Krishna in Eighth-century Kanchipuram* (New York: Oxford University Press, 2008), p. 73.

32 For works in the group, Felten and Lerner, *Thai and Cambodian Sculpture*, pp. 224–27.

33 Baptiste and Zéphir, *L'Art khmer*, no. 43, pp. 150–51.

34 Inscription K.266–68: George Cœdès, "Les inscriptions de Bàt Čuṃ," *Journal Asiatique* 10th ser., 12 (1908), pp. 213–54; some passages translated; David Snellgrove, *Angkor—Before and After: A Cultural History of the Khmers* (Trumbull Conn.: Weatherhill, 2004), pp. 74–77.

35 Woodward, *Art and Architecture of Thailand*, pp. 150–51.

36 One attractive theory posits that the link between Phimai Buddhism and the later state Buddhism was the temple of Preah Khan, Kampong Svay, east of Angkor, and that the future Jayavarman VII was raised there. See Claude Jacques, "The Historical Development of Khmer Culture from the Death of Sūryavarman II to the 16th Century," in Joyce Clark, ed., *Bayon: New Perspectives* (Bangkok: River Books, 2007), pp. 30–49 (esp. pp. 30–35).

37 Woodward, *Art and Architecture of Thailand*, p. 151; Wibke Lobo, entry no. 76 in Jessup and Zéphir, eds., *Sculpture of Angkor*, p. 273.

38 I thank Brice Vincent for making this distinction. It is possible that the two types are distinguished in Khmer epigraphy: *śaṇka* (for a trumpet); *ardhaśaṇka* (for a conch-shell holder). See Dominique Soutif, "La monture de conque inscrite du Musée national de Phnom Penh: Relecture de l'inscription angkorienne K.779," *Aséanie* 22 (December 2008): 52 (inclusive, pp. 47–61).

39 For an introduction to some of the controversies concerning the history of the period, Michael Vickery, "Bayon: New Perspectives Reconsidered," *Udaya* 7 (2006): 101–58.

40 The pedestal of this sculpture bears an inscription, inventoried as K.1013 and thought to be in Sanskrit but still unpublished.

41 Information concerning the other images, courtesy of Brice Vincent.

42 T. S. Maxwell, *The Gods of Asia* (Delhi: Oxford University Press, 1997), pp. 49–55.

43 Inscription K.834, stanza 88: Cœdès, *Inscriptions du Cambodge*, vol. 5, pp. 256, 267.

44 Bhattacharya, *Les religions brahmaniques*, p. 87.

45 Yoshiaki Ishizawa, *Special Issue of the Inventory of 274 Buddhist Statues and the Stone Pillar Discovered from Banteay Kdei Temple, Renaissance culturelle du Cambodge* 21 (2004), 2 vols. (Tokyo: Sophia Asia Center for Research and Human Development, Institute of Asian Cultures, Sophia University).

46 Inscription K.241: Cœdès, *Inscriptions du Cambodge*, vol. 3, pp. 77–78.

47 Maṇgalartha inscription, K.488: Louis Finot, "Inscriptions d'Aṇkor, XI, Temple de Maṇgalārtha à Aṇkor Thom," *Bulletin de l'École française d'Extrême-Orient* 25 (1925), pp. 393–406. The Pali inscription, K.754: G. Cœdès, "Études cambodgiennes, XXXII, La plus ancienne inscription en Pāli du Cambodge," *Bulletin de l'École française d'Extrême-Orient* 36 (1936), pp. 14–21. The inscription of 1327 CE, K.470: G. Cœdès, *Inscriptions du Cambodge*, vol. 2, pp. 187–89.

48 Coiffure: Woodward, *Art and Architecture of Thailand*, pl. 85; Baptiste and Zéphir, *L'Art khmer*, p. 388 (MG 18912, Preah Pithu pediment).

49 Hiram W. Woodward, Jr., *The Sacred Sculpture of Thailand* (Baltimore: The Walters Art Gallery, 1997), fig. 156, p. 155.

A Technical Study of the Kampong Cham Figure Group Paul Jett

1 Thermoluminescence test performed by Oxford Authentication Ltd., report no. N208d77, dated 9 December 2008.

2 Hiram W. Woodward, Jr., *The Sacred Sculpture of Thailand* (Baltimore: Walters Art Gallery, 1997), pp. 68–70.

3 David Bourgarit et al., "A Millennium of Khmer Bronze Metallurgy: Analytical Studies of Bronze Artifacts from the Musée Guimet and the Phnom Penh National Museum," in Paul Jett et al., eds., *Scientific Research in the Field of Asian Art* (London: Archetype Publications, 2003), pp. 103–26.

4 Paul Jett, "A Study of the Gilding of Chinese Buddhist Bronzes," in S. La Niece and P. Craddock, eds., *Metal Plating and Patination* (Oxford: Butterworth-Heinemann Ltd., 1993), pp. 193–200.

5 The results were compared to bronze standards, and the accuracy for the stated amounts of the individual elements is estimated as follows: copper ±2%; tin ±10%; lead ±30%; zinc ±5%; and iron ±10%.

6 Paul Jett and Janet G. Douglas, "Chinese Buddhist Bronzes in the Freer Gallery of Art: Physical Features and Elemental Composition," in *Materials Issues in Art and Archaeology* III, Materials Research Society Symposium Proceedings, vol. 267 (Pittsburgh, Pa.: Materials Research Society, 1992), pp. 205–23; Edward V. Sayer, Paul Jett, and Emil Joel, "A Technical

Examination of the Chinese Buddhist Bronzes in the Freer Gallery of Art, Part B: Stable Lead Isotope Analysis," in *Materials Issues in Art and Archaeology* III, Materials Research Society Symposium Proceedings, vol. 267 (Pittsburgh, Pa.: Materials Research Society, 1992), pp. 225–37.

7 P. A. Lins and W. A. Oddy, "The Origins of Mercury Gilding," *Journal of Archaeological Science* 2 (1975), pp. 365–73; Emma C. Bunker, "Amalgam Gilding in Khmer Culture," in E. A. Bacus, I. C. Glover, and P. D. Sharrock, eds., *Interpreting Southeast Asia's Part: Monument, Image and Text* (Singapore: NUS Press, 2008), pp. 296–305; Emma C. Bunker and Douglas A. J. Latchford, *Khmer Gold: Gifts for the Gods* (Chicago: Art Media Resources, 2008), p. 130.

8 Woodward, *Sacred Sculpture of Thailand*; Bourgarit et al., "Khmer Bronze Metallurgy"; Donna Strahan, "A Technical Study of 11th–12th c. Khmer Bronze Sculpture," in *The Fourth International Conference on the Beginning of the Use of Metals and Alloys (BUMA-IV)* (Sendai, Japan: BUMA-IV Organizing Committee and the Japan Institute of Metals, 1998), pp. 97–102; Chandra Reedy and Pieter Meyers, "New Methods for Analyzing Thin Sections of Casting Core Materials: A Case Study with Southeast Asian Bronzes," in Janet Douglas, Paul Jett, and John Winter, eds., *Scientific Research on the Sculptural Arts of Asia* (London: Archetype Publications, 2007), pp. 103–14.

Angkorian Metalwork in the Temple Setting: Icons, Architectural Adornment, and Ritual Paraphernalia John Guy

The author thanks Hab Touch, Ang Choulean, Im Sokrithy, Hiram Woodward, Ashley Thompson, Brice Vincent, and Louise Cort for conversations on aspects of this paper and for responding to specific questions.

1 Zhou Daguan, in Chou Ta-kuan, *The Customs of Cambodia* (Bangkok: Siam Society, 1993), p. 2.

2 Bernard Philippe Groslier, *Angkor and Cambodia in the Sixteenth Century according to Portuguese and Spanish Sources* (Bangkok: Orchid Press, 2006 [1958]), p. 57.

3 A *triśūla* prong of this scale was excavated by the Apsara Authority near the north gate of Angkor Thom in early 2007; personal communication Christophe Pottier.

4 The Sanskrit name given is Hemasringagiri, inscription K.277, stanzas 29, 31; George Cœdès, *Inscriptions du Cambodge*, vol. 4 (Hanoi and Paris: École française d'Extrême-Orient, 1952), pp. 155, 159. The 'K' numbers refer to the French system of inventorying Cambodian inscriptions, in both Sanskrit and Old Khmer, as published by Cœdès, *Inscriptions du Cambodge*, 8 vols. (1938–66). This inventory is actively maintained by the École française d'Extrême-Orient (EFEO), Siem Reap and Paris.

5 Fragmentary *triśūla* in the Wat Raja Bo museum collection, Siem Reap, have been identified and catalogued by this author for integration into a larger project underway with the Apsara Authority, forthcoming. A mercury-gilt bronze *triśūla* discovered in 1953 within Preah Khan (National Museum of Cambodia, Phnom Penh, Ga4266; inventory records courtesy of Brice Vincent) also may have been a tower antefix, but its relatively small scale (height 25 cm) allows for it to have been mounted on a staff carried by a Saivite ascetic or used as a fitting for a guardian sculpture; both uses are depicted in reliefs.

6 H. Parmentier, "L'Architecture interpretée dans les bas-reliefs du Cambodge," *Bulletin de l'École française d'Extrême-Orient* 14 (1914), pp. 1–28.

7 Pierre Baptiste and Thierry Zéphir, *L'Art khmer dans les collections du*

musée Guimet (Paris: Editions de la Réunion des musées nationaux, 2008), cat. 43, a kneeling male attendant holding an offering basin, tenth century or later; a bronze kneeling female devotee, hands raised in *anjali*, is in the Metropolitan Museum of Art, New York (1972.147).

8 Chou Ta-kuan, *The Customs of Cambodia*, p. 5.

9 Mirrors were recovered in the excavations conducted around the royal platform at Sras Srang in 1964 by Bernard Philippe Groslier, in what he identified as a funerary deposit; Paul Courbin, *La Fouille du Sras-Srang. Collection de Texts et Documents sur l'Indochine* 17 (Paris, École française d'Extrême-Orient, 1988), pp. 21–43, pls. 17, 24.

10 Since its installation in the Royal Palace, this sculpture has become the focus of ongoing worship; worshipers routinely visit it prior to going to the main sanctuary; Ang Choulean, "Nandin and his Avatars," in Helen Ibbitson Jessup and Thierry Zéphir, eds., *Sculpture of Angkor and Ancient Cambodia* (Washington, D.C.: National Gallery of Art, 1997), pp. 62–78.

11 Bernard Philippe Groslier, *Indochina. The Melting Pot of Races* (London: 1962), pl. 134.

12 Jean Boisselier, "Notes sur l'Art du Bronze dans l'ancien Cambodge," *Artibus Asiae* 29 (1967), figs. 10–14; the massive head is now displayed at the National Museum, Bangkok.

13 M. C. Subhadradis Diskul, "The Bronze Portal Guardian Masterpiece of Prasat Sa Khamphaeng Yai," *Muang Boran* 15, no. 4 (1989), pp. 76–81 (in Thai). See also Hiram Woodward, *The Art and Architecture of Thailand, from Prehistoric Times through the Thirteenth Century* (Leiden: Brill, 2003), pp. 126–27 and pl. 34.

14 For this creation myth and an astrological interpretation of its meaning and ritual significance proposed in the context of the rock-cut sculpture of the subject at Udayagiri, Madhya Pradesh, early fifth century, Michael Willis, *The Archaeology of Hindu Ritual* (New York: Cambridge University Press, 2009). For the lineage of stone lintel versions of this subject in pre-Angkorian Cambodia and Champa, Jean Boisselier, "Arts du Champa et du Cambodge préangkorien. La date de Mi-So'n E-1," *Artibus Asiae* 19, no. 3/4 (1956), pp. 197–212.

15 Mary Shepherd Slusser, *Nepal Mandala: A Cultural Study of the Kathmandu Valley*, 2 vols. (Princeton: Princeton University Press, 1982), pl. 376.

16 Boisselier, "Notes sur l'Art du Bronze dans l'ancien Cambodge," figs. 26–28, 30–32.

17 Richard D. Cushman, *The Royal Chronicles of Ayutthaya*, ed. David K. Wyatt (Bangkok: The Siam Society, 2000).

18 Cushman, *The Royal Chronicles of Ayutthaya*, p. 15.

19 The account does not specify that they were bronze, but other passages confirm the installation of large-scale "gold icons," and it is highly unlikely that large stone sculptures would have attracted the same attention or survived transportation.

20 For issues on the restoration of Khmer rule, Claude Jacques, "The historical development of Khmer culture from the death of Suryavarman II to the 16th century," in Joyce Clark, ed., *Bayon: New Perspectives* (Bangkok: River Books, 2007), pp. 30–49.

21 Boisselier, "Notes sur l'Art du Bronze dans l'ancien Cambodge"; also John Guy and Richard Richards, "The Architectural Ceramics of Sukhothai Province," *Transactions of the Oriental Ceramic Society* 56 (1993), pp. 75–100.

22 For this group, Wolfgang Felten and Martin Lerner, *Thai and Cambodian Sculpture* (London: Philip Wilson Publishers, 1988), pp. 225–26; summarized in Emma C. Bunker and Douglas Latchford, *Adoration and Glory:*

The Golden Age of Khmer Art (Chicago: Art Media Resources, 2004), p. 238. The hand gestures of the Phnom Bayang figure are those displayed by the gilt bronze standing male figure in the Metropolitan Museum of Art, to which it is closely related.

23 For a discussion of temple festivals in a South Indian context, John Guy, "Parading the Gods—Bronze Devotional Images of Chola South India," in Vidya Dehejia et al., *Chola: Sacred Bronzes of Southern India* (London: Royal Academy of Arts, 2006), pp. 12–26.

24 For example, inscription K.276 at Prasat Ta Kev, Cœdès, *Inscriptions du Cambodge* 4, pp. 153–54; thanks to Hiram Woodward for this reference.

25 For a discussion of the concept of *Neak Ta*, Ang Choulean, *Les êtres surnaturels dans la religion populaire khmère* (Paris: Cedoreck, 1986). Also Paul Mus, "Cult Indiens et Indigenes au Champa," *Bulletin de l'École française d'Extrême-Orient* 23 (1934), pp. 367–410, a study of ancestor rock worship in mainland Southeast Asia (English translation published as *The Religious Ceremonies of Champa* [Bangkok: White Lotus, 2001]).

26 John Guy, *Indian Temple Sculpture* (London: V&A Publications, 2007), pp. 90–96.

27 Jean Filliozat, "The role of the Saivagamas in the Saiva ritual system," in Fred W. Clothey and J. Bruce Long, eds., *Experiencing Siva: Encounters with a Hindu Deity* (Columbia, Mo.: South Asia Books, 1983), pp. 81–86.

28 Inscription K.569: Alexis Sanderson, "The Śaiva Religion among the Khmers (Part I)," *Bulletin de l'École française d'Extrême-Orient* 90–91 (2003), p. 353.

29 Inscription K.661: Sanderson, "The Śaiva Religion among the Khmers (Part I)," p. 354.

30 Richard H. Davis, *Ritual in an Oscillating Universe: Worshipping Siva in Medieval India* (Princeton: Princeton University Press, 1991).

31 E. Hulzsch, ed., *South Indian Inscriptions*, vol. 1 (Calcutta: Government Press, 1890), p. 24.

32 George Cœdès, "La stèle du Práh Khan d'Ankor," *Bulletin de l'École française d'Extrême-Orient* 41, fasc. 2 (1941), p. 255.

33 The issues surrounding the structure and symbolism of the Bayon are explored comprehensively in Joyce Clark, ed., *Bayon. New Perspectives* (Bangkok: River Books, 2007).

34 Cœdès, "La stèle du Práh Khan d'Ankor," p. 266.

35 Cœdès, "La stèle du Práh Khan d'Ankor," p. 267; George Cœdès, "La stele de Ta-Prohm," *Bulletin de l'École française d'Extrême-Orient* 6, nos. 1–2 (1906), p.77.

36 Pierre Baptiste and Thierry Zéphir, *Trésors d'art du Vietnam. La sculpture du Champa, Ve–XVe siècles* (Paris: Réunion des musées nationaux, Musée des arts asiatiques Guimet, 2005), p. 196–97; Robert L. Brown, ed., *Ganesh: Studies of an Asian God* (Albany: State University of New York Press, 1991), pp. 171–233.

37 Claude Jacques, "Notes sur l'inscription de la stele de Vat Luong Kau," *Journal Asiatique* 250, no. 2 (1962), pp. 249–56; see also Oliver W. Wolters, "Khmer 'Hinduism' in the Seventh Century," in R. B. Smith and W. Watson, eds., *Early South East Asia: Essays in Archaeology, History and Historical Geography* (Oxford: Oxford University Press, 1979), p. 438.

38 Boisselier, "Arts du Champa et du Cambodge préangkorien," fig. 1.

39 A rare conch shell in a bronze setting has survived; dedicated to celebrating Hevajra, it is now in the Cleveland Museum of Art. John Guy, *Ceramic Traditions of Southeast Asia* (Singapore: Oxford University Press, 1989), pp. 23–24.

40 Louis Finot, "Manuscrits sanskrits de sadhana's retrouvés en Chine,"

Journal Asiatique 225, no. 2 (1934), pp. 1–85. Carved conch shells have been recovered, along with other liturgical equipment, from recently discovered shipwreck cargoes in the Java Sea attributable to the tenth and eleventh centuries—clear evidence that such conch shells continued to circulate in the Hindu-Buddhist diaspora of Southeast Asia. The conch shell lent itself to trumpeting, while the high-value metal copies were more likely for worship activities, such as the lustration of icons. Both functions are liturgically appropriate.

41 In Cambodian imagery, Hevajra's sexual union with his *sakti* Nairātmā, personification of wisdom, from which generates the *dakini*s, is rarely represented, unlike in the Himalayan tradition where it is the standard iconography. For the pioneering study of Hevajra ritual in Khmer culture, J. J. Boeles, "Two Yoginīs of Hevajra from Thailand," in *Essays offered to G. H. Luce by his colleagues and friends in honour of his seventy-fifth birthday*, ed. Ba Shin, Jean Boisselier, and A. B. Griswold (Ascona: Publishers Artibus Asiae, 1965), vol. 2, pp. 14–29.

42 David Snellgrove, *The Hevajra-Tantra* (London, Oxford University Press, 1959).

43 A mold of identical composition is in the National Museum Bangkok: Boeles, "Two Yoginīs of Hevajra from Thailand," fig. 4; molds attributable to the Jayavarman VII reign excavated at Sras Srang in 1964: Courbin, *La Fouille de Sras-Srang*, pls. 20, 34, 44–45.

44 The most important such image, from Angkor Thom, is in the Metropolitan Museum of Art, New York: Martin Lerner and Steven Kossak, "The Arts of South and Southeast Asia," *Metropolitan Museum of Art Bulletin* 51, no. 4 (spring 1994), pl. 89.

45 For recent work exploring the significance of the Hevajra cult in the reign of Jayavarman VII, see Peter D. Sharrock, "Hevajra at Banteay Chmar," *The Journal of the Walters Art Museum* 64/65 (2006–2007, published 2009), pp. 49–64.

46 Dominique Soutif, "La monture de conque inscrite de Musée national de Phnom Penh," *Aseanie* 22 (2008), pp. 47–61.

47 Baptiste and Zéphir, *L'Art khmer dans les collections du musée Guimet*, cat. no. 119.

48 A lotus of similar design supports the throne of a seated Buddha on a bronze mold for producing miniature clay icons, National Museum of Cambodia, Phnom Penh, Ga5657.

49 George Cœdès, *Bronzes Khmers* (Brussels: Ars Asiatica, 1923), pl. XIXb.

50 As witnessed in the An-thai inscription of 902, Quang Nam province: Jean Boisselier, *La Statuaire du Champa. Recherches sur les Cultes et l'iconographie* (Paris: École française d'Extrême-Orient, 1963), pp. 121–22.

51 Woodward, *The Art and Architecture of Thailand*, pp. 46–51; see also Boreth Ly, "Protecting the Protector of Phimai," *The Journal of the Walters Art Museum. Essays in Honor of Hiram W. Woodward, Jr.*, vol. 64/65 (2006–2007), pp. 35–48.

52 Chou Ta-kuan, *The Customs of Cambodia*, p. 72.

53 The weights mentioned equate to approximately 1,500 metric tons of copper, Cœdès, "La stèle du Práh Khan d'Ankor," pp. 270, 294.

54 K.906: Cœdès, "La stèle du Práh Khan d'Ankor."

55 Similar features are visible at Preah Ko, Roluos (880), and on the brick towers on the upper terrace of the East Mebon temple (953).

56 These findings are based on this author's field work in January 2006. A fuller study of this research is in preparation.

57 Iron fittings for securing textile canopies survive in situ in some temples.

Glossary

Angkor "Sacred city" (from Sanskrit *nagara*, city). The capital of Cambodia, circa 900–1431.

Angkor Thom "The big city." The walled city-within-a-city constructed by King Jayavarman VII in the closing decades of the twelfth century.

Angkor Wat "The city with the monasteries." The Vishnu temple built by King Suryavarman II (reigned 1113–after 1150) and, centuries later, the site of two Buddhist monasteries.

Apsara (Sanskrit) "Cloud maiden," heavenly nymph. A term sometimes applied to the celestial females who adorn the walls of Angkor Wat.

Avalokiteshvara (Sanskrit) The lord (*īśvara*) who looks down (*avalokita*) (upon the world with pity for the sufferers). The most prominent of the bodhisattvas, an embodiment of compassion. Also Lokeshvara ("lord of the world," *loka*) in Cambodian inscriptions. Guanyin in China; Kannon in Japan.

Baray (modern Khmer) The artificial rectangular lakes constructed at Angkor.

Bodhgaya The site in the modern state of Bihar, India, where the Historical Buddha Shakyamuni achieved the state of complete enlightenment, enabling him to escape reincarnation and to teach the Buddhist truths.

Bodhisattva (Sanskrit) A human being (*sattva*) on his way to enlightenment (*bodhi*). Originally, the Buddha Shakyamuni prior to his enlightenment or in one of his previous lives. Subsequently, a Buddhist practitioner following the Bodhisattva path. Plus, on the celestial plane, a divine embodiment of Buddhist virtues. Avalokiteshvara is such a bodhisattva.

Brahma The four-faced creator god; one of the three chief gods in Hinduism.

Brahman In India, the priestly caste. Cambodia never adopted a full-fledged caste system, but Brahman priests performed Brahmanical ceremonies (involving ritual offerings, for instance) in temples and, presumably, at home.

Dakini (Sanskrit *dākinī*) In Tantric texts, a female being whose powers are absorbed by a male practitioner. Frequently depicted dancing, with a ferocious demeanor. The *yoginī* is more or less equivalent.

Dvāravatī A kingdom in central Thailand, probably centered at Nakhon Pathom, attested in the seventh century. Sometimes applied to the Buddhist culture of the greater part of modern Thailand, sixth to eleventh centuries.

Ganesha In Hinduism, the elephant-headed god, a son of Shiva. Lord of his troops and lord of beginnings.

Linga (Sanskrit) Phallic emblem, the form in which the god Shiva is generally worshiped. The linga (or Shivalinga) is considered a fiery cosmic pillar, infinite in dimension.

Lokeshvara See Avalokiteshvara.

Maitreya A bodhisattva, the Buddha of the future, now residing in Tushita Heaven.

Nandin (Sanskrit) "The gladdening one." An epithet for the bull ridden by the Hindu god Shiva and his spouse.

Prajñāpāramitā (Sanskrit) The perfection of wisdom. Complete insight into the nature of existence, as understood by Buddhists; the highest of the perfections. Personified, especially in Cambodia, as a female goddess.

Prasat (Sanskrit *prāsāda*) Temple, palace. In Khmer, temple names are generally preceded by Prasat, as in Prasat Bayon, "the Bayon temple."

Pre-Angkor, pre-Angkorian The period in Cambodian history (sixth–eighth centuries) prior to the coronation of Jayavarman II in 802 (according to a later inscription).

Rishi (Sanskrit *rsi*) A hermit, especially an adherent of the god Shiva devoted to ascetic practices.

Sampot (Khmer) The term applied to the long rectangular piece of cloth wrapped around the waist, seen on male divinities.

Shakyamuni (Sanskrit) The sage of the Śākya clan. The Historical Buddha ("enlightened one") who taught the doctrines later codified as Buddhism in about the fifth century BCE.

Shiva One of the three chief Hindu gods (with Brahma and Vishnu); the volatile god of destruction. To his followers, a supreme god responsible for both the periodic creation and destruction of the universe.

Shivalinga See linga.

Tantra A class of Buddhist and Hindu texts, increasingly influential from about the ninth–tenth century onward, mostly outlining secret rituals that were a means to convey spiritual virtues from master to pupil.

Tushita Heaven In Buddhist cosmology, one of many heavens. See Maitreya.

Vajrayana (Sanskrit) The way of the *vajra* (a ritual instrument). A Buddhist movement that developed in the seventh to eighth centuries, advocating, among other things, a shortcut to enlightenment by initiation into a circle of divinities (a mandala). Sometimes the terms Vajrayana and Tantric Buddhism are considered synonymous.

Vishnu The third member of the Hindu trinity, the god of stability. Generally depicted standing, with four arms, but after the death of one world era and prior to the birth of the next, he reclines in deep sleep upon a cosmic ocean.

Yasodharapura The city (*pura*) established by King Yasovarman, circa 900, that is, Angkor.

Suggested Readings

Baptiste, Pierre, and Thierry Zéphir. *L'Art khmer dans les collections du musée Guimet*. Paris: Editions de la Réunion des musées nationaux, 2008.

Boisselier, Jean. *Trends in Khmer Art*. Ithaca, N.Y.: Cornell Southeast Asia Program, 1989.

Bunker, Emma C., and Douglas Latchford. *Adoration and Glory: The Golden Age of Khmer Art*. Chicago: Art Media Resources, 2004.

Chandler, David P. *A History of Cambodia*. Boulder: Westview Press, 2008.

Coe, Michael D. *Angkor and the Khmer Civilization*. New York: Thames and Hudson, 2003.

Cœdès, George. *Bronzes Khmers*. Brussels: Ars Asiatica, 1923.

Dalsheimer, Nadine. *Les collections du Musée national de Phnom Penh: l'art du Cambodge ancient*. Paris: École française d'Extrême-Orient, 2001.

Felten, Wolfgang, and Martin Lerner. *Thai and Cambodian Sculpture*. London: Philip Wilson Publishers, 1988.

Giteau, Madeleine. *Khmer Sculpture and the Angkor Civilization*. New York: Abrams, 1965.

Guy, John. "The Temples of Angkor." Introduction to Steve McCurry, *Sanctuary: The Temples of Angkor*. London, Phaidon, 2002.

Jacques, Claude, and Philippe Lafond. *The Khmer empire: cities and sanctuaries, fifth to thirteenth centuries*. Bangkok: River Books, 2007.

Jessup, Helen Ibbitson. *Art & Architecture of Cambodia*. London: Thames and Hudson, 2004.

———. *Masterpieces of the National Museum of Cambodia*. Norfolk, Conn.: Friends of Khmer Culture, 2006.

———, and Thierry Zéphir, eds. *Sculpture of Angkor and Ancient Cambodia*. Washington, D.C.: National Gallery of Art, 1997.

Khun Samen. *Preah Neang Tevi: collections of the National Museum*. Phnom Penh: Department of Museums Ministry of Culture and Fine Arts, 2006.

Lerner, Martin, and Steven Kossak. "The Arts of South and Southeast Asia," *Metroplitan Museum of Art Bulletin* 51, no. 4. New York: Metropolitan Museum of Art, 1994.

Woodward, Hiram. *The Art and Architecture of Thailand*. Leiden and Boston: Brill, 2003.

Woodward, Jr., Hiram W. *The Sacred Sculpture of Thailand*. Baltimore: The Walters Art Gallery, 1997.

Contributors

Louise Allison Cort. Curator of Ceramics, Freer Gallery of Art and Arthur M. Sackler Gallery, Washington, D.C.

Ian C. Glover. Emeritus Reader in Southeast Asian Archaeology, University College, London

John Guy. Curator of South and Southeast Asian Art, Metropolitan Museum of Art, New York

Paul Jett. Head, Department of Conservation and Scientific Research, Freer Gallery of Art and Arthur M. Sackler Gallery, Washington, D.C.

Hiram Woodward. Emeritus Curator of Asian Art, Walters Art Museum, Baltimore

Board of the Freer Gallery of Art and Arthur M. Sackler Gallery as of September 2009

Ms. Diane H. Schafer, Chair
Dr. Catherine Glynn Benkaim, Vice-Chair
Mrs. Masako Shinn, Secretary
Mrs. Sunandini (Nunda) P. Ambegaonka
Ms. Susan Beningson
Mrs. Jane Bernstein
Mr. John R. Curtis
Mr. Richard M. Danziger
Mr. Michael de Havenon
Dr. Robert S. Feinberg
Mr. Michael E. Feng
Mrs. Hart Fessenden
Mr. Martin J. G. Glynn
Ms. Merit E. Janow
Ms. Shirley Z. Johnson
Mr. Gregory Kinsey
Mr. James Lintott
Mr. H. Christopher Luce
Mrs. Constance C. Miller
Mrs. Susan Pillsbury
Mr. David Solo
Mr. Leopold Swergold
Mrs. Patricia P. Tang
Mr. Ladislaus von Hoffman
Honorary
Mrs. Cynthia Helms
Sir Joseph Hotung

Photo Credits

Photographs of the exhibition objects in this catalogue (see the checklist, pages 130–41) were taken by Darren Campbell and Ocelus Productions and are reproduced courtesy of the National Museum of Cambodia, Phnom Penh. Credit lines for all other images are listed below.

Fig. 2. Fifteen vessels. Image courtesy of Joel A. Greene.

Figs. 6 and 6A. Lakshmi or Uma. Angkor period, early 10th century. Sandstone; 124.2 × 37.5 × 24.3 cm. Gift of Arthur M. Sackler, Arthur M. Sackler Gallery, Smithsonian Institution, S1987.909.

Fig. 7. Stele with eight-armed Avalokiteshvara. Anonymous, Cambodia, 900–950. Sandstone; 36 × 22 cm. Walters Art Museum, gift of Yoshie Shinomoto (25.194). Photo © The Walters Art Museum, Baltimore.

Fig. 15. The Bodhisattva Avalokitesvara. Cambodia, late 7th century–early 8th century. Sandstone; 80 × 28 × 15 cm. MG14885. Photograph by Thierry Ollivier. Réunion des Musées Nationaux / Art Resource, NY. Musee des Arts Asiatiques-Guimet, Paris, France.

Fig. 22. Ensemble with images of the dancing Shiva. Cambodia, Angkor period, second half of the 12th century. Metal alloy; 15.3 cm (h.). Bangkok National Museum, Thailand, acc. no. 9th. Photograph by Hiram Woodward.

Fig. 40. Architectural ornament. Cambodian, Angkor period, 11th century. Bronze. Museum no: IS.87-1993. ©V&A Images/Victoria and Albert Museum, London, Gift of the Anthony Gardner Estate.

Fig. 41. Offering dishes. Cambodia, Angkor period, early to mid 12th century. Gilt silver; diam. 9 and 9.5 cm. Photograph courtesy of Christies, New York.

Fig. 43. Composite reconstruction of Angkorian shrines and palace architecture. Line drawing after H. Parmentier, "L'Architecture interpretée dans les bas-reliefs du Cambodge," *Bulletin de l'École française d'Extrême-Orient* 14 (1914). Courtesy of John Guy.

Fig. 46. Life-size silver-copper alloy sculpture of Nandin. Silver Pagoda, Royal Palace, Phnom Penh. Photograph by John Guy.

Fig. 47. Vishnu sleeping on the serpent Ananta. National Museum of Cambodia, Phnom Penh. Photo reproduced with permission from École française d'Extrême-Orient (EFEO), Siem Reap and Paris.

Fig. 48. Two monumental bronze guardians, Arakan Pagoda Monastery, Mandalay, circa 1900. After V. C. Scott O'Connor, *The Silken East: A Record of Life and Travel in Burma* (London: Hutchinson, 1904). Courtesy of John Guy.

Fig. 52. A Khmer monarch and his two queens venerating an icon of Vishnu. Bayon, Angkor Thom, second half of the 13th century. Photograph by John Guy.

Fig 53. Thanksgiving ceremony, Banteay Srei temple, 1999. Photograph by John Guy.

Fig. 59. Relief from the pedestal of a now-lost icon. Bodhgaya, eastern India. Pala dynasty, circa 12th century. (After A. Cunningham, *Mahabodhi*, London, 1896.) Courtesy of John Guy.

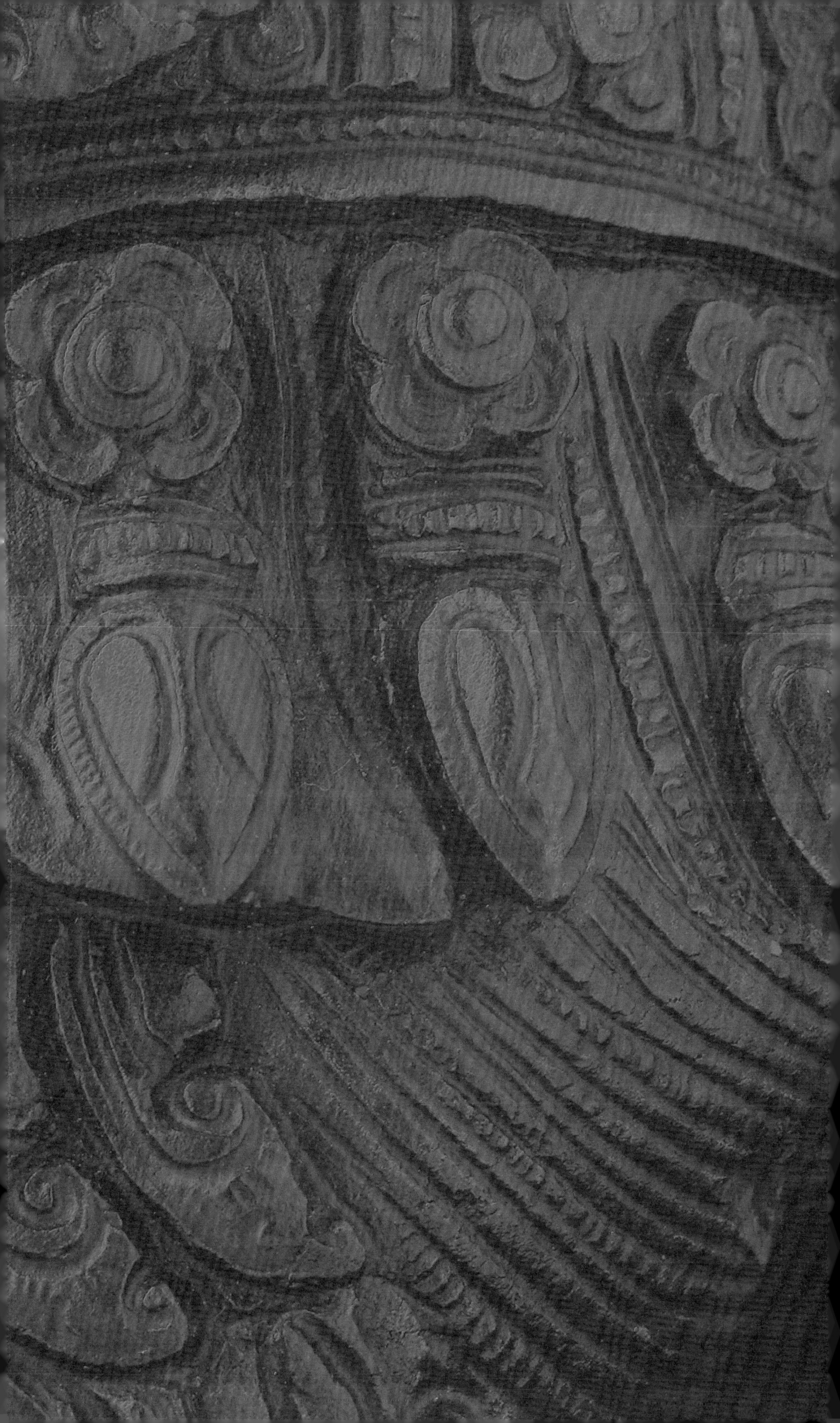

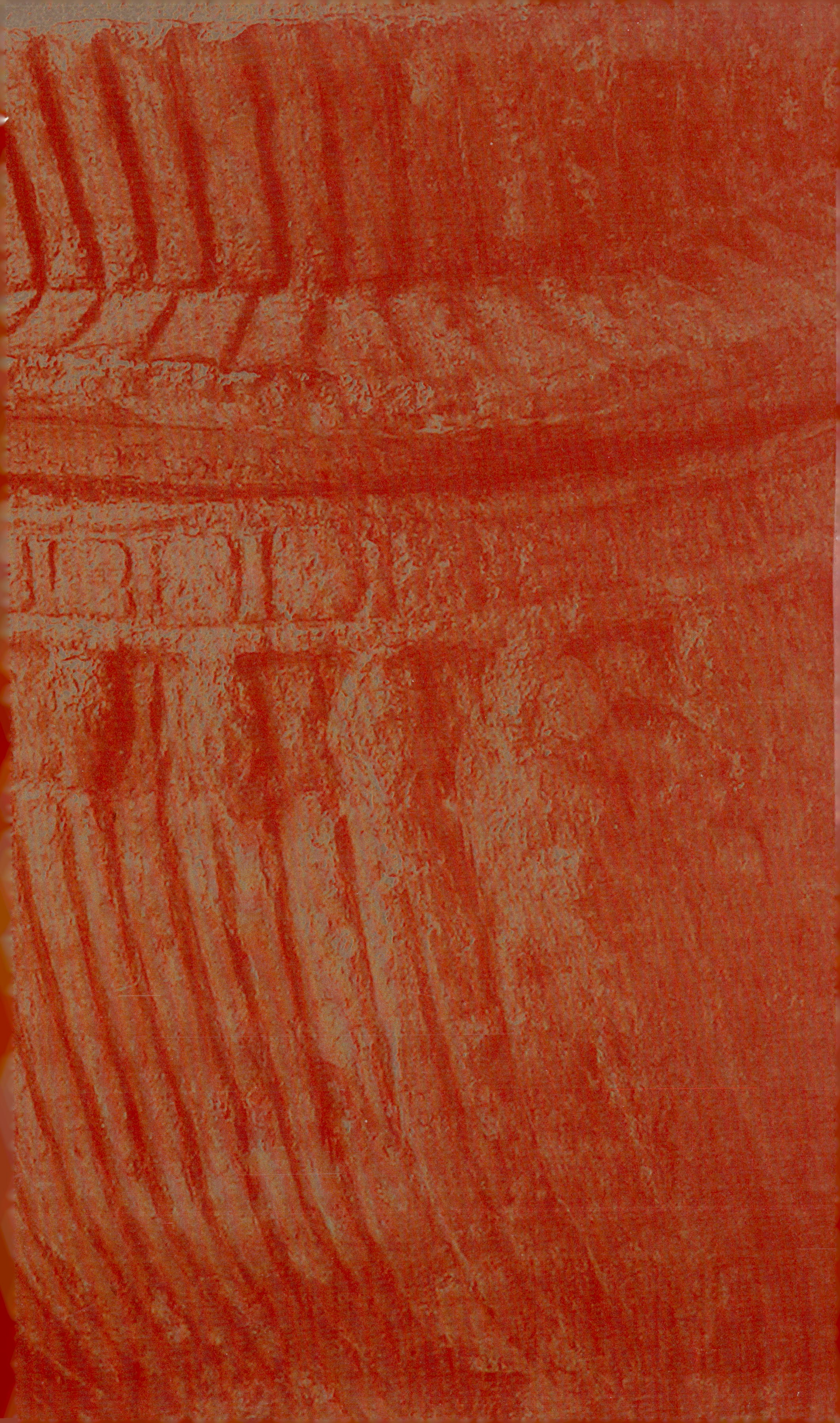